Alexina Mackay Harrison

Mackay Ruthquist

Singing the Gospel among Hindus and Gónds

Alexina Mackay Harrison

Mackay Ruthquist
Singing the Gospel among Hindus and Gónds

ISBN/EAN: 9783337281328

Printed in Europe, USA, Canada, Australia, Japan

Cover: Foto ©Lupo / pixelio.de

More available books at **www.hansebooks.com**

Alexina Mackay Harrison

Mackay Ruthquist
Singing the Gospel among Hindus and Gónds

ISBN/EAN: 9783337281328

Printed in Europe, USA, Canada, Australia, Japan

Cover: Foto ©Lupo / pixelio.de

More available books at **www.hansebooks.com**

A. MACKAY RUTHQUIST

OR

SINGING THE GOSPEL AMONG HINDUS AND GÓNDS

BY THE AUTHOR OF
"A. M. MACKAY, PIONEER MISSIONARY OF THE C.M.S. TO UGANDA"

"Take my voice, and let me sing
Always, only for my King."
FRANCES RIDLEY HAVERGAL

London
HODDER AND STOUGHTON
27, PATERNOSTER ROW

MDCCCXCIII

PREFACE.

ALEXINA MACKAY RUTHQUIST proved herself a true missionary. Her work was thorough, and its fruits are manifest.

Combined with an invincible devotion to the work she undertook, she possessed a fearless yet winning manner, and a marked strength of character which gave her staying power and made her a stay to others.

Women, and not women only, but very frequently fathers of families, young soldiers and little children, gave her glad welcome, because she carried sunshine and song with her wherever she went. She was a living epistle, full of good tidings, clearly and brightly written, and many of all classes read her to their own profit and the glory of God.

Her last call came to her when executing a self-denying work which she undertook from pure

Christian compassion, and thus her missionary career ended as it began—in the spirit of perfect consecration to the will and service of our Blessed Lord, and now she has her reward.

Her letters reveal her mind and heart, and vividly set forth her work. Some people may think them too revealing, and would prefer that they were pruned and trimmed; but, in a Biography, readers have a right to know, and increasingly demand to know, the real mind and heart of its subject. So the letters have been left as they were. For this they are much the better, as they portray her in all the sincerity, and beauty, and ardour of her character.

May this record of a bright, sunny, self-sacrificing life help to turn the eyes of many to a heathen land whence twelve hundred souls pass every hour into eternity!

J. W. H.

September, 1893.

CONTENTS.

CHAPTER I.
ON THE BEACH 1

CHAPTER II.
A BEAM OF SUNSHINE 6

CHAPTER III.
A YIELDED LIFE 11

CHAPTER IV.
WAITING 16

CHAPTER V.
THE CRADLE OF FABLE AND SONG . . . 27

CHAPTER VI.
"THE CITY OF SERPENTS" 38

CHAPTER VII.
CAMPING OUT 66

CONTENTS.

	PAGE
CHAPTER VIII.	
IN AND OUT OF THE ZENANAS	78
CHAPTER IX.	
THE SOLDIERS AT THE FORT	120
CHAPTER X.	
ALONE	131
CHAPTER XI.	
OPEN DOORS	158
CHAPTER XII.	
ON AND AFTER FURLOUGH	219
CHAPTER XIII.	
"THE TRUTHFUL GÓNDS"	265
CHAPTER XIV.	
SORROW AND SERVICE	283
CHAPTER XV.	
IN THE RED SEA	326

CHAPTER I.

ON THE BEACH.

*"And nearer voices, wild or tame,
Of airy flock and childish throng,
Up from the water's edge there came
Faint snatches of familiar song."*

ON the rocky Banffshire coast of the Moray Firth, midway between the busy fishing towns of Portsoy and Cullen, is a long stretch of beautiful silvery sand, terminating in a cove or creek, around which nestle some forty homesteads, forming a hamlet known as "Sandend."

These cottages were evidently not built with any desire to command the prospect of the changeful ocean, for not infrequently the gable-end in which there was not the slightest pretext of a window, was directed to the bay. No! these busy fisher-folk preferred to "gang furth" to see the view; and on an autumn evening, some thirty years ago, when the day's work of repairing and drying the nets was over, seated on a bench at a point of vantage, would be found the elderly inhabitants of the place.

"The tough old boatmen, half amphibious grown,"

with horny hands, and faces tanned and seamed from exposure in all weathers, smoked their pipes and gazed right sea-wards, interrupted only by an occasional glance overhead, while the women, whose knitting needles seemed to go by magic, more wistfully even than their companions scanned the briny deep.

No homeward bound mail steamer or troop-ship was in sight, but a fleet of open herring boats, drifting with the tide, manned, several of them, by their kith and kin—able-bodied men of the hamlet. Some of these grand-sires had sunk far into the infirmities of age, but as the sun set, their dim eyes saw in imagination the drift net "shot" into the sea, and murmuring the prayer,—

"O God of might, O God of right!
Go with Thy children where they go;
Be Thou their guide, their beacon light,
And keep them safe from every foe,"

they retired indoors to rest, and to dream of toiling at the long labyrinth of ropes, meshes, bladders and cork-floats, in the darkness of the night, and of the "glow of living light" in the boats caused by the phosphoric properties of the newly-hauled herring.

On an August evening, in the year 1859, a little group of people had spent a quiet hour on a bench at the end of the "big hoose," when a pleasant-looking old woman, dressed in a dark serge gown (about which was a strong "savour of the sea") and a white kerchief neatly arranged across her bosom, suddenly exclaimed, "Sandy! isna it gettin' late, an' time thae bairns had gaen their ways hame?"

The individual addressed, gave a look at the sky, continued chewing his tobacco, but vouchsafed no remark. The woman eyed him nervously, for well she knew that

> "In moons and tides and weather wise,
> He read the clouds as prophecies,
> And foul or fair could well divine,
> By many an occult hint and sign."

After some minutes he quietly replied, "Dinna fash yersel', gudewife; they're a' richt; saut water winna hurt them;" but evidently discerning that this remark failed to re-assure her, he continued, "Lat the little anes alane. What for wud ye spile their play? Bless their little herts! they'll niver be sae happy again, niver in this warld."

"That's nae to the pint, Sandy," the woman rejoined. "Their folk will be fay aboot them, sae they maun gae hame this vera meenit;" and suiting the action to the word, she jerked her knitting wires into a straw sheath which the string of her apron fastened to her waist, and with an air of decision, she marched off in the direction of the sands.

* * * * *

I think I see them still—a happy little party of sun-brown children. They had dropped their shoes and stockings, and like the clanging sea-gulls in the distance, were gambolling in the water, the chief fun being to meet the white-maned waves, which rolled in swift advance towards the beach, and then to turn and rush back, so as to escape a soaking from the spray. Tired of that, a bonnie, winsome little maid of some ten summers, a very "bundle of fun," mounted the sandwich basket on her shoulders in imitation of a Newhaven fishwife, and to the great amusement of her companions, sang out, in a clear, rich voice :—

> "Wha'll buy caller herrin'?
> They're bonnie fish and halesome farin',
> Wha'll buy caller herrin,'
> New drawn frae the Forth?"

Had Thomas Edwards passed by, on one of his evening excursions along the coast, in quest of moths and butterflies, or to visit his sea-traps in some deep rock-pool, most probably he would have been too much occupied, crooning an old Scotch air, to have even noticed the children, nor is it likely that any stray pedestrian on the sands gave them more than a passing glance; but a pretty picture they made that evening, and one whose value and interest has been enhanced by time. For no fewer than three of that little group faithfully redeemed the opportunity of life's brief day, and became pioneers of progress, and light-bearers to the dark places of the earth.

That fair, curly-headed boy, in the kilt of variegated tartan, is Alexander Mackay, whose name will ever be associated with the early days of Christianity in Uganda, while his cousins, the little singer and her younger sister by her side, consecrated their voices to the service of Christ, and responded to the call :—

> "Go tell thy dusky kinsman,
> As he bows by Ganges' tide,
> Of the sacred stream that courses
> From a Saviour's riven side."

With the exception of the boy, the group hailed from the Free Church Manse of Fordyce, about two miles inland. They had crossed "the haughs" and the foot-bridge, and run down through the fragrant bean fields and the waving corn for a frolic on the beach; and now, with their friend's not too gentle reminder that it was "gettin' dark," they made their way home,

> "And sped the time with stories old,
> Wrought puzzles out, and riddles told,
> Or stammered from their school-book lore
> The chief of Gambia's golden shore."

CHAPTER II.

A BEAM OF SUNSHINE.

"Bright be the skies that cover thee,
　Child of the sunny brow—
Bright as the dream flung over thee
　By all that meets thee now.
Thy heart is beating joyously,
　Thy voice is like a bird's,
And sweetly breaks the melody
　Of thy imperfect words.
I know no fount that gushes out
　As gladly as thy tiny shout."

MRS. ALEXINA RUTHQUIST, the subject of this sketch, and the little singer of the preceding page, was the third child of the Rev. M. Mackay, Free Church Minister of Fordyce, and was born there on September 8th, 1848.

Her maternal grandfather was the Rev. John Robertson, Minister of the parish of Gartly, in the famous presbytery of Strathbogie, who cast in his lot with the Free Church of Scotland at the Disruption, while her grandmother, Mrs. Robertson, was a gracious, highly cultured, and strong-minded Christian of a type of the old Scottish gentlewoman, now, unhappily, well-nigh passed away.

The village of Fordyce is a dreary enough place in winter; but to a lover of nature its very solitude is charming. No railway-whistle or coach-horn is heard in its precincts, and not a sound reaches the ear but the bubbling of the brook, the whispering of the trees, the carolling of birds, the lowing of cattle, or, mayhap, the lashing of the waves against the distant rock-bound coast.

> "A place of idle eyes and ears,
>   A cobwebbed nook of dreams;
> Left by the stream whose waves are years,
>   The stranded village seems."

In such environments Alexina grew in grace and sweetness. A merry little girl, full of rhyme and repartee, she was not only a very sunbeam in the home, but her brightness extended also to the cottages of the villagers. At a very early age it was her wont to spend the play-hour every morning in a round of visits to the blind, deaf, and afflicted old people of her acquaintance, to "give them a cheery word, and brighten their lonely day," which, judging from the welcome she received, it no doubt did, although it seldom amounted to more than a kindly greeting or a humorous remark.

> "For to children oft is giv'n
> A grace like habitants of heav'n,
> Gems of God's infinite art,
> Flowers from the Eternal Heart."

One night when Alexina was in her fourth year, an incident occurred which might have proved disastrous, especially if the brook had been frozen, or a high wind blowing. She and her sisters had been commended to the care of the Good Shepherd, and "tucked" in their little cots by their mother's loving hands, when, some hours afterwards, the nurse entered the room in search of something from a cupboard.[1] In a moment of abstraction she left the burning candle on the shelf, and having locked the cupboard door, quitted the room. Unfortunately the shelves contained quantities of the *Witness* and other newspapers filed for reference. By-and-by the family became alarmed by the extraordinary smoke, and hurrying upstairs, extricated the children, who awoke to find themselves little white-robed figures by their father's study fire. Some of the older ones were nervous and frightened, but "four year old," although she confessed afterwards that she "felt eerie enough," so soothed and comforted her companions, and made fun of the whole affair, that they had quite a good time, and on retiring again to rest, expressed the

---

[1] Called in Scotland, a "press."

hope "that there would soon be another fire, as it was *such fun!*"

Yet there was a thoughtfulness about the little girl, and a quiet depth of character, which many wondered at.

The love of Jesus Christ ruled and reigned in the home, and from early infancy her parents had taught her that

> " God wants the girls, the happy-hearted girls
> The loving girls, the best of girls.
> *   *   *   *   *
> God wants to make the girls His pearls,
> And so reflect His holy face,
> And bring to mind His wondrous grace,
> That beautiful the world may be,
> And filled with love and purity."

In the year 1860 a great wave of revival of religion passed over Scotland, and about that time Mr. Duncan Matheson and Mr. James Turner, well-known evangelists in the North, held meetings at Fordyce, and were guests at the Free Church Manse. Mr. Reginald Radcliffe and Mr. Grant of Arndilly had also similar evangelistic services at Portsoy, to which Alexina was taken as a little girl, and she generally also accompanied the other members of the family to the revival services held every summer in the grounds of Huntly Lodge, kindly lent for that purpose by the sainted Duchess of Gordon. But it is not known when she was first awakened. It is questionable if she herself knew of any time when she did *not* love her Saviour, for she seemed to have been specially consecrated for the Lord's work from her early infancy.

A well-known writer says :—" The secret of happiness here and hereafter, the gold thread of youth, lies in loving God, and loving our neighbour; loving them early if it be yet possible, loving them well; losing one's own life in theirs, becoming guileless, meek and reverent in our intercourse with them, loving them long, yea, for ever."

At a very early age Alexina learnt this secret, and she grew up into young womanhood like a beautiful myrtle tree, imparting a sweet fragrance all around, and delighting the eye with its white fairy-like bloom.

CHAPTER III.

A YIELDED LIFE.

"Use me! and let my weapon be
The clear brook's polished stone;
The weakness of the work be mine,
The glory all Thine own."

HER grandfather, the Rev. John Robertson, had his sympathies enlisted in the cause of Christian missions in the early part of the century, in days when little was known of the condition of the heathen, and consequently little zeal or enthusiasm manifested in their behalf. The Jesuits had imparted new life into the decrepit Roman system and had, since the founding of their Society, in 1534, been working, with exemplary devotion and intensity of purpose, "for the greater glory of God," in every known region of the earth, and John Knox had, as far back as the year 1560, pledged the Reformed

Kirk "to preche this glaid tydings of the Kyngdome through the haill warld," yet the Church [1] of Scotland did not awake to her duty with regard to the heathen, and did absolutely nothing for them as a Church, until 1829, when she sent out the noble Alexander Duff as her first foreign missionary, the centre of his labours being Calcutta.

Many influences were, doubtless, fashioning and moulding Alexina for her part in life, and she may have inherited some of her grandfather's enthusiasm for missionary work. At all events it is worthy of notice that no fewer than four of Mr. Robertson's grand-daughters have devoted the best part of their lives to the foreign field.

Perhaps also, as she sat at the drawing-room window of the Manse, poring over a volume of the *Free Church Children's Missionary Record*, in its gay binding of blue and gold, and looked out on the rippling ocean below, and thought of India, of its hoary superstitions, its child sacrifice, its widow burning, and its blood-stained opium traffic, the tender heart may have been stirred until the very sails covering the horizon seemed so many handker-

---

[1] One of her ministers, however, has the honour of being one of the chief originators of the London Missionary Society, in 1795, and Robert Morrison, the founder of Protestant Missions in China, in 1807, was of Scottish parentage.

chiefs waving and beckoning to her, and she heard the voice :—

> " Bane instead of blessing
>   Britain pours to-day,
> Over India's millions,
>   Under Britain's sway.
> Asia's sons are dying,
>   Pierced by Britain's hand ;
> Blood to God is crying :
>   *Can ye listless stand ?* "

Anyhow the idea of devoting her life to the work of God in India sprang up and matured, unknown to her friends, until at last, while she was at school[1] in Edinburgh she was enabled to say,—

> " Jesu, Master, take me, use me ;
>   I belong to Thee ;
> Thou art mine ;—my life shall serve Thee
>   Through eternity ! "

She immediately wrote home and acquainted her parents of her resolve. They were far from being surprised, yet—

> " Her mother could not speak for tears ; she ever mused thus,
>   The bees will find out other flowers,—but what is left for us ? "

Like Eli of old, her father " perceived that the Lord had called the child," and exclaimed with heartfelt thanksgiving, " It is the Lord ; let Him do what seemeth Him good," yet the mother, although

---

[1] Miss Milne's Seminary, 26, Palmerston Place.

by example and precept she had ever striven to give the noblest direction to the lives of her children, and continually kept the Lord in remembrance of His promise, "I will bless thee, and thou shalt be a blessing; and in thee shall all families of the earth be blessed," could not part with her treasure. Little had she dreamed, as she and her husband had patiently, and with much wrestling with God in prayer, not only sought to make their children choose the better part, but had also, with quite exceptional care, endeavoured to fashion and mould their lives after the Divine Pattern, that in the dim horizon of the future there was awaiting Alexina a lone bungalow, in the outskirts of a dirty city, teeming with idolaters, under a tropical sun, and in a land of pestilence, storm and cyclone!

The Rev. E. Lombe, in his admirable paper,[1] "How is the Present Need of Missionaries to be met?" says, "One," and he might have said *The* "great source of supply is the *home* of the Christian parents."

"Parents," he continues, "train your children, not for God only, that they may be saved, *but for God's work, that they may be employed by Him in it.* Seek place, seek high honours for them. Seek them with

---

[1] Published by the Church Missionary Society.

all your powers, but let it be place in the household of God, to do His work, high honours, such as attach to him who goes forth to enlarge the dominions of the King of kings and Lord of lords."

Yes! To every home in Christendom,—to every mother-heart in such—the question comes :—

> "What gifts for Christ, then, bring ye with the rest?
>   Your hands have worked well; is your courage spent
> In handwork only? *Have you nothing best*,
>   Which generous souls may perfect and present,
> And He shall thank the giver for? no light
>   Of teaching, liberal nations, for the poor
> Who sit in darkness when it is not night?
>   No cure for wicked children? Christ,—no cure?
> No help for women sobbing out of sight,
>   Because men made the laws?"

To Alexina's mother this was plaintive music borne ashore by a summer zephyr, from a distant ship, but much too far off for the ear to catch the tune. Like Mary at the sepulchre, that which she had so diligently sought and ardently longed for, she did not at first recognise for her tears.

CHAPTER IV.

WAITING.

" I look without; how great
Earth's enmity to Thee, how dense her gloom!
I would restore her to an Eden's bloom,
Save her from present woe and future doom,
And yet Thou bidd'st me—wait."

IN deference to her mother's feelings Alexina agreed not to apply to any missionary society, nor take any step whatsoever to further her desire. On the other hand, should a call to the Foreign Field come, the maternal sanction was to be no longer withheld. This was to be the test of whether or not the matter was of the Lord, and subsequent events abundantly justified the wisdom of the arrangement.

An eminent writer says, "How will you find good? It is not a thing of choice; it is a river that flows from the foot of the invisible Throne, and it flows by the path of obedience." Alexina faithfully kept her promise, believing that those

> "Who may not strive, may yet fulfil
> The harder task of standing still,
> And good but wished with God is done!"

She needed the sorrows and discipline of life to strengthen and deepen her beautiful character—"a taking root downward, as well as a bearing fruit upward."

*   *   *   *   *

Eight "long harmonious years" passed, and it is in 1876, in the little town of Alva, in Stirlingshire. Here we find Alexina, teaching in the family of Mr. Cowan, banker. Since the new year had dawned her heart has been greatly stirred, and the old longing for service in the foreign field revived, for Alexander Mackay, the playmate of her childhood, and with whom she was still

> " One in kind,
> As moulded like in Nature's mint;
> And hill and wood and field did print
> The same sweet forms in either mind,"

has been accepted by the Church Missionary Society, as one of the pioneers for their new mission to the heart of the "Dark Continent." The winter had been severe, and had lingered late, and although it is now April, there are still patches of snow on the Ochils, but the first herald of spring has come at last, and

> "There is an upward movement in the heather,
>   Night drops down starry gold upon the furze,
> Wild rivers and wild birds sing songs together,
>   Dead Nature breathes and stirs."

Subtle influences are at work; the sun's rays are touching every tree and bush into life, and the bright aspect of Nature accords with Alexina's feelings; and her hope

> " Becomes an April violet,
>   And buds and blossoms like the rest."

For, strange to say, she has received a letter from her home, stating that a friend of the family, who knew nothing of her wishes, had been asked by a member of the Acting Committee of the Free Church of Scotland "Ladies' Society for Female Education in India and South Africa," whether she knew of any consecrated young lady who would be willing to leave home and kindred to carry the gospel to her dusky sisters in the far-off East.

The Aberdeen Auxiliary of this Society had been for some time pushing to the front, and now felt that they ought to have a representative of their own as visitor and religious teacher to the prison-like seclusions of the caste women of India. A well-educated girl with a good linguistic turn; a good singer; but one especially alive to the opportunities and possibilities that are open to women for extending the kingdom of Christ in the homes of the Hindus was wanted. Where was she to be found?

One of the greatest of living preachers says: "It is not out of every roadside quarry that you can cut and polish a corner-stone for a king's palace. And it is not to every so-called Christian family that you can come to look for a Christian lady. . . . It is a common saying among us, indeed, that boys and young men are often seen to rise in talent, and in manners, and in refinement of mind far above their extraction; but girls and young women seldom or never. And thus it is that, in our delineation of a Christian lady, we are more dependent on our knowledge of her father and her mother than we are in the case of a Christian gentleman." Accordingly, this friend replied without any hesitation,—"Yes! I know the family of a Free Church minister, where there are several girls—all pious, for they have the inestimable blessing of a mother who spends much of her time in secret prayer. If you can secure one of them you will do well." One daughter was named as being considered eminently suitable, but she is not the subject of these pages.

Immediately the Rev. Mr. Mackay was communicated with, and the letter was forwarded to Alexina. Her reply to a sister, preserved more by accident than design, runs as follows:—

"OCHIL BANK, ALVA,
"*April*, 1876.

" MY DEAREST ——,

"Many thoughts have been stirred within me since I received your kind letter, charged with such weighty contents. I will tell you simply how I feel in regard to this most important subject, and may God overrule the whole matter for His own glory and our good. Well, when I read your letter, a burst of grateful surprise took possession of me, since it seemed to me that here, at last, I had got the call to go forth to the work I had many a time longed to be permitted to engage in! and at once I submitted the matter to God's hands, that He might dispose of it as He saw fit. With Him, then, I desire that it may rest. I think this is pretty much my attitude of mind, in regard to the answer to the question—

> 'As a little child relies
> On a care beyond his own;
> Feels he's neither strong nor wise,
> Fears to stir a step alone—
> So let me with Thee abide,
> As my Father, Guard and Guide.'

"I feel that it would be a great privilege (I shrink from viewing it in the bare light of *a duty*) to be permitted to enter the lists with those favoured few who have been called to bear the 'lamp of life' into the dark corners of the earth, and if, in the providence of God, I am being called to that honour, I desire to respond, 'Here I am,' and to venture forward on the unknown, untried path, in the spirit of the hymn that says,—

> 'I know not the way I am going,
> But well do I know my Guide"

(there is much need I should get to know Him better, and to trust Him more);

> 'With a child-like trust I give my hand
> To the mighty Friend by my side.'

"I believe I am physically and morally constituted, so as to be equal to such an undertaking (do not set me down as being *heartless*, if I am *stronger* of heart than some are, according to natural constitution),—the question is how am I constituted *spiritually?* To this I can give no satisfactory answer, but He is *able* to make all grace abound; and, after all, my labours (should I indeed enter upon them) would be more of a secular nature than purely missionary, so that the question of personal devotion, in the highest sense of the term, need not necessarily be the hinge on which my decision turns.

"Now write to me very soon again on the subject, and do not fear to express the opinion of each one of you on the subject. I am in no excitement in regard to this suggestion, longing to be off, etc., etc., but I am a little in the attitude of Eleazar when he watched to see what was to be the result of his master Abraham's mission.

"Don't, don't think me indifferent in my affections! but all of you consider yourselves as much deciders in this matter as myself, and so we shall understand and sympathise with each other aright.

"Please thank Miss Patton cordially in my name for the honour she has put on our family in communicating with us as she has done.

"Your affectionate sister,
"ALEXINA."

When this reply reached her home, her mother now clearly saw the hand of God in the matter, and she herself carried the letter to the monthly committee meeting of the Aberdeen Auxiliary Branch of the Society. At the very moment she arrived, prayer was being offered for a suitable missionary, and the committee regarded the visit as a direct answer from on high.

After some correspondence, Alexina went to Edinburgh to see the General Committee, and on May 2nd, the very day Alexander Mackay first sighted the coast of Africa, and the thirtieth anniversary of the founding of the Hislop College at Nagpoor, we find her writing home the following description of this interview :—

"OCHIL BANK, ALVA,
"*Tuesday, May 2nd,* 1876.

"MY DEAREST MOTHER,—

"I returned last night from a most successful visit to Edinburgh. Yes, 'successful' is the right word in reply to the one inquiry present, I am quite certain, in all your minds, for God seems to be prospering my way. It is now virtually settled that, nothing unforeseen occurring, I go to India! But, mother, only on an engagement of three years! This fact is to me a great relief, and is it not to you? I thought I might have to go on as long as my health stood out, and I calculated that I had a good deal more than a three years' stock! In this, however, I am probably mistaken; but, be this as it may, I feel that faith and fancy can easily bridge over such a separation, though it is at the same time true, at home or abroad, that we know not what a day may bring forth. What do you think Miss Angelica Fraser requested, in the course of the beautiful prayer she offered up, at Mrs. Lumsden's request, when our interview was closing? It was that if I were not the right person to be sent, or if it were wrong for me to go, God would raise up some insurmountable wall of difficulty! This wonderful request was, however, immediately followed by words like these:—

"'But, O Lord! let it be otherwise. Be pleased rather to make the way very plain to Thy young servant, to go before her, and to prepare a place for her in that distant land, which she will feel to be of Thine own appointment.'

"I can't tell you whether Calcutta or Nagpoor is, D.V., to be the scene of my labours. This depends on the reply Mrs. Lumsden gets to a letter she is to send to Calcutta, inquiring whether a vacancy that had occurred there has been filled up or not (as I understand). If it has been, Nagpoor will be my destination, as there *is* a place awaiting *some one* there. A Mr. and Mrs. Cooper are at the head of the little Free Church Mission there, and a Miss Berrie has been provided as one of two assistants who were required! I hear that Mrs. Cooper is a delightful, energetic, cheerful woman, who enjoys good health out there. By the bye, I will need to conform to the rule of submitting to be reviewed by one of that highly inquisitive class — doctors! although Miss Fraser remarked that she thought they might quite risk sending *me* out independently of this. She seemed to think I carried my certificate in my face (unusually flushed, of course!) October would be the time of departure. No one can corroborate my statement as to Dr. and Mrs. Murray Mitchell's intention to return to India in the end of the year.

"Good-bye, dear ones,

"Your own

"ALEXINA."

The Rev. W. D. Moffat, late United Presbyterian Minister at Alva, now of Rose Street, Edinburgh, writes concerning this time:—

"Alexina was foremost in every kind of service that lay open to her in Sabbath School, Bible Class, Mission District, and in warm interest in the poor, the sick, the distressed, and the intemperate in the general community.

"Her services in leading the praise, both in Sabbath and Bible Class, won for her the love of young and old, and the parting present she received when leaving for the foreign field was a proof of how much her work in that direction was appreciated.

"Indeed, she was always singing. There was a note of praise in her eyes as well as in her voice. She was the picture of a *happy* Christian. Always bright, sunny, hopeful, and brimful of a mirth that was contagious, a cheerfulness that had its roots in the love of God, and a buoyancy that left room for neither depression nor despair.

"Everything she did was done so naturally and

with such a quiet repose of soul, that no one could have guessed, by casual observation, the amount of work she did for the Master. Her very activity was restful.

"It was no astonishment to me when I learned that she had consecrated herself to service in the foreign field. When I think of her life as I knew it, I can see just how the Spirit was leading her out into the higher service, and how, finding her faithful in a few things, the Lord made her ruler over many things. On her first visit home on furlough she called on me in Edinburgh, and I can never forget how, as she sang the sweet native hymns and described her work in the zenanas, her soul seemed on fire with enthusiasm and love for her work.

"To me, one of the mysteries of the Kingdom is the removal of such beloved and fervent workers from the place where they are so much needed and sorely missed. 'Even so, Father, for so it seemeth good in Thy sight.' Sad as the circumstances of her death were, they were only in keeping with the whole of her life. She never seemed to think of herself. Her self-sacrifice reminded one continually of Christ. It was the secret, not only of her joy, but of her power in winning others."

CHAPTER V.

THE CRADLE OF FABLE AND SONG.

" Light for the darkened earth !
Ye blessed, its beams who shed,
Shrink not, till the day-spring hath its birth,
Till wherever the footstep of man doth tread,
Salvation's banner, spread boldly forth,
Shall gild the dream of the cradle-bed,
And clear the tomb
From its lingering gloom,
For the aged to rest his weary head."

FROM the earliest dawn of history a halo of romance has surrounded the land of the Hindus. Poets sang of its "ambrosial fruits and vegetable gold." Crusaders craved the treasures of its hoary temples. Emperors and kings cast envious eyes towards the dazzling throne of its Great Mogul. In search of its gorgeous products, navigators sought to compass the ice-bound shores of Labrador, and even the frozen steppes of Siberia, and in every direction the spirit of maritime discovery was stimulated to effect a quick and easy passage thither, and—

> "Joy was upon the lonely seas,
> When Indian forests pour
> Forth to the billow and the breeze
> Their fragrance from the shore."

But at length the spell was broken. Britain had been slowly and surely gaining supremacy over the country from the latter end of the reign of Queen Elizabeth, when the East Indian Company established themselves at Surat.

It was in truth the "clime of the sun;" the trees were never destitute of flowers; diamonds were still cut and polished at Golconda; and the court of the Emperor of Delhi realised all the wonders of the "Thousand and One Nights." Yet it was a land of moral darkness, where the most cruel and revolting rites were practised, and where, on the sacred days of festivals to the gods, the very temples reeked with blood. The mass of the people were sunk in the deepest ignorance and superstition, although they rank among the most ancient and civilised of nations, and can boast of their Homer, their Shakespeare and their Milton!

To this benighted and joyless land, a century ago, Carey and other missionaries of the cross heard the call—

> "Go, break the chain of caste;
> Go, quench the funeral pyre, and bid no more
> The Indian river roll its waves of gore;
> Look up, thou East, thy night is overpast."

Since then the British Government has "abolished the cruel 'suttee,' the casting infants to the alligators of the Ganges, the human sacrifices offered to the goddess Kàli, the Meriah sacrifices of living victims in the Madras Presidency, the car of Juggernaut and its blood-stained wheels, 'Thuggee,' and many other atrocities."[1]

Hinduism is the religion of nine-tenths of the whole population, and numbers among its votaries fully 207,731,000 of people, of whom only one out of twenty can read. As a system Dr. Duff has aptly applied to it Milton's words,—

> "An unfathomable ocean, without bounds,
> Without dimensions, where length, breadth and height,
> And time and space are lost!"

The law of caste is the basis of this ancient superstition, and is *the* great hindrance to all missionary endeavour. Having its root in the home, it sends its ramifications into every grade of society, and is carried into the pettiest affairs in life. Originally there were but four castes. The highest in dignity

---

[1] See "Infant Marriage and Enforced Widowhood in India," *C.M.S. Intelligencer*, December, 1890.

and privilege is that of the Brahmans or Priests, who form the learned order of the community. To them belong the exclusive right of *teaching* the Vedas or sacred books, and of officiating at sacrifices. The second caste is the Kshutryas, or military. Then come the Vaisyas, or agriculturists and merchants. All these three castes are denominated "twice born." The last and lowest is the Sŭdras, or "once born," whose highest honour is to wait on the Kuleen Brahmans, although they *may* humbly serve any of the twice-born. In one respect they have an advantage over their honoured neighbours, inasmuch as they may sojourn where they choose, whereas the limits of the other castes are prescribed. Besides these, there is a variety of mixed castes, according to trade and occupations, and these refuse to eat, drink, or intermarry with any other class than that in which they are born. It is generally said that when once caste is lost, it is irrecoverable, and that "to attempt to pass from one caste to another is impossible and absurd ; a donkey might as soon expect to become a butterfly, or a frog to be transformed into a humming-bird !" The priests, however, will give back caste on payment of an enormous sum of money, and "in some cases, impure families may, in process of time, regain the place from which they have fallen ; and the base-born, by the performance of certain meritorious acts, may hope to attain final beatitude."[1] One-fifth of the entire population are said to be outcasts, or persons who have forfeited the privileges of their original class. These poor creatures are denied the common rights of humanity; they are turned out of their homes, required to wear only the clothes of the dead, and for ornaments only rusty iron, and to use only broken vessels for their food. They are denied all intercourse with their friends, and have to roam from place to place, until death releases them from hopeless misery.

But the cords of caste are being untied all over India. Sir C. U. Aitchison[2] says, "It will be easily understood how the connection of India with England has resulted in a great awakening. We are not referring at this moment to the direct effect of Christianity, though that is very marked; but to the general effect of contact with Europe and Western civilisation, of education, science, railways, trade, and the thousand material improvements introduced into the country during the last three-quarters of a century, and especially since the assumption of the government of India by the Crown. . . . The practices of Hinduism may be submitted to by

---

[1] Thornton's "British Empire in India," vol. i. p. 9.
[2] See "The Brahmo Somaj, or the New Dispensation," *C.M.S. Intelligencer*, March, 1893.

educated men in their homes, to please their wives or their mothers; *outside* the home they are fast losing hold upon the life. The regulations as to food and marriage are probably the only ones that are now at all generally observed, and even these are being gradually relaxed."

We shall now take a peep *inside* the homes, or zenanas, as they are called, where the wives and mothers lead a life of absolute seclusion, and of utter subjection to their husbands,—

> " Pining in the silence of a woe,
> Which from the heart shuts daylight."

Here, for centuries, the women, who have moulded the character and opinions of millions of the Hindu youth have been hidden away behind the " purdah," where "all life dies and death alone lives." Down-trodden and degraded by traditional customs, they have been immured in these prison homes.

In the year 1834 the " Society for Promoting Female Education in the East " was established for the purpose of restoring the women of the zenanas to the image of God, and the following year access was gained to a native home in Calcutta by one of the lady agents of this Society. In 1852 the "Indian Female Normal School and Instruction Society " was originated, and since the mutiny many similar societies have been formed, and hundreds of Christian ladies from Britain and America have spent their lives in visiting these homes, and in endeavouring to mitigate their "time-honoured social wrongs." After the first fright is overcome, they are eagerly welcomed

> "By the eyes that watch and weary
> For the morn that does not wake,
> By the hearts with nameless longings,
> That in darkness beat and break."

Many of these ladies (for they are the upper class women) have never seen a tree, nor a river, nor a mountain, nor anything at all beyond the precincts of their own quarters, their "outing" consisting of the daily ablutions in a walled-in pond in the courtyard. Miss Abbie B. Child, Secretary, Woman's Board of Missions, in connection with the American Board of Commissioners for Foreign Missions, in an able paper read at the Centenary Conference on Protestant Missions, quotes the following remarkable prayer, expressing the soul longings of a Hindu lady:

"O Lord, hear my prayer. For ages dark ignorance has brooded over our minds and spirits; like a cloud of dust it rises and wraps us round; and we are like prisoners in an old and mouldering house, choked and buried in the dust of custom, and we have no strength to get out. Bruised and beaten, we are like the dry husks of the sugar-cane when the sweet juice has been extracted. Criminals confined in jails are happier than we, for they know something of Thy world. They were not born in prison, but we have not for one day, no, not even in our dreams, seen Thy world; and what we have not seen we cannot imagine. To us it is nothing but a name; and not having seen Thy world, we cannot know Thee, its Maker. We have been born in this jail; we have died here, and are dying. O God of mercies, our prayer to Thee is this, that the curse may be removed from the women of India."

Many Hindu ladies begin their secluded life at six years of age, and they must all be betrothed before they are eight, although the wedding may be delayed until they are ten. Their years are spent, for the most part, in doing their hair, and in making curry and sweets. Some, more favoured, may say to their lords,—

> "We sew, sew, prick our fingers, dull our sight,
> Producing what? A pair of slippers, sir,
> To put on when you're weary—or a stool
> To stumble over and vex you . . . 'Curse that stool!'
> Or else at best, a cushion, where you lean
> And sleep, and dream of something we are not,
> But would be for your sake."

There are twenty-five millions of widows in India and seventy-seven thousand of these are actually not ten years of age! The results of this cruel system of child-marriage are inconceivable. The plaint of a young widow who has learned to write is a fit accompaniment to the prayer given above [1] :—

"If by chance my face is seen early in the morning, I prove a curse. If through haste or by accident my veil falls from my head, I am chained with a hundred bands of scolding. Every visitor to the house speaks of me ironically, and treats me with disdain. From every word I speak, offence is taken. My heart has become sore from the piercing of these bitter words. I am deprived of every pleasure. While every one else in the house puts on dresses of different colours, and plays, laughs and talks among the company, I alone, the most wretched and full of grief, am deprived of such enjoyments. If even by mistake a spot of colour is seen upon my raiment, it causes trouble. In the house one woman will be engaged in adorning herself in fine robes, another will be busy combing her hair, blacking her eyes and teeth, another will be making the house ring with the tinkling of her foot jewels and ankle ornaments, while I am condemned to sit in a corner and weep alone with my broken heart. Even this comfort it is difficult for me to indulge in, for if any one should happen to see me weeping, he would consider it a bad omen, and

[1] See *Regions Beyond*, May, 1893.

curse me for it. The will of my persecutors is that I should neither scream nor weep, but die quietly in my misery. While the whole family enjoys eating delicious food, I am served with *fried dal* and coarse bread. I am strictly forbidden the comfort of sleeping upon a bedstead, but a mat upon the floor and a coarse piece of carpet is my bedding. The wretched barber's wife shaves my head daily. On every festive occasion and at weddings every one is present but me. The women whose husbands are alive take the lead in all ceremonies. One sings, one plays on the musical instruments, another puts on the holiday costume, another primps with pride before the looking-glass, while I am shut up in my room to prevent the ill omen which would be the result of my face having been seen. Who can be more wretched than I? Death comes to all, but I am deprived of that blessing also. This is the rainy season, the rain falls heavily; my equals, dressed with gay skirts and coloured veils, with their fingers dyed red, are singing gaily the songs of this season of the year. Showers of tears flow from my eyes. I feel that some one has broken my heart; it is withered like the kammal (lotus) flower. I exist, but my life is useless; no flowers, no fruits. I have no rest, not even for a single day. I am as thin as a thorn; my body has become like a skeleton, and yet I am abhorred by others, and they are disgusted at the sight of me. I look upon all sides, but find no comforter. There is no one to inquire into my condition, and no one to wipe away my tears. Our Gracious Queen Victoria takes pity upon all others. The cries of unfortunate widows like myself have not yet reached her ears. The Lord Jesus Christ gave life to the dead, but His followers do not attempt to relieve us from our sufferings. In what hope shall I spend the days of my life? How can the ship be anchored in the midst of the tempest? 'The boat is in the midst of the river, but there is no captain.' The Government prosecutes the person who shows cruelty to animals deprived of utterance, but no notice is taken of the sufferings and cruelties which we poor women endure Alas! that dear comforter, Hope, can do us no good.

"A Christian widow hopes to meet with her husband in heaven after death, but in our Hindu religion there is no hope of such a meeting. No one listens To whom shall I complain? Before whom shall I go? O God! what shall I do?"

CHAPTER VI.

"THE CITY OF SERPENTS."

> "*But he whom Heaven*
> *Hath called to be th' awakener of a land*
> *Should have his soul's affections all absorb'd*
> *In that majestic purpose, and press on*
> *To its fulfilment, as a mountain-born*
> *And mighty stream, with all its vassal-rills*
> *Sweeps proudly to the ocean, pausing not*
> *To dally with the flowers.*"

IN the year 1811, Carey finished the Marathi translation of the New Testament. Six years later he records the baptism of the first convert at Nagpoor, the capital of the empire of the Berar Marathas. In this year (1817) not only did the village of Blantyre, on the Clyde, give to the world an eminent missionary and explorer, but at Duns, in Berwickshire, was also born one who was to be to Central, and then unknown and unexplored India, exactly what Livingstone was to become to Central Africa. This man was Stephen Hislop. In 1845 he commenced his pioneer work, in connection with the

Free Church of Scotland, at Nagpoor, *i.e.* "City of Serpents," a great idolatrous city, situated on a plain 1,200 feet above the sea level, in the very heart of India, and 580 miles north-east of Bombay. Amid successes and discouragements he laboured on until we find him, on the 8th September, 1848, the day on which the subject of this sketch was born, and the anniversary also of his own birth, in fear lest the door at Nagpoor was to be closed against him, and he would have to flee. This was owing to the controversy which arose on the persecution and lengthened imprisonment of a Brahman lad, Baba Pandurang, who had openly professed Christianity. A few months later, ere Alexina had emerged from the cradle, Hislop had opened the first girl's school in Nagpoor. "The undertaking was a bold one, and was commenced not without much hesitation; but it has succeeded fully better than we had ventured to hope." "Such," says his biographer, "is the ardent evangelist's description of the beginning of what has proved to be one of the most successful Woman's Missions in the East."[1]

The Edinburgh committee having approved of the choice of Alexina by the Aberdeen Auxiliary as

[1] See "Stephen Hislop, Pioneer Missionary and Naturalist in Central India," by Dr. George Smith, p. 79. London: John Murray.

their Zenana agent at Nagpoor, she was formally set apart for this work to be under the care of the zealous and experienced missionaries, Rev. J. G. and Mrs. Cooper, who, since the lamented death of the noble Hislop, had been at the head of the Mission there.

Alexina had a long time to wait since she wrote those lines in p. 21. It is now 1877—

> "A wintry blast
> Was hurrying wildly o'er land and sea;
> The glory of spring time was long gone past,
> And the branches were bare on the trembling tree,"

ere she sailed from England; yet after all the delay[1] she reached her destination many months before Alexander Mackay sighted the silvery waters of the noble Nyanza. Compared with the pioneer difficulties which he encountered on his wearisome march from Zanzibar, and subsequent voyage across the lake in an open boat to Uganda, or with the eight months of continuous peril and disaster experienced by the first missionary sent to India by the Free Church of Scotland, her voyage was uneventful. Reaching Bombay by the *Italia* on November 9th, she found kind friends awaiting her, who took her on to Nagpoor by rail—a different rate of progress from the twenty miles per day by which the pioneer mis-

---

[1] Unfortunately there are no letters of this period extant and no one remembers the reason of her detention.

sionary party accomplished the tedious journey of 580 miles, in the year 1845!

Soon after her arrival Mrs. Cooper wrote:—" I feel sure Miss Mackay will write to interest the Aberdeen ladies; each morning at breakfast she describes her experiences in the city, and if she only writes as she tells us, they cannot fail to be satisfied. The more we know her, the more we love her, and thank God for giving us such a helper in the work of labouring among the zenanas of this benighted country."

Another lady writes:—" Miss Mackay is very delightful—a favourite with everybody, and always pleasant. How the women like a bright happy face when you go to see them!"

Again Mrs. Cooper says:—" At the close of a year I cannot help writing again to thank you for the valuable help you gave us when you sent dear Miss Mackay, and the wisdom you showed in selecting her. We truly needed help, and Miss Mackay has proved herself equal to the work, and been able to carry it on with vigour, so that we have every cause to thank God for so guiding you, and inclining your hearts to help us."

About this time Alexina addressed the following lines to her dear mother:—

Grieve no longer, O my mother,
   Sitting 'mid the shadows dim;
See the Saviour stand beside you,
   Lift your tearful eyes to Him.

He will soothe your every sorrow,
   Hush you in His arms to rest;
None who pillow on His bosom
   Are with cares or fears opprest.

Said you in your hasteful moments,
   He had robbed your happy nest?
Nay, but listen, He will tell you
   All He did was for the best.

Souls were sitting in the darkness,
   Jesus knew a table bright,
Where the lamps so thick were crowded,
   That they killed each other's light.

Well He knew each lamp was valued,
   Well He knew each had its place;
But He yearned o'er homeless wanderers,
   And would have *them* know His grace.

"Lend one lamp," He whispered gently,
   But His voice seemed far away;
Jesus comes in strange disguises,
   And we often say Him "Nay."

Many a heart-beat, many a tremor
   Suffer weak disciples here;
All because the Master's accents
   Are not heard distinct and clear.

"Fear not! It is I who love you;
   Fear not! You to Me are dear;
With My precious blood I bought you
   Shed for you full many a tear."

*   *   *   *   *

"Yes, Lord Jesus! Yes, my Master,
   Thou shalt never ask in vain;
Take my children, keep them for me;
   Thou wilt give them back again."

    *   *   *   *   *

Hark! I hear the Saviour singing—
   Singing 'mid the choirs above:
"She who sparéd not her loved one
   Loves *Me* with her deepest love!"

Before leaving Aberdeen Alexina had four lessons in Marathi from Mrs. Dr. Anderson, Old Aberdeen, and formerly wife of the late Rev. Robert Nesbit, of Bombay, who is described by Mr. Hislop as "the best Marathi scholar and the best preacher in that language in all the Bombay Presidency." These lessons enabled Alexina to study a good deal on board ship, and knowing well that the only way to reach the hearts of the people is through their language, she resolved to master both Marathi and Hindustani; and so quickly did she acquire the former, that her pundit wished her to pass a Government examination in that tongue. She considered the proposal, but declined it, as the class of words needed would not have proved helpful in mission work. Within six months she was able to sing native hymns and to read the Scriptures to the inmates of the zenanas to which she gained access. Generally speaking the female portion of the Hindu community among Marathi-speaking people—even those of the highest caste—are not "in purdah," and enjoy much more freedom than their Bengali and Madrasee sisters, who are very strict—never venturing to shop for themselves, nor being seen in the street, and only allowed out for a drive when carried in a "palky," which resembles an ordinary travelling-trunk, in the floor of which the victim has to sit, squeezed up into as small dimensions as possible; and as there is neither window nor ventilator to the box, there can neither be change of scene nor air.

Marathi-speaking women, however, go freely on the public road for water, or to visit each other; only before their husbands, even in the house, there is a great deal of feigned modesty. On the entry of her lord, the wife rises from her seat and turns away her head!

Hindu homes are very dirty and dusty. Even the ladies' apartments have no appearance of culture, or even of comfort, and are most meagrely furnished. Hideous pictures of gods and goddesses (and there are three hundred and thirty millions of these) adorn the walls, but there are seldom flowers or ferns, or books, or musical instruments, or anything to suggest the presence of the gentle sex. Dogs swarm in the rooms, and hens, chickens, and even crows are allowed to roam unmolested, and perch on the bedsteads or anywhere they choose, as part of the Hindu worship is that beasts and birds are to be fed. The homes of the Mohammedans are equally unattractive, but of course with them "no dogs are admitted!"

In the Royal Zenana of the late Rajah of Nagpoor, there were, at the time of his death, six queens, two of whom sought access to Mrs. Hislop's school in order to escape the persecution and cruel treatment invariably shown to widows in the upper circles. The queen-mother, however, of this zenana was a bigoted Hindu, who daily worshipped and feasted the Brahmans, and drank the water consecrated by their great toes! This was not because she loved them, but the poor heathen believed that unless she honoured them and treated them well, they would not aid her entrance into heaven. This queen-dowager, Baki Bay, expired on Alexina's tenth birthday, and Mr. Hislop thus graphically describes her last hours :—

"Five sacred humped cows were brought into her sick chamber, and to the tail of each successively the woman's hands were applied, the priest meanwhile holding it by the head, and ready to lead it away, together with a handsome donation in rupees. It is believed that the invalid at the moment of death is thus dragged into heaven at the tail of the cow, under the superintendence of the holy Brahman."

On the same day the dying queen "called for a cow, and falling at its feet, as far as her now fast-failing strength would permit, offered it grass, which she invited it to eat under the venerated name of mother!" This may cause a smile, but is there no lesson to be gathered from Baki Bay's anxiety to enter the golden gates? Like all Hindu women she was deplorably ignorant and fond of her religion, and she knew of no other way to the city than

> "By the helplessness that bowed her
> 'Neath cold custom's heartless sway."

There had only been one zenana agent in Nagpoor prior to Alexina's arrival, and as this lady was obliged to return to England at the end of twelve months, through failing health, it was really pioneer work for a long time that Alexina found herself engaged in. The following letters, sent to her family during her first year's service, describe her efforts to disperse the shadows from the hearts of her dusky sisters by telling them—

> "When He findeth as He seeketh
> Access where His love may show,
> How God makes the sweets of heaven
> Out of bitterness below."

AT WORK EARLY.

(To her Sister J——.)

Zenana Mission Bungalow, Nagpoor,
March 23rd, 1878.

I am beginning to feel as if I were in my proper sphere of action. I have got my mornings all filled up now, and really a spirit of interest in my proceedings is being manifested, as well as in some cases great regard for myself. This morning, about six o'clock, when I was seated in an old rickety, wicker-work armchair, placed for me in the courtyard in front of the home of one of my lady pupils, as I was busily engaged reading aloud to the gathered company, the sun was observed to peer inquisitively upon me from behind the trees, and a "bhoy" was sent into the house for a punkah, an ornamental fan, made in this case of paper roses! and the umbrella which I opened to shade myself with was considerately taken from my hand, and given to a servant to hold. Notwithstanding this deference paid to me, however, Rebekah, the girl I had with me as interpreter, remarked to me afterwards that a mat had not been spread for Amundai, the Bible-woman, or herself to sit upon, the bare ground consequently becoming their seat. If the same omission is made next day, I will take notice of it. I did observe the look of disgust which passed over the face of

Lodookai's mother when poor Amundai (an elderly, rather toothless, somewhat cross-looking, but good woman) was about to sit down beside her, on the bedstead she was occupying! This was on account of the difference of caste, I understand. You would be amused at the attempts I make to teach politeness to the women. There seems to be no word synonymous with "Thank you" in Marathi, so, as the utterance of the word "Salaam" is the nearest approach to it, I get them to make use of this form; only one feels amused to see it accompanied by the graceful token of obeisance wedded to it in saluting superiors! It is the same with "If you please," their own substitute for which, when literally translated, means, "Mercy making!" We had an addition to our number of two very respectable-looking young wives, both of whom had been taught to read; but they wish to learn to work. The pleasing thought is that, in coming for this, they will be in the way of receiving Christian instruction, both by listening to the reading, singing, and explanation that precedes the work, and by means of the Christian books put into their hands. Again, at Gujerabai's house we found a nice, working, elderly woman, who had come in from a village fourteen miles off, on business of her own. She had seen Mrs. Cooper there in the course of one of her district visiting tours, and had heard of God ; but she is still very ignorant, although much interested in the subject. I read for her benefit the chapter in the " Peep of Day," beginning " When did God begin to live in heaven?" and every now and then, as I read, she signified her assent audibly. Amundai reasoned with her afterwards on the subject of worshipping idols, and the poor woman was very amenable to instruction, only she explained that because they cannot see God they worship through an image. Of course we tried to meet this from God's Word.

March 24*th.* I have just returned in excellent spirits from my visiting. The encouragement I have had this morning has been very great. There were upwards of twenty gathered in the " long room," the greater part of whom were women, but there were some children, and some four or five of the male sex. One young man had begged a holiday from his heathen schoolmaster, so anxious was he to be present! We read and sang " Jesus of Nazareth," after which I read the chapter in the " Peep of Day " about Jesus being sent into the world to redeem mankind from the consequences of the fall. Then, by the request of one of the women (who can read, and had been looking over the native hymn-book), we sang a hymn entitled, " Mary's Lament." As its title denotes, it treats of the anguish of the mother of Jesus when she saw her Son nailed to the cross. As we proceeded with it I could hear every now and then a little sympathetic moan from one of the mothers. After this we reasoned with them on behalf of the worship of God instead of images, and then we read the introductory chapter of the most valuable "Reading-Book for Females." This chapter speaks of the opinions concerning women-children by the male sex in India, and points out how efforts are being made by Christians to raise their condition. A ready assent is always granted to this statement. Before I left I was asked "if I would eat anything they gave me." I replied that "I would with pleasure." In fact, I had been feeling faint, as I had not eaten anything since getting up. The question was put with an eye to the future, however, for as I was stepping into the bullock-coach it was intimated to me that they were going to make a *feast* for me. I felt much gratified, as you may suppose, only I had to say that it would need to be in the morning, as I could not go out in the heat of the day. They were rather nonplussed on hearing this, but finally declared that they could manage it. Is it not nice to have gained their love?

On leaving this house I was conducted by Amundai to another she had found entrance into, and again I found myself in most interesting circumstances. We were introduced to a homely dyeing establishment, where the male sex predominated, the women hanging diffidently back. Scarcely were we seated ere the goodman of the house (who has three wives) placed on the ground before me a large brass salver, with a sort of egg-stand upon it, containing cardamoms, betel-nuts, etc., from which, before I left, I helped myself to a few. After a little talk we sang a hymn, the burden of which is synonymous with our "Nothing either great or small." It asks, "Why do you go on pilgrimage and wash in holy water?" etc. I asked mine host if he thought it pretty, and he answered in the affirmative, with a pleased expression of face. Next I asked Rebekah to tell them I had been learning their language for a few months, and to ask if they would like to hear me read a little in it. To this a most cordial assent was given, and again I lifted up my voice. I was soon interrupted by the question put by one of the men as to "whether Satan can be seen by us?" "Naku," was the answer, and immediately the questioner made use of the Marathi word for spirit to describe him. My rendering of their language met with a hearty eulogium, and the conviction was expressed that I would soon be able to speak it well. Indeed, they complimented me on doing that already, because I gave fluent utterance to a few stock phrases! A marriage is about to come off in the house, and preparation for this makes them busy; but they are to call for me after it is over, and they assured me of the pleasure my visit had given them.

Last night, as I was preparing to go to bed, having shut the doors of my little bungalow on my two girls and myself, I was startled by an excited knocking at the back-door, and the impatient voices of some of the girls from the orphanage, calling loudly for one of my companions. I asked who were there, and what had happened, and was informed that Virima's mother was dead! She had been in her usual health up to a few minutes before, when she took a fit of coughing, and, complaining that she could not breathe, immediately expired. To-day Mrs. Cooper took me to Virima's home, that I might see the remains put in the coffin; and truly I was never present at such a scene. There was a Roman Catholic Sister there, who gave the most frantic expression to her grief. She expanded her arms over the bed on which the body was lying, and poured out endearing terms, in her own language, with an expression of ecstatic grief, so to speak, on her face. Then she brought down her hands lightly on the body, over and over again, as if embracing it. She even kissed the feet! and, finally, on the removal of the coffin, she ran out after it, presently returning to throw herself on the floor and toss her arms about! It seems, however, that though her grief was most violent, she had not been the best of daughters.

The old husband's grief was very affecting. On taking his last look, and bestowing a farewell kiss, he retired from the side of the coffin, striking such blows on his chest as might well have seriously hurt him, had he been in a less excited state of mind.

Virima was deeply moved, but in a quieter way. Mrs. Cooper appeared in a very good light on the occasion. She improved the opportunity by talking away in Marathi on the subject of death to a visitor, who presented a most interesting spectacle, as she stood, with her tall, erect figure and large, wondering soft eyes, taking in what was being said with the simplicity of a child, and asking questions where she could not understand. She seemed to wonder how one could be in heaven, and yet lying in the grave. *Atma*, the soul, I explained!

And now I have a suggestion to make, and it is this, that M—— should take lessons in Marathi, if possible, from Mrs. Anderson's *protégée*, her pupil! Perhaps, dear mother, you will "grow in grace" so much yet as to let her join me sometime, on a three years' engagement, if the Aberdeen ladies can afford to maintain two agents. She could come out with

Mr. Whitton, and the understanding would be that she would return with me at the end of three years! I am sure she would gain the affections of these women; as I told Mr. Whitton, she is beloved by every creature she comes near! and I and a Higher would take care of her. Don't take fright, dear mother; I have merely dropped a seed-thought. Cover it up and see whereunto it will grow, or if it will grow at all. Even were Miss Duncan to continue an agent, if the work increases as we would like it to do, there will be room for many more hands! Forgive me, dear mother, I am all alone, though I am cheery enough in my *personal* solitude. I know the grief and anxiety I have caused you in the past, and pray, pray for me.

If you had seen me this morning telling the gospel story to an old man, ready to worship the angelic-looking (because white) declarer, you would have felt wonderfully moved! But the story itself seemed to reach his heart. He, to all appearances, believed the things that were said, and declared with enthusiastic simplicity that he would never any more worship idols!

(*To her Brother.*)

SEETABALDI, NAGPOOR,
April 29*th*, 1878.

I got up this morning at 4.30. As Mr. Cooper has made the usual hot-weather change of school hours down in the Institution from eleven o'clock to six, and as Miss Duncan and I both visit in the early morning, and there is only one Zenana Mission conveyance, we will have to avail ourselves of the spare seat in the bullock-coach (a sort of omnibus, and a good protection from the sun) which conveys the three gentlemen, Messrs. Cooper, Whitton, and Clubb; and as each of us needs to be accompanied by one or two native helps, my companion girl will have to sit outside with the driver. We enjoyed our drive to the city under the light of the remaining quarter of the waning moon, and the few stars bearing it company, and alighted in one of the narrow lanes. After some delay caused by the explanations volunteered by some men who were about, to the effect that the female community we had come to see had been up all night at a marriage, and had gone to sleep, Amundai went in to inquire, and came to say that they could see us. Well, in we went to the place set apart for our reception—literally what I call a shed. In the far end was a noisy cock, whose clamour had to be stilled by a basket being thrown over its head; albeit said basket was very mercifully constructed, for it had a large circular hole in the top, large enough to admit of the bird's exit, were he to become very impatient. Then there was a bunch of sugar-cane straw on the floor as another piece of furniture, while saddle-girths or such-like hung on the wall. Nevertheless a wickerwork armchair was provided for me, and another for Amundai, only she preferred to sit on a native seat, exactly like a baking-board, with feet of an inch or two in length, so that Mrs. Gujerabai herself occupied the chair. We had three grown women, all more or less done out with jewelry—the nice-looking one, whose lesson (out of an advanced book, called "Summary of Christian Doctrine") I heard, had a pearl-studded nose-jewel and massive-looking twisted anklets, etc. Then there were two much younger wives, a toddling, perfectly nude little child, and quite a circle of outsiders, mostly men. This does not answer to the picture sketched for us by Mrs. Murray Mitchell, does it? But of course her picture holds good in regard to women occupying a superior position in life, in Calcutta especially. After a little talk we explained and sang a hymn called, "The Way of Salvation"; then, as the women had been telling us that the bride whose marriage they had been at was only a very little girl, and that she had been crying for her mother, I got Amundai to read aloud, from the book purposely written for Indian females, the chapter on the subject of marriage. Of course it points out all the abuses of this institution, etc. Then we each took a pupil, and as the one I had was reading about the creation and the Creator, and our duty to Him as such, I afterwards read it aloud for the benefit of the whole group.

In regard to the Eitwarree women, it was believed that some of them were living immoral lives. All the more need they have of light, don't you think? It seems as if it is to be my lot to go out into the highways and hedges in quest of souls, while Miss Duncan attends to the better class of people! Well, she filled up the breach made by Miss Berrie's departure, while I did not mean to begin active work till I had become in some good measure acquainted with the language. The appeal of the "man of Macedonia," however, made me change my resolve. Said man, I may remark, is showing remarkably little interest in his charge, now that I have consented to visit at his house. It is suspected that he had interested motives in being so active formerly, that he expected to be paid for his trouble in gathering the women; but since no personal good is accruing, his zeal is evaporating. Meantime my services are highly prized by "Sonnabai," my foundling; but, on account of my visiting her, I am forbidden access to the house of a well-to-do neighbour, an educated man, whose wife I had begun to visit. I cannot help this. Indeed, it was only after having turned away three times from his door without having seen his wife, who was ill, that I cast my eyes about for another opening, and got hold of "Sonnabai." If the latter does not give up her evil ways, I don't say that I will go on visiting her; but I will certainly try to let her know that they are evil. Two dear little boys always join the company gathered in her house. They listen eagerly, and crowd quite close to see the fancy-work stitch. One of them had brought Sonnabai on capitally with her letters, in the interval between my two visits. Both boys are attending the school of "Mark," one of the native Christians, and they can read English very nicely. It was delicious to hear their ringing little voices giving such distinct utterance to the English words.

Mr. Browning, who is General Inspector of Government Schools in the Central Provinces, has kindly volunteered to get an introduction for me into a good house he has access to. The head of it is a well-educated man, who can speak English beautifully.

SEETABALDI, NAGPOOR,
May 11*th*, 1878.

MY BELOVED FATHER,—

* * * * *

I am getting into a good deal of work now Amundai, the Bible-woman, hunts up the houses, and then I go forward as general of the party! To-day the gathering at a new house was most interesting. The head of the house is a widow (but not being a Brahman, she is not deprived of her hair, etc., etc.), and one or two other widows came, as well as quite a little assemblage of mothers, with children, and two or three men, one of whom had a beaming smile of satisfaction on his face all the time! "Kurry Gōsht," he kept saying from time to time as the "new doctrine" fell on his ears. He laughed aloud when Amundai pointed out how vain it was to think that though water can cleanse the body it can cleanse the soul from sin—in acquiescence, of course. The husband of one of the widows present had received instruction from the late eminent missionary, Mr. Hislop. There is a road in Nagpoor named after him, and a kind of fossil discovered by him to be seen in the Museum. He was a great geologist.

We have been introduced to one of the grand houses (as things go here) this week as well. The first day I went I enjoyed myself *very* much. We had a splendid opportunity of making known the good news to a large promiscuous gathering of the men, women, and children connected one way or other with the household. One man, the head of the house, I think, seemed perfectly delighted with the hymns. He told me they were "*gord*" (roll the *r*), *i.e. sweet*, to him. Beautiful work in beads was displayed; it was all brought in on a sort of shovel, and formally placed at my feet by a servant! I duly inspected and unfeignedly admired the various knick-knacks; but I find that the young woman who made them (she can read well, too, and I have given her the nice "Book for Females") is rather conceited—she does not appreciate the favours bestowed on her sufficiently. To-day we found them all very busy. A marriage had been on the *tapis*, only of a male servant, however. Very soon, however, the verandah got well peopled by a company of *men*, quite ready to become listeners! Unfortunately we had to ask them to retire, as the women stood shyly peeping out of a doorway, and would not come forward on account of them! After all, we had to proceed, in spite of noise and interruptions, as work had to be done, and one and another ordered away, etc., because they were servants. But we must not regard the clouds or the winds, but continue to labour in season and out of season.

REPORT TO THE HOME COMMITTEE.

Perhaps the most interesting mode of giving in the report of my first year's experience of zenana visiting in Nagpoor will be by asking my friends to accompany me in imagination on my various rounds in the city, taking up each day's work as it comes in connection with the successive days of the week.

To begin with Monday! A pleasant drive along a country road, skirted with trees, and lying at the city end of it, along an extensive, picturesque-looking tank, leads us into the city; and after threading our way through a couple of streets, a lane, and an alley, we reach our first house. On entering the narrow old wooden door leading into the yard, the first thing that meets the eye is a mass of weedy luxuriance, occupying a spot in the yard which might be turned to better account (by our advice something of improvement was effected for the sake of health on the spot in front of the house), while in another corner stands a painted clay model of a sacred bull, in close proximity to which two women are busy grinding the morning's supplies by turning, in conjunction, a round, flat stone, with a handle in the middle, upon a similarly shaped one beneath. "Salaam," we say, and pass on round the house to the outside room we occupy while teaching. Something in the shape of a carpet has been thrown down on the floor, and an old chair, in preparation for the arrival of " Missi Baba," as I am termed ; and, after a few minutes' waiting, we are joined by Sukyabai and her mother, Lodubai, both nice-looking women, and both pupils, the mother having first urged on her daughter to acquire the art of reading, and requesting latterly to be taught herself. Four little girls from the neighbouring houses attend here as well, and listeners often drop in. We begin by singing a hymn, and explaining the meaning of it; and the effect of this opening exercise is wonderful upon those who are present for the first time. Times are surely changed, when we can fearlessly open fire upon a group of heathen men, women, and children, and attempt to storm their prejudices by singing out such words as these: "Why do you toil in vain? Bathing and going on pilgrimage, and all your many ceremonies, will profit you nothing"—the only result being an interchange of looks of pleased surprise, with perhaps an attempt at argument afterwards on the part of some zealous believer in the "Shasters." After we have sung, I am in the habit of reading aloud either a passage from the New Testament, or a portion from some nice tract or adaptation of Scripture; but for the most part I have as yet to hand the explanatory part to

Amundai, the native Bible-woman, who accompanies me, or to employ my young friend from the Orphanage, to convey my thoughts to the listeners. It is not easy for one living among English people to acquire a foreign language conversationally. Still, I do not scruple to make attempts to converse with my native friends, and I may report, for the comfort of my friends, that I am well understood.

On Tuesday we visit in another and very distant quarter of the city, where eight houses are open to us. I cannot overtake all of these in one morning, so I mean to divide the labour and go once a week to each four. In this way we shall be able to spend more time in the various houses, and to get more satisfactory work done, though our visits must be less frequent. In the first of these houses, separated in some cases by considerable distances, live a most respectable Brahman family, father, mother, widowed daughter, and some others, related I don't quite know how. There is another widow, with such a sweet-looking little boy. Besides these, several friends come in from time to time, amongst others a very respectable-looking man, a son of the old Brahman, at the head of the house, who keeps a school next door, and some of his boy-pupils. A very interesting feature of the work in which I am engaged is, that ever and anon opportunities of spreading the good news occur unexpectedly in connection with the comers and goers in the homes we visit; and here I must remark that, so far as I have seen, the women of Nagpoor are not kept in nearly such seclusion as those in other parts of India are. It is true that my work lies at present amongst the humbler class of people, but I remark this even in exceptional cases. Certainly, so much the better. But I must hasten to look in on the other houses. A few yards down the lane we find another open door, but here the " frooshkal kám," *i.e.*, much work of the mother and grandmother, together with the business calls paid to the head of the house, who is a goldsmith, I am told, prevent our doing any very steady work in the way of giving instruction. We persevere in visiting, however, and it was through this house we heard of several others. A little way off lives another Brahman widow, such a happy-looking old woman, in spite of her shorn head. In her house we have four pupils, one of them her little pet, a grandchild, in whose lesson on the alphabet she eagerly joined one day, by way of encouraging the child, who was rather shy. Near this house is another, where a number of showy-looking women assemble, some of whom are avoided by their neighbours on account of the low platform of morality they occupy. I am not supposed to know their private character, however; and, in any case, our religion teaches us to stoop and try to lift up the fallen, and to sow beside all waters.

But it would be tedious to enumerate all the houses visited. I shall therefore take the liberty of asking my friends to content themselves with the glimpse into various homes already given. I have access at present to sixteen houses. In many of these our work is purely evangelistic; but, on adding up the number of those who are learning to read, I find that I have twenty-nine pupils. In consideration of the fact that these numbers represent ground gained since this time last year (with one exception), I think there is good cause for encouragement in the prosecution of the work. Will the friends at home then continue to remember us specially in their prayers, in answer to which already a certain amount of success has been granted?

A. MACKAY.

CHAPTER VII.

CAMPING OUT.

" ' In the highways and hedges go seek for the lost,
Gather them into the fold'—
Was the earnest command that our Saviour Divine
Taught His disciples of old.

Urge them to come, show them the way,
Tenderly, lovingly bring them to-day;
Urge them to come; why should they roam?
Bring them along to our dear Sabbath home."

FROM the report of Alexina's labours during her first year in Nagpoor it will be seen that the greater number of the zenanas, in the common acceptation of the term, were closed against her; but, nothing daunted, she went wherever she could find an open door, believing that God is no respecter of persons, and that the soul of the poor outcast is as precious in His sight as that of the lady clothed in her richly embroidered sarree, and bedecked with jewels from head to feet. She thus gained access not only to the women of the humbler classes, but to hundreds of working men and boys, whom otherwise the gospel story might never have reached. This sort of work found great favour at the late decennial conference at Bombay, and had many advocates. The Rev. James Smith, of Simla, says:—" In my deliberate judgment the higher castes will be reached and converted through the lower, and not through higher education"; and he goes on to tell how the sons of low-caste parents are already competing with rich Brahmans, and acquiring positions of trust and responsibility in both Government and mercantile services.

Sitting on a mud-wall enclosing the courtyard of some gold-filigree worker, or of one who styled himself an artist, but in reality was only a painter of heathen gods! and addressing and singing to the motley group gathered around, Alexina was perfectly happy. She was a thorough evangelist, and embraced every opportunity of speaking for her Master. Going along the road, it mattered not whether she met lepers, strolling beggars, or religious devotees; she engaged in conversation with them, lest they might never have another opportunity of hearing the gospel story. She ever lived in full view of that eternity which lies in the shadowy distance to most people, recalling to mind the words of the sainted Henry Martyn: " Live more with Christ, catch more of His spirit; for the spirit of Christ is the spirit of Missions, and the nearer we get to Him the more intensely missionary we become." Therefore, when Mr. and Mrs. Cooper invited her to join them on their cold season itinerancy in the villages, in the jungle of the Weingunga valley, she gladly accompanied them, and realized the words of the ancient record:—" These were they who dwelt among plants and hedges; there they dwelt with the King for His work."

The real life of the Hindu is seen more in the villages than in the towns, and there also one thoroughly understands the immense hold which idolatry and superstition have on the minds of the natives.

The following letters to her father describe the valuable experience which she obtained on this tour.

THE TENT, PATTON SAONEE,
December 14*th*, 1878.

Yesterday morning saw us make an early start for "the district," before daylight. Mr. Cooper, Timothy and Elisha had set out on foot. Take a peep at us as we turn out of the avenue into the road. In front are Virima and a band of the bigger girls, all looking very comfortable in their bright shawls. Mrs. Cooper and I follow, and the rear is brought up by "the ark," or large coach-like gharree, my tonga, and a Madras cart for the girls. It was a lovely morning, keenly cold, but so clear and bright that all nature looked glad. We passed beautiful fields of "zewaree," a native grain, with stalks resembling that leafy reed always to be seen in the picture of Moses and the ark of bulrushes! Each head of corn resembles in massiveness a bunch of the lilac flower, only that this is grain, not blossom; and when ripe, it bends over the stem, like a matured but humble Christian nearing his end. To protect these fields men are stationed here and there in little boat-like structures, elevated several yards above the ground by means of long supporting poles, and reached by ladders. Farther on were fields of tobacco and cotton plants, and a species of oil-plant, with delicate green leaves and a tiny blue blossom, which I much admired. Milestone after milestone we passed, as we journeyed on, and still we did not seem to near our purposed place of encampment; for instead of eight miles it turned out to be fourteen, as our pedestrians found to their cost. When we did draw up, hard by a fine grove of large mango trees, there lay poor Mr. Cooper, not indeed like a stranded wreck, but his bronzed countenance suggesting the possibility that he felt footsore and weary. He looked more like a well-seasoned East India coffee planter, however, in his buff corduroys, stout shoes and ample headpiece (large brimmed sun topee or pith-hat, covered with grey muslin), than a way-worn missionary. It was good to see that he could comfort himself over a twist of the "Indian weed" in the absence of the luggage carts conveying our victuals, for they had fallen behind. When they did come up, it was most interesting to watch the lively scene that followed. Two or three groups busied themselves over getting ready the morning meal. The others, with all haste, got out the tent-gear, and set to work erecting the same into these wonderful patriarchal tenements, so suggestive of olden times. First, the stakes on which the cords were to be fastened had to be driven into the ground. Just before being reared, the tent looks like a folded umbrella, but by a long pull, a strong pull, and a pull all together, it is gradually induced to expand itself generously for the accommodation of the houseless ones seeking its shelter. I have a little Noah's Ark-like tent for myself, by way of a bedroom—a little pet it is, with its quaint brown canvas walls, figured with a perpendicular coral-like pattern. I cannot say I spent a very comfortable night in it, however, for do what I might, I could not get warm.

In the afternoon we all set out for the neighbouring village to do a little evangelistic work. Mr.

Cooper and his assistants went by themselves, to minister to the men, while Mrs. Cooper and the rest of us went to seek out the women. I had fallen behind with one or two of the girls, and this led to our ultimate separation from the rest of the party, as a woman beckoned me to speak to her, and we soon found ourselves surrounded by a group of her neighbours, along with herself, to whom we sang and told the gospel story. Passing on in search of Mrs. Cooper, but not finding her, we again gathered a group around us, and did what we could amongst them. This morning I wandered into the city, and not knowing in which direction to turn, I was looking about me, when I discovered Mr. Cooper surrounded by a little band, to whom Timothy was preaching. I quietly joined them, and was greatly pleased to have an opportunity of hearing this good young man address his fellow countrymen in their own tongue. I felt quite touched when he told them that he was just a simple man like themselves until he became a Christian, thirteen years ago, and how he became so happy by believing in Jesus—his sunlit countenance and mild expression giving beautiful emphasis to his words. One man, sitting just before him, kept up a kind of thinking aloud conversation with his instructor, asking for fuller information on this and that point, giving his whole attention to the things being told him. He came to the tent afterwards to get a little book, that he might instruct himself more fully, as he could read.

RAM TEAK,
December 17*th.*

We have made two other marches since I wrote the above. We stayed over Sunday at the first place, Patton Saonee, going into the town every day to hold meetings, and getting access to really a great many. On Sunday afternoon I asked Mrs. Cooper to let me have Virima (the Biblewoman) with me, as well as my usual quota of the girls to help with the singing, and she was quite agreeable. In passing up the street we were called by a woman (beside whose house we had taken our stand, or rather our seat on the little mud wall of the courtyard, on two previous occasions). She wanted to hear us again, as she had "forgotten what we had told her the day before!" Poor woman, the "certain strange things" brought to her ears had not been sufficiently grasped by her. She was a woman in very humble circumstances, trying to spin cotton, though her arms and hands were sadly deformed and shrunken! A good many neighbours gathered round, and we had a nice little meeting, which was brought to a close by our telling them that we must go farther up the street and tell others what we had been telling them. Where were we to locate ourselves next? was the question. It is really like drawing a bow at a venture, this walking along through the streets of a strange town, looking about to see where we can get an opening. I suggested our seeking permission to sit down on the ledge of a nice clean courtyard near the Bazaar, in which hundreds of people were congregated, engaged in buying and selling. Virima said that if we sat there we would be surrounded by a number of men, but I didn't think that was any objection; so there we located ourselves, and by-and-by were engaged in ministering the gospel to a large concourse of people—men, women and children—the first class largely predominating. I was pleased to recognise one earnest-looking young man, who had been with us in another place in the morning. He pushed his way through the crowd, and stationed himself in the front row, listened with marked attention, and asked questions with a view to his better understanding the things spoken. In the next village we went to, I again chose for our site the threshold of a house very near the teeming bazaar. The women in the verandah we made up to were engaged in spinning cotton, and they began to make excuses when asked to allow us to sit down beside them, saying, "they could not understand," etc. We still urged our plea, however, telling them that all we wanted was a seat on their doorstep, that they need not listen unless they liked, but others might wish to hear! We were backed up by some men standing near, who said to us, "Bei-ta!" "Bei-ta!" *i.e.* Sit, sit; and so we did, and began to sing one of our hymns, the signal, as you may suppose, for the motley gathering we succeeded in surrounding ourselves by! And we had, indeed, a satisfactory meeting. Of course my white face was the grand primary attraction. The gloaming had set in before we rose to go, and the babel that sprang up on my announcing that I would give a book or two to any amongst them who could read, made us fain to tear ourselves away after distributing some to those who came forward first.

We are finding wonderful opportunities, too, at Ram Teak, though it is quite a Brahman seat. Yesterday, on visiting the lovely temple built on one of the picturesque wooded heights in the neighbourhood, to reach which 480 steps had to be climbed, we saw a god, in the shape of an enormous hog, under the belly of which the worshippers pass, in order to leave their sins behind them! It seems that stout Brahmans have such difficulty in doing this, that they have either to pay handsomely for assistance, or provide themselves with substitutes. The very fat ones are thought to be the greatest sinners.

Good Timothy intercepted a few of the worshippers, as they passed along with their garlands of flowers, and preached Christ to them. I entered into conversation myself with a nice-looking man at the head of the long stair, gave him a little book, and proceeded to read a few sentences to him from another, in answer to his objections; but after he had listened for a few minutes, he said he "would need to go and do his Pujah (worship), or he would be too late!" He promised, however, to read the little book at home. Don't think, however, that all are equally docile. One conceited young Brahman quite contradicted the contents of a little book I set him to read aloud last night, affirming that "to drink the water in which the feet of a Brahman had been washed does purify the soul!" etc., etc. At the same time a friend by his side looked all attentive and receptive.

Our next march is on to Bandhara. We will have to break it into at least three days' journeys. I like camp life very much. The taking down the tents in the early morning, pursuing our way in the twilight, on foot, in the clear cool air, the conveyances following; then emerging into a new landscape with the dawn of day; the fording of bridgeless rivers, the re-erection of the tents; the preparation of breakfast in the open air, gipsy fashion, the partaking the meal under a tree, etc., etc., all have a charm for me.

Had I only faith and love in *large measure*, I could "rejoice in the Lord."

The day before the last of the old year, *i.e.* December 30*th*, 1878.

Mr. and Mrs. Cooper's tent, pitched beside a few trees on the roadside, on the outskirts of a small village whose name I don't remember!

We are a little beyond Bandhara, which you will find in a map of India. It will be marked as situated near the Weingunga River, which we crossed to-day. I must tell you in what circumstances your letter found me, for they were novel enough! Well, you must know that we were spending a few days at a place called D'Orabella's Village, away from the haunts of men, in a retired nook in the "jungle," shut in from the outer world by lovely hills covered with " bush," much of which bore a tassel of honey-scented blossom, on a background of small white leaves, which lit up the green shrub very prettily. The owner of this village is a quiet, worthy man, a native Christian, who dresses, however, like a European. He taught in the Mission School in Nagpoor, in Mr. Hislop's time, but he has since taken to farming. He was very anxious that Mr. Cooper should visit him and his family in their retirement, especially as he had a little grandchild to be baptised, and his wife's brother wished to make a profession of his faith in

Christ at the same time. Well, this simple-minded, unpretending man treated our whole company with the courtesy and munificence of a king. He and his wife knew that they could not entertain Mr. and Mrs. Cooper and myself comfortably at their own place, consisting of huge shed-like enclosures for his numerous family; so they sent bountiful provision down to our tents for us. We were there over Sunday, and Mr. Cooper had two services, held under the shade of a thatched canopy, supported on wooden poles all round, the walls being of ether, and the poles merely acting as props to the roof. In the morning the baptisms were performed in presence of a good many of the unreclaimed natives, who had come together to see what was going on. These were addressed afterwards by Timothy, in Marathi, and the sight of one man seated on the ground, just in front of the speaker, his face softened into the heavenly beauty begotten of believing adoration, affected me considerably, together with the beautiful statement of the gospel story being made by Timothy, who gets quite enthusiastic as he narrates instance after instance of the power put forth by Jesus while on earth. The old man looked quite "drunk up" with what he was hearing, as he sat slowly moving his head in rapt contemplation. I thought how such a sight would affect dear —— who covets the possession of such a simple faith.

CHAPTER VIII.

IN AND OUT OF THE ZENANAS.

" Rise and lift the yoke that earth-power
Lays upon weak woman's neck,
And with wreath of regal vantage
Womanhood's meek brow bedeck."

AS time went on Alexina was admitted into Brahman and other superior homes, and her work continued to advance with many tokens of encouragement. Sometimes she found the husbands greatly averse to their wives being taught the true religion, but her bright winning manner generally overcame their prejudices. She says:—"The following is the copy of a letter (in pencil) put into my hand by the husband of a woman I was visiting in the city the other day:

"'MY DEAR MADAM,—

"'I hope you will excuse me to express my opinion in regards teaching of our women. I am strictly of opinion that no books or sermons on matters adverse to the religion in which the learner is brought up should be taught or preached, unless and until they have acquired sufficient strength of mind not to be led away by the superficial light. This strength, I perceive, cannot be obtained unless they advance in their study. For the present, I think you will kindly stick to rudimentary teachings and needlework, and such other fine things which are essential to a family woman.

"'Yours faithfully,
"'NILKANTTKAO.'

"'My reply, written there and then:—

"'MY DEAR FRIEND,—

"'I am very sorry to find that your mind is so prejudiced against the religion of Jesus Christ, the Saviour of the world. I cannot consent to keep silence on this all-important subject, on the occasion of my visits to your house. I suppose I must, therefore, discontinue my visits till your *own* mind becomes enlightened.

"'Sincerely yours, etc.,
"'A. MACKAY.'

"I was not allowed by the wife to leave the compound till I had an interview with her husband, in his private office, surrounded, as he was, by a number of business friends! I found him a most pleasant man, and we had a long talk on the subject in hand. As he had been educated in the city or Government School, he had read a little of the Bible, so I am going to give him one. That day I gave him two Gospels in Marathi to begin with, and he promised to study them."

After a little time Alexina was asked to return to this man's house, as his wife missed her visits so much.

It is most difficult to get Hindus to comprehend the meaning of sin. They never ask their gods to take away their sins. When they offer their idols flowers and fruit, grain, or even animals, these are as *presents*, not in the sense of sacrifice for sin. The picture of heaven as a holy place is unintelligible to the dark minds of the women; but when told that there "God shall wipe away all tears from their eyes; and there shall be no more death, neither sorrow, nor crying, neither shall there be any more pain," then rapt attention is at once gained.

Gospel stories and the parables are particularly suited to their modes of thought, but nothing so commends itself to them as sacred song. Mr. C. E. Chapman (late of the Indian Civil Service), in an address at the discussion on the Missionary in Relation to Literature, in connection with the Centenary

Conference on Protestant Missions, says:—" Let me also remind you how important a part hymnology must play—how important it is to take the native lute and to train up men who go into the villages with their lutes to sing the gospel. We want the gospel sung in such a way that every native, high or low, shall listen to it—not to go in a stilted form, just as a preacher will preach infinitely above the heads of his audience, but to go right down and take their modes of thought, and communicate to them. We want to get down to the masses, to their everyday life, and if we can, to saturate that with the blessed principles of the gospel of Christ." The Rev. John Hesse (Calw, Würtemberg) also says:— " As to adapting our methods to the native taste— singing the gospel, I once came to the great city of Tanjore, and there I saw a fine building, half Oriental and half European in style. I was told it was the house of a native Christian singer and poet, a member of the Lutheran Leipzig Missionary Church in India. This man and his whole family were given to singing the gospel. They had evening meetings, chiefly during Passion Week, and the natives used to flock in and hear the whole story of the Passion of Christ, by singing."

Regarding this subject, Alexina writes:—" Two incidents I may mention. One was my being promised *a pice* (a copper coin, less than $\frac{1}{2}d.$ in value), if I would sing a hymn to a crowd of people gathered in and around the verandah of a house we had just passed, towards which I had been looking with longing eyes, feeling as if I should make up to it. Of course the strolling native singers and the Gurus, too, are paid for their services!

"'Without money, and without price' has, on more than one occasion, been a recommendation of our message! We had such a delightful time amongst these people. One old blind man, sitting beside me, had a long story to tell me, in the course of which he was checked by his neighbour, who wished to hear the end of my story about why I had left my own land, etc. The blind man said that he had heard me sing somewhere else, and had been longing to hear me again!

"The second incident is, that as we were leaving this house, a woman came up and regretted that she had heard nothing. I said I would go to her house if she would lead the way, and presently, hemmed in by a mob which accompanied us, we found ourselves in a beautifully clean outer room, facing the street, into which we were welcomed by a devout-looking old man, who proceeded to pay us homage, as if we had been goddesses! I had repeatedly to check him, and tell him not to worship me! He said, 'Is not God in you?' 'No,' I replied, perceiving the fallacy underlying his question, for he would have invested a consecrated stone with the same honours, 'but God is near me. He is present with us, but Satan is in the hearts of some people in the sense that God is in the hearts of others.' I don't remember particularly the order of my remarks. Suffice it to say that in return for the tender veneration in which I was held by this saintly-looking old man, I tried to enlighten his mind in some measure, while in his company, and left an instructive little book with him, as he could read. Do not think that I am well pleased with myself, and self-satisfied, as I narrate these incidents. My imagination is pleased, but oh, the heart knoweth its own bitterness—and I am often 'ready to halt.' What sweet, choice passages those were father sent me for my birthday! The first: 'Be careful for nothing,' etc., seems to be dear Mr. Cooper's life motto; he so often quotes it in prayer."

May 1st, 1879.

SOME MORE OF MY EXPERIENCES IN THE CITY.

The other day, on entering the large Brahman house I have often spoken of, we found it the scene of an unusual amount of business. We were asked to go upstairs, however, and, on getting seated, I soon discovered what was going on.

In the lower verandah a couple of little boys were seated, tailor-fashion, on a pair of square wooden footstools, being taught their prayers, etc., by an old Brahman! They had newly been invested with the Brahminical thread, which thread they must prove themselves worthy of! The little fellows were quite devoid of clothing, only their bodies were stained yellow all over with saffron, and their foreheads painted red, and ornamented with a white pattern laid upon the background. Their heads were shaved, too, all save the crown-lock, I suppose. If you could only have seen the farce their teacher was putting them through! Let me try to describe it. Before them are arranged several brazen vessels, some of them containing clean water, which the little novices are directed to ladle out into the left hand, which has immediately to be waved round the head, and applied to the forehead and ear in quick succession. After this the hands have to be quickly clapped together, and the body whirled quickly round. These ceremonies concluded, a number of "muntras" have to be uttered, etc., etc.

The old Brahman teaching the little boys resembled an old experienced nurse, who might be excused taking liberties with her dull children, rather than a sacred teacher; for, not only would he indulge in a self-satisfied laugh in connection with a mistake made, but he would firmly shake into obedience the uninitiated little hand of the younger boy.

But, apart from the grotesqueness of the sight, it was a sad one, and I tried to tell the older boys who were looking on from the upper verandah, along with myself, how valueless, in the sight of God, all such external ceremonies are.

In a little while, a highly respectable English-speaking young man came upstairs (we had been asked to forego our instructions for once, and look at what was going on), and entered into conversation with me. I shall describe part of our conversation:—

Indian youth—" How long have you been in this country ?"

" For about eighteen months, now."

" I suppose you are in employment ?"

" How do you mean? Yes, I go from house to house to instruct the women."

" Yes, I know. You are a missionary, are you not ?"

" Yes."

" You are not married, I suppose ?"

" No. In our country we don't marry until we are quite grown up, and sometimes not at all."

"What is your age? I suppose you are about sixteen or seventeen?"

(Aside.) (Oh, I did feel this rich!)

"Well, I am not in the habit of telling my age. I will keep that to myself, if you have no objection."

"Oh, I have no objection. Do you belong to the Unitarian or the Trinitarian party?"

"Oh, the Trinitarian; but we don't call ourselves by that name. The Unitarians don't hold right doctrine."

(The doctrine of the Trinity was a great mystery to him. I told him no human mind could understand it, that the finite mind could not grasp the Infinite, and told him the story of the gentleman who used the simple illustration to a friend of the clover-leaf, which, though divided into three, is still one.) Then, he could not get himself to believe, he said, that a merciful God would punish the innocent, in the person of His own Son, for the guilty. Why could He not have forgiven man without this? I told him that God could not lay aside His *justice*, and pointed out to him that Jesus *willingly* offered Himself in our room. The question of original sin, too, he took up. He told me they believe that we inherit no sin, and that if we act according to conscience, we will be saved. I asked him what he made of the fact that little children, before they know right from wrong, give way to angry passions, striking their own mothers when they are crossed? He replied that they were not responsible at that age, but he couldn't deny that it proved that sin was in them. As to acting according to the light of conscience, I told him that since sin came into the world, our consciences had become darkened, referring him (for he was educated in the Mission School) to the persecution of the Christians conscientiously carried on by Saul of Tarsus, etc.

Then he asked me what came of all the people who lived in the world *before* Jesus Christ came. In reply, I told him that as soon as man fell, God intimated the coming of a Saviour, and appointed sacrifices as a symbol of the Great Sacrifice that would one day be offered, and that all who believingly looked forward to the coming Saviour were saved. After this and much more had passed between us, I told him I did not think he should ask any more questions to unsettle his mind, adding, that I would like to make one remark in closing our conversation, namely, that the religion of Jesus Christ taught men to care for the salvation of *others*, whereas they were content to be saved themselves! To this he replied: "No. If I had been able to instruct in our religion from the *beginning*,. I think I would have got you to believe it ; but you have grown up in the Christian belief." I asked him if he did not himself think it a great delusion to teach the two little boys to depend for salvation on the absurd outward ceremonies they were being initiated into, seeing that God, who is a Spirit, looks to the heart! He said these ceremonies were not necessary, and that many additions had been made to their religion—that it was originally much purer. To this I replied: "Well, do you not see that whatever has its origin in man gets into a more and more corrupted state?"

We parted very good friends. I showed him my likenesses, and offered him any book he might fancy out of my bag. He wished for an English book, however. He said it was no matter on what subject it was, and I mean to give him a copy of "The Pilgrim's Progress." He occupies a very good position, under Government, in a neighbouring town. Mr. Cooper says he used to be very well behaved and a good scholar when at school, and it seems he once showed the mission party great kindness when they were out on tour, if I mistake not. He told me he liked very much to have a conversation on religious subjects, and that there was no one he could speak with where he is settled. I assured him I was very glad we had met. The book is to be sent to him through his mother or wife, who lives in Nagpoor (the latter is only betrothed, as yet, I understand), and is about to visit him. I hope God will bless it to him.

(*To her Sister M.*)
ZENANA MISSION BUNGALOW, NAGPOOR.
July 9th, 1879.

I have just bid good-bye to a native woman I brought up with me, along with her little girl, from the city, that they might see my bungalow!—Motyabai, whose name you may remember, and Laonybai. Motyabai had long promised herself this treat, but her husband's gharree is not always at her command, as it is required away at a village owned by him; therefore Cheenie and I gave her a seat in our own. She was greatly pleased with everything she saw. First, I brought her in with me to Mrs. Cooper's attractive-looking bungalow, asking her and the little girl to sit on a couch and look about them for a little, while I ate my breakfast. (Of course, to have partaken with me would have been fairly to break their caste, though their prejudices are greatly broken down.) I may mention that, true to the Eastern fashion, my friend didn't come empty-handed, but brought with her a few mangoes, and a small wicker-work basket, full of "meetáe," native sweetmeat, as an offering, to be shared by Mrs. Cooper and myself. I showed her, as the first curiosity, a piece of loaf (*dooble rotee*) as they call it, then the wheat porridge I was breakfasting off (called by her, *gungee*). Meantime, Mrs. Cooper had come in to speak to my visitors, who had the politeness of feeling to stand when she entered! Mrs. Cooper graciously received the abovementioned offerings, much as a queen might do, she, the stout lady, sitting, quite at home, on a chair, while her courtiers, a pair of timid, barefooted native women, approached, offering them to her in a couple of plates, hastily removed from the breakfast-table for the purpose! Then Mrs. Cooper gratified their curiosity by taking them into her bedroom, the study, etc., all the time speaking away to them in their own language (according to her rendering of it) in just those cheerful, re-assuring tones you use when engaged in conversation with little children, to whom the uneducated natives bear a striking likeness in their simplicity. After this they were taken out to the schoolroom, to see the children in their nice building, and hear them sing a hymn, and then I ushered them into my little mansion, and showed them everything, letting them peep into my chest of drawers, etc., with a view both of entertaining them and developing their intelligence. Afterwards I played to them on Mrs. Cooper's beautiful harmonium, time still being on our hand (for we had to wait for the return of Ram Chunee, my gharree-man, to drive them back to the city, when it would be time for Miss Duncan to go on her rounds).

I trust I am really on the fair way to speak Marathi now, for I got on unaided with Motyabai, during that hour or two, wonderfully well, and I do launch out at some length every now and then, in the city, in the hearing of a considerable company! Of course I have always one of the girls at my elbow, upon whom I can fall back, when I am in want of a word. I was quite pleased, one day, lately, to overhear an active-looking, elderly Brahman, who took his seat in the midst of a company gathered round us, remarking, with pleased astonishment, that I was reading just like one of themselves! I do not feel at all proud of my acquirements in connection with the language, but I am glad to be assured that my pronunçiation is pure, and my utterance distinct, and therefore intelligible.

I have had such a nice little experience, lately, in connection with a house I asked leave to enter! The lad coming out of the gate, to whom I addressed myself, was willing enough, but the few people sitting in the verandah did not understand what I could have to say to them! Not easily overcome, however, we maintained the footing we had got, offering to sing a hymn, and presently quite a little gathering took place, amongst which was one intelligent boy, who attends our Free Church Institution. His little sister, with such a superior little Brahman face, was there, too, and we secured her as a reading pupil. She had begun to learn with me, as I recognised, in a neighbouring house, but had been withdrawn almost immediately. The other day, yesterday, on calling there, we found that the morning meal was going on, a ceremony neither to be disturbed nor hastened, being considered a religious act (a lesson to us). A messenger who had been despatched from another house entered the yard, just on our arrival, however, and asked us to follow him, which we did, anon finding ourselves the centre of attraction in a large company gathered in a roomy verandah! I immediately recognised my friend, the Brahman school-boy, whose home this was, not the other house, and around him were the various members of a most respectable household, besides some Brahman boys from an adjoining house. The father, whose portly figure I caught sight of as he stood, taking his bath in a small adjoining room, the door of which was wide open, called out quite frankly: "Salaam! salaam!" making some of the others laugh by doing so in the circumstances;

for, of course, except that he had on a kind of "bathing pants," he was devoid of any other encumbrance. I used to wish to turn up this lane, fancying from the buzz of voices there must be a school there, or, at least, a gathering of some kind! We sang, and I read a capital chapter from "The Summary of Scripture Doctrine," arguing with the listeners on the subject of idolatry, as best I could, afterwards, and no one opposed us. Then the little girl got her lesson. Her brother had been helping her, so that she did remarkably well. She is to get a "dollie" when she can read. "Gungubai" is her name.

(*To Mrs. Colonel Young.*)

NAGPOOR,

July 18*th*, 1879.

I have been very much cheered in connection with my visiting, within the past few days, so that I feel inclined to tell you a little about my experiences.

Some time ago you may remember that we made bold to go up to a Native School, which was held in a large verandah facing the street, in hope of securing some openings through the influence of the master, or, at least, of being allowed to sing a hymn or two to the assembled children (all boys, of course). Well, we were allowed to sing, but, although we paid a second visit soon after, to inquire as to the result of the intimation made to the children of our readiness to visit their homes, we had no encouragement given us, as no one wished to learn!

On a subsequent day, however, we heard that a woman living in an upper storey of the building was very anxious to see us. This was good news, and we soon presented ourselves in the large verandah, from which the school had adjourned somewhere else, to inquire after her. We got rather a rough reception, however, from an old Brahman, who had lain down to sleep there. He told us we "had no concern with them, indeed," so that we had to withdraw, concluding that the poor woman who wished to see us must have her difficulties in getting her desire gratified. On hearing that it was still her wish that we should call, we returned on another day, but though not repulsed as before, we had again to retire, as a feast was being given to a company of Brahmans within!

Well, once again, a few days ago, we had a direct call from the woman herself, as we were passing, and soon we were surrounded, not only by a little company of women with such kindly faces, in the centre of which was our own special friend, in the shape of a Brahman widow; but a large gathering from outside, consisting of men, youths and children, grouped round us, and listened very quietly to some of the most stirring hymns selected by us, as well as to a plain statement I read to them from a little book, concerning the true way of salvation.

As we were taking leave of this company, several of the women from other houses urged us to visit their homes too, which we were only too glad to do, finding new opportunities in the circle of friends connected with each.

The young native teacher of another school to which we introduced ourselves came up to our gharree the other day, and asked us to visit his mother-in-law (Sassoo), sending a boy along with us to show the way. Here we had a capital opportunity, a number of women crowding in, while several men and boys seated themselves in the little courtyard. The teacher himself joined us, and graciously granted permission to his shy-looking wife to learn to read, along with another member of the company, who had consented to become a pupil.

Several wished to be taught to make topees, but our general rule is that reading (in its preliminary stage) must be acquired first. We make an exception in the case of elderly women and Mussulmanees, who do not always care to learn to read Marathi, Hindustani being their language. I hope, if spared, to acquire this second very important language after I have got a better hold of Marathi.

While sitting in a certain house one morning, about to begin our first hymn, a young minstrel, a religious beggar of some sort, appeared in the yard. He had a tambourine, or some such musical instrument, in his hand, and we allowed him to treat us to one of his songs, afterwards asking him to listen to us. He had been singing about one of their heroes, Sukaram by name, as he informed me. I told him our song was about the true God, who filled heaven and earth, and had created us and everything. When we had finished singing, he asked us for a hymn-book. Now these hymn-books cost four annas, *i.e.* about 6*d.*, and on ordinary occasions we insist on the payment of this small sum, if the person soliciting it seems to be in comfortable circumstances, otherwise there would be no end to our gratuities. In this case, however, in consideration that the young man in question could read (in itself a rare accomplishment) and moreover, that he made his living by song-singing, and might himself unconsciously become a propagator of the true religion if he took to singing our hymns, or even carrying them about with him, I made one over to him, as well as the little First Book, containing so much Christian instruction. Meeting him since at another house, I was able to give him a little book written by one of our missionaries, containing the history of *his* hero, Sukaram! We frequently invite these strolling musical or other mendicants to sit down and listen to a hymn, when they call at the houses we are visiting, and some of them are really attentive, intelligent and interesting-looking, living, as they do, a simple, dependent life, in conscientious conformity with the manner of life of their forefathers. Their stated visits to their neighbours are taken as a matter of course—the handful of grain being at once brought out and bestowed as well as received in silence!

We began to visit such an interesting little household, lately, consisting of the head of the house, a most respectable man, his delicate wife, and two fine boys, who attend our Free Church Institution. The father is, I think, the most interested listener. He seats himself quite docilely in our midst, his little family round him, just like some decent Scotchman at a "Diet of Catechising," acquiescing in every statement made, and even supplementing a little from his own conviction of what is the truth. The house this man lives in is not at all like a native's. It resembles rather one of these small, box-like observatories, occupied by the pointsmen on the "line," and is so clean and well-lighted. The room we generally sit in is reached from without by means of a narrow stair along the wall. Our friend learned his business—that of a scientific mechanic, in

Bombay, and one day, after having bestowed the most lovely wreaths of fresh red roses upon us, together with a large parcel of native sweets, wrapped up, according to custom, in withered leaves, we were treated in his little garden to a rather entertaining sight, namely, the action of a jet of water made to play, fountain-like, by means of machinery constructed by himself, upon a metal ball thrown into the centre of the little net-work contrivance. The water was utilised as well, for a bed of healthy-looking cresses lay at the bottom of the fountain, and got nicely watered while we were being entertained.

It was rather amusing to discover that Mr. Douglas, whose gharree we had shared, had found his way to the house of our native friends in quest of us, as we were being detained longer than usual! Of course his appearance in our midst, or rather the news that he was approaching, was a signal for the mother to beat a hasty retreat to the house! She looked out upon us from the window, however—a grated opening, it must have been—and seemed to enjoy seeing the sahib, to whom Amundibai immediately transferred her wreath of roses. The funniest custom is the presenting one with a tiny piece of wadding at the end of a splinter of wood, dipped in sandal-wood oil, that you may squeeze out the contents and anoint yourself therewith. If you feel reluctant to do this, the kind hands of your hostess soon perform upon you instead! I was urged to transfer the little scented sponge to my ear (the upper part of it) by one friend, but I preferred lodging it in my handkerchief.

Visitors of the male sex frequently come to see my bungalow! One day six men honoured me with a visit, simultaneously. I knew one of them, as we visit his wife. After we had conversed for a little, the request for a hymn was proffered, and it was suggested that the young friend from the Orphanage, who usually accompanies me to the city, should be sent for to help me! Accordingly my friend himself stepped over the way to ask Dnyanapoo to come, and soon we were doing our best to entertain and edify our friends. To gratify curiosity I had to favour them with one or two specimens in English as well! I do so like to come across the school-boys in the city, and we are often sought out by them, and even followed here and there. They are intelligent, and can read.

Yours affectionately,
ALEXINA MACKAY.

(*To a Young Friend.*)

ZENANA MISSION BUNGALOW, NAGPOOR,
January 18*th*, 1879.

Thank you very much for your loving and lovely gifts, so unexpectedly discovered in the heart of my home parcel. It was delicious to find myself all at once surrounded by such a dear little family of pussies and doggies, and to feel that somebody, all unknown to me, had been thinking so kindly of me.

I would like to tell you about the marriage of a native Christian here, at which I was present the other day. The bridegroom was Elisha, who teaches in Mrs. Cooper's Orphanage, and his bride's name was Martha. She seemed quite pleased to become his third wife, for two former wives have died! After the usual admonitions were given, and the marriage knot tied, the little bride's-maids hurried forward, laden with long wreaths of white jessamine-like flowers, and presently all the principal people in the room looked quite grand. Then a tray of "*pán*" (that funny roll of leaves from the betel-nut tree, with spices inside) was handed round, and afterwards a bottle of perfume was freely lavished upon us. While this was going on, Virima, the matron of the Orphanage, assisted by some of the girls, sang some lively sacred songs, suitable for the occasion, and after a good deal of shaking of hands, etc., we dispersed. I daresay there would be a supper given in the bride's house in the evening, but the guests would feel more at home without us, as we could hardly manage to sit and eat in their way.

Some of the women I visit in the city have been extra kind to me just now, because they are glad to see me back from the district. In one house a tray full of strange-looking fancy cakes of their own making, as well as a good deal of fruit, was presented to me. How to carry it home I didn't know, but the difficulty was soon got over by a mantle being brought out—a large cloth or kapura, as they call it—which had evidently been worn by some one! Into this the fruit was unceremoniously turned, and duly stowed away in our gharree. The native children in the Orphanage thought it very good, I have no doubt, for I made most of it over to them.

I greatly amused some of my friends this morning by trying to turn the large, heavy upper mill-stone, at which two of them were engaged grinding wheat. They called out that I could never manage it, but I did make at least one round, by dint of a great deal of effort.

Yesterday such a nice little boy led the way for us to his home, where we found his mother and some other friends waiting for us. Almost immediately a wreath of splendid roses was thrown round my neck, and this the month of January, remember! and the usual refreshment of betel-nut offered, after which we sang and explained a nice hymn. A little baby of a month old was shown to us. The mother wishes to be taught to read and make topees soon. The boy is very anxious to learn English, but his father will not pay the school fees. He is a selfish man, and spends the money on himself. The grandfather was an educated man ; he taught in a school founded by a famous missionary, now dead, a Mr. Hislop. He almost made up his mind to profess Christianity. I do hope the way will be opened up for my little friend, for he has a very interesting face, and I would like him to become a good man, and to preach to his countrymen. I would give something for his schooling myself, but Mr. Cooper says the fees are so small that any one anxious can meet them, and those who are educated for nothing do not prize their privileges. We'll see! He can read Marathi very well. I gave him a religious little book one day ; I hope it will be blessed to him.

Good-bye, dear,

Your loving friend,
ALEXINA MACKAY.

(*To her Father.*)

MY LITTLE BUNGALOW,
September 3*rd*, 1879.

I have had my heart cheered to-day by the kindness shown me in a Mohammedan house which it used to be a trial to visit, on account of its dirt and disorder. I was invited to *a feast* there! and I felt it right to accept of the invitation. Well, Karoona and I, on our arrival, went through the usual lessons and instruction, though the cold part of our collation was already spread for us on a wooden *couch* covered with a clean duster-like cloth! I made the pleasing discovery meanwhile, that several nice-looking young women amongst them could read fluently in Urdu (though of course not in Marathi) from a Gospel I had brought in my bag in that character; and as I had also taken a copy of the New Testament in the Roman character with me, we were able to follow each other wonderfully well! Another pleasant experience I had when a hymn (wholly unintelligible to me, because in Hindustani, not Marathi) brought tears into the eyes of a stout woman amongst the listeners, who had been trying to show me that the Koran is the revelation to *them* as the Bible is to us! I begin to reap the firstfruits of persevering in visiting all who call me, be their language what it may, and their motive what it may, in inviting me. My impressions on this head were a little shaken on discovering how certain others had resolved to stick to Marathi-speaking people, with a view to doing more efficient work, and also (which does not commend itself to me) with a view to keep oneself in pure Marathi; but the bright idea occurred to me lately, that I could order copies of Gospels in all the different lauguages spoken around us, and use *them* in exceptional circumstances. In carrying out this idea I have been able to give Gospels in Gujerathi to the Parsees while teaching them English, in Telugu and Tamil to the Madrasees, and so on, in this way meeting the exigency in some measure, and having an opportunity of "holding forth the word of life" to the very mixed population in this centre of the Central Provinces!

The other day I found that in a round of visiting, Dnyanapoo and I had been using as mediums six different languages, viz., Marathi, Hindustani, Bengali, Telugu, Tamil, and English! Dnyanapoo knows something of all these, strange to say (for she came originally from Southern India), with the exception of Bengali. Besides these languages one occasionally meets with a mixed kind, spoken by Purdeshis, and some can read Hindi, but not the kindred Marathi character.

I have got such an interesting photograph to send you of a newly married native girl, who is likely to be my pupil one day. She is the young ten-year-old wife of the Kali Baboo's eldest son. The marriage has taken place, but she will remain in her parents' house in Calcutta for a year or two; yet I was saying to the Baboo, that if she adorns her mind as liberally as she has done her body, she will be an accomplished lady! Mrs. Lumsden and the ladies attending the Monthly Prayer Meeting would like to see it, no doubt, and when they have seen it, I think you might send it on sight to Mrs. Col. Young, to whom I mean to write anon. The girl can read and write Bengali, but she has probably never read a Christian book. I hope she will come on *a visit* before she comes to stay.

I forgot to finish up about the feast provided for me in the Mohammedan house. It was really a very creditable one, and pressed upon me very affectionately. I wished dearest mother and all could have had a peep at us. Water was poured on my hands before and after the meal by one of the serving women, and garlands ornamented with silken paper hung round my neck thereafter.

Much love to you all, my very dear ones.

(*To her Mother.*)

My Little Bungalow, Nagpoor,
September 30th, 1879.

I will write to you to-day, and give you some account of my experiences since yesterday morning, as they have been more varied than usual! Well, shortly after seven o'clock in the morning I set out in my little bullock-gharree for Kampthi, having still some business to attend to there, connected with my proposed visits to Punah and Bombay. The morning was cool and pleasant, and I was in rather a happy rame of mind. On I went then, enjoying my own thoughts, circling round nice re-assuring texts for the most part; for, were it not that "in the multitude of my thoughts within me, God's comforts delight my soul" from time to time, it would be indeed ill with me!

At last I neared the "Halfway House," as it is called, where people often change bullocks, etc., but meantime my youthful gharree-man (his brother Ram Chun's substitute, as the latter had "fever") began to look suspiciously at one of the wheels of the vehicle, and on inquiry I found that a breakdown had occurred! What was wrong I did not exactly know, but the black fluid tar that ought to have been retained as a lubricating lotion for the wheel's axle was pouring down on the road, while the wheel itself was ajee. There I stood, revolving in my mind what was to be done, and demanding of my boy driver, "Ky kālā pohejoy?" (What is to be done?) Just at this juncture two natives came along in a smart tonga, drawn by a horse, and judging from the appearance of one of them that he was an educated man, I asked if he could speak English! I found that he could, and this set me more at my ease, so that I at once explained my dilemma to him, and asked if he would very kindly give me a seat back to Nagpoor in his conveyance. To this he consented with the utmost possible politeness and suavity, expressing himself as feeling highly honoured in having me in his gharree, and only afraid I would not be comfortable! (A bit of affectation this, since his was superior to my own!) He made his footman, who had before been sitting behind, run alongside of us; but this is the custom here when style is kept up. Sometimes there are two of these runners keeping a look-out in case of obstructions being in the way.

We left directions with Kágo, my driver, to try to get the wheel temporarily repaired, and then to follow me home—neither of which (perhaps impracticable) directions the little man attended to, as will be seen hereafter! On entering into conversation with my new friend (a distant connexion of the Good Samaritan, I should say!), I found that he was not an idolater like his countrymen, but neither was he a Christian. He belongs to a sect calling itself the Theosophistic Society, concerning the tenets of which I began to read in a magazine he had with him. I did not get far enough on with it to enable me to discover these; but I read one sentence in which the opposition of the system to Christianity, in common with every other professed religion, was undisguisedly stated. This led me into a conversation with my companion on the true source of spiritual light, and I urged him not to rest satisfied until he had examined into the claims of the Christian religion, and I assured him that if he was really anxious to be led into the light, and besought God to guide him, he would be directed into the right path. He promised me so to do, and in consequence of a desire I expressed to get a copy of the magazine he had showed me, he promised to try to supply me with one. In speaking of the various opinions men hold in regard to what is the true system of religion, he used the figure of a man's feeling puzzled on hearing three different verdicts as to one and the same colour (reminding one of the story of the chameleon). I suggested to him that the fault might be, and is, in the diseased eyes of the onlookers, which need to be enlightened by the Holy Spirit of God, the Source of all truth.

At length I was deposited at Mr. Cooper's door. We all thanked the stranger for his kindness, after which he asked and obtained permission to take his leave.

"The casualty did not prevent my carrying out my plan of going to Kampthi, for Mr. Whitton's old tonga was at my service, and the other pair of bullocks, so that, after taking a little breakfast, I set out again, and this time reached my destination all right. On arriving at the part of the road where the breakdown had occurred, we found the little *gora wala* (driver), nothing abashed, about to eat his morning meal, which he had prepared in my absence! I saw a huge *chupatti, i.e.* scone, as thick as a "harvest-roll," in the distance, and he seemed to have something in the shape of *kitchie*, probably in the curry line, to eat with it. After he had breakfasted by my permission, for I gave him ten minutes' grace (not looking at my watch in the matter, however), he resumed the journey with me, the other driver being deemed more competent to see after getting the broken gharree home. I was brought into giving the latter a rupee to get himself a new "puggery" (turban), as he had to use his own (probably a rag, many years ago) to tie up the wheel with! I did not grudge it to him, however, poor creature, only that I wondered at the amount he mentioned as necessary to obtaining it, when I asked him, thinking smaller things might do with him! Like a wise man he determined to make hay while the sun shone, however, and he even added two annas himself, that he might get just what he wanted!

(*To her Sister J*——.)

MY LITTLE BUNGALOW, NAGPOOR,
October 11*th*, 1879.

It now occurs to me to tell you something tragic, with which I was brought into contact the other week! You remember that I had to set out a second time for Kampthi, on account of the break-down of my gharree? Well, before leaving the station (Seetabaldi as ours is called, Nagpoor being the name of the *city*) I drove up to Mr. Douglas's bungalow, to tell him of my fortunes, and while talking to him, my attention was turned to a crowd of people at the corner of the road I was to take. The explanation of it was that two dead bodies, that of a man and woman, respectively, had been discovered in an adjoining compound, victims of the midnight murderer! who had deprived them of life to get hold of some jewels they had on. The bodies were being carried to the hospital, under supervision of some policemen, and I passed first one and then another! The words: "He (Satan) was a murderer from the beginning," occurred to me, as I contemplated the awful spectacle, and I said to myself, "So this is the character of him who would insinuate himself as the indulgent guide of the soul, and lead it to depart from God, as from an austere master! Well may we turn with loathing, from the author of such deeds of darkness, and follow the Light of the world, who may, indeed, lead His children along a narrow, strait, uphill path; but who promises that it will end in perfect day. You will be glad to know that the perpetrators of the shocking crime were arrested soon after, in the train, being intercepted as they thought to effect their escape.

But what I wanted specially to tell you was this. On my return from Kampthi, next day, I felt inclined to be a little "eerie" at the thought of spending the night alone in my little bungalow*; but I suppressed the thought, saying to myself, Is not God able to take care of me? You remember, dear sister, your directing my attention to the ninety-first Psalm, with a view to my taking it as my Indian

---

* For three years, she was quite alone at night, as her native assistants and the servants slept in their own homes.

pillow of repose in all times of peril? Well, after this, I had occasion to emerge into the moonlight for the purpose of opening a door from the outside, as the bolt had fallen into the socket, so that I could not enter from the inside; and having done this, I prepared for bed, and retired, finding, on getting up in the morning, that I had forgotten to fasten my large outside door, which stood half-open, just as I had left it on the preceding night! Only the thin purdah, or curtain, on its iron slide, had separated me and all my property (and it is very pilgrim-like in its appearance), from the eye and hand of any member or members of the heathen public.

Next letter must be a "missionary" one. I have lots to tell. Good houses are being opened, and much favour is being granted me in the eyes of their occupants. But poor A—— *officially* and *personally* are two very different beings!

> "For still I watch and struggle,
> And still I live in hope,
> And still I in my agony
> With Babylon (Apollyon) must cope."

But you know what follows. *May* it be the happy experience of all!

(To her Sister M——.)

FREE CHURCH MISSION, PUNAH,
  October 25*th*, 1879.

The scene is once more changed for me, you see. I arrived here, two days ago, after a wonderfully pleasant journey. Mr. Douglas got up early on Wednesday morning, and accompanied me to the station, to meet the train that left at five o'clock. I got into a carriage all by myself, my return ticket costing R. 45 = £4 10*s*. I have Pikoo with me, too, but he travelled third class, his single ticket costing R. 11. It was only the recognition of the fact that in this country every one is expected to have his or her own servant, that led me to take him. There is one comfort, however, in the reflection that I save my month's *board*, while away visiting, and should I be away for *two* months, this would save R. 60 = £6, so greatly helping to defray my expenses.

Apart from this monetary view of the matter, I am sure you will all think it well I should be adding to my missionary experience, as I will have a glorious opportunity of doing, in the course of my stay both here and in Bombay, not to speak of any directly personal gain I may acquire. I will tell you a little about my journey. I enjoyed the first stage of it perhaps, best. I was feeling well, happy and hopeful. The complete change, too, was so nice. Everything looked so bright and beautiful in the clear morning air. The sun rose like a huge ball of burnished gold, from behind a mountain summit in the distance, reminding me of P.'s appreciative rejoicings over celestial sights far less imposing.

In an adjoining carriage were Mrs. Col. M—— and her daughter from Nagpoor, and they were very kind and mindful of me. Miss M——, the handsome, fashionable, but bright, unaffected girl, looked in on me, now and then, to see how I was getting on, asking me if I had had a cup of tea, bringing me a quilt to lie down upon, and finally handing me over a beautiful tender fowl, her mother and she did not want, as they were nearing their journey's end. These kind attentions awoke feelings of the warmest gratitude in my heart, and I thought how much obliged my father and mother would also be, were they aware of it. Miss M—— and I got weighed at one station—she turning out to be about nine stones (she is tall, but thin, just a growing girl), while I have shaken down into the ladylike proportions of six stones and twelve pounds.

A party of natives came in beside me at one station, by some mistake, for the carrriage was meant for the use of ladies only. Miss M—— got this put right for me by an appeal to the guard.

Wasn't she kind? A little further on, two Eurasian girls joined me, but their presence was rather a diversion to me. These East Indians, occupying as as they do, a middle platform, between the European and native element in society, are quite a study in dress, etc. One of these "young ladies" had what I consider a Jewish style of face, and she had on an elegant gold chain, fine earrings, rings and bracelets. Her companion was more commonplace, but she also had some pretensions to being fine. I soon entered into conversation with them, offering the finer of the two the little sketch of Frances Ridley Havergal's life, and telling them why I had come to India, etc. I was able to relieve the nervous headache of the other, by saturating her handkerchief with Rimmel's toilet vinegar. In return, I was asked to partake of a beautiful dish of curry and rice they had brought with them for their dinner! The meal had been prepared by the fashionable one herself, and the rice was so perfectly cooked that I inquired how it was done.

On reaching, late at night, a certain junction, and having to change carriages, I was put in beside a distracted Irish woman, who was proceeding to Bombay with her three children, loudly lamenting the death of her husband, who had succumbed to an attack of dysentery on the way, having started with her on the journey. He was on his way to Ireland, to Cork, actually, to enjoy the pension he had earned. Truly an opportunity was here afforded me of showing mercy to the distressed, and I was glad to embrace it by drawing her thoughts upward to the God of the widow, and ministering to her bodily wants a little, for I could get the fasting woman a cup of tea, which she drank off greedily, though she could not eat, lend her a warm wrap, etc. I bethought me of pencilling a note for Dr. Townsend, whose name she knew quite well, in hope of engaging his interest on her behalf, thinking the circumstance of her having come across my path in the heart of India might, in itself, interest him. Mrs. Sheehan was her name. She is a Roman Catholic, and remarked, at the beginning of our interview, that there was nobody now to look after her and her children but "God Almighty and His blessed Mother!" I told her God had put it into my heart to be kind to her, and urged her to pour out her sorrows to Him, through the one Mediator appointed by Him, the Man, Christ Jesus.

On parting with her, my next companions were a soldier (not a nice specimen, morose and dour), his wife, a young woman, the worse of drink, with a child at the breast, and an elder little girl, to whom she spoke so harshly for crying, repeatedly saying: "That'll do, miss."

I asked her to speak kindly to the child, but she told me that would only make her worse.

This family was bound for New Zealand, where the young woman's mother lives on a farm. Her husband, young as he was, had already earned a pension.

I had a little talk with this unhappy-looking creature, too, after the man had been ordered into another carriage, in the course of which I urged her never to drink beer, for which she had been calling, without eating something solid with it.

The last stage of the journey found me in the company of a good-looking Parsee lady and her two children. She had scarcely seated herself, ere she began to pull out tiffin for themselves out of a hamper, and she made me a sharer, handing me various specimens of scone-like preparations and a hard-boiled egg. I discussed the former, and found them not bad. I think it was Gujerathi my companion spoke. Whatever it was, it was a language unintelligible to me, as Marathi was to her, for the most part; but the language of *kindness* is universally understood. The border of this lady's sarree was all embroidered with flowers by her own hand, as were also the borders of her children's silk trousers and the boy's topees, one of which, with swans, etc., worked on it so prettily, he allowed to fly out of the window. For this carelessness he did get a little rebuff, but his previous bad conduct, expressed by screwing his face, crying, and kicking with his feet, etc., was allowed to pass, almost unreproved. He was very angry because we could not get a second supply of *ice* supplied to us before by his father. He seemed to think his mother should stop the train and get it for him!

At length, after passing through a great deal of lovely scenery, that of the *Ghâts*, as the Indian ranges of hills in this neighbourhood are called, we reached Punah, where I found Mrs. Small and Janie ready to give me a most hearty welcome. They had come out in a little gharree, in the heat (at 3 o'clock) to meet me, having with difficulty restrained Mr. Small, who was very poorly, from coming too. This is a delightful home, and I am urged just to make myself at home. Below are a few verses I composed the other night.

TO THE FIRE-FLIES

Tune, " Twinkle, twinkle, little star.'

SPARKLING gems of living light,
Pleased I mark your airy flight,
In and out the silent trees,
Softer than the evening breeze!

Came ye from the Upper Sphere?
Us to comfort, us to cheer?
What your mission? Whence your birth?
Sure ye sprang not from the Earth!

WINGÉD GLOW-WORMS.

Dropped ye from yon glittering star,
Shining in the heavens afar?
Dewdrops are ye from the moon?
Sure to vanish all too soon!

Hush! my soul, the answer hear,
Whispered softly in thine ear :—
" We are earth-born, just like you,
Darkness brings our light to view.

" Wingéd glow-worms, such our name,
We're no aspirants to fame,
But the Hand of love and power
Framed us into Beauty's shower.

" Humble be, and *ye* shall shine,
Lighted up by grace Divine;
Lowly be, and *ye* shall rise
To the Home beyond the skies."

CHAPTER IX.

THE SOLDIERS AT THE FORT.

" O God, for a man with head, heart, hand,
Like some of the simple great ones gone
For ever and ever by;
Some still strong man in a blatant land,
Whatever they call him, what care I ?
Aristocrat, autocrat, democrat,—one
Who can rule, and dare not lie !"

"OH that Thou would'st bless me indeed, and enlarge my coast!" was Alexina's frequent prayer, and she was ever on the outlook for opportunities to win souls.

One day, while recovering from a severe illness, a dear friend requested her to jot down her thoughts, there and then, on the subject of the disciples toiling all night and catching nothing.

She had been resting on the sofa, but sat up, and at once pencilled the following :—

"Jesus here teaches His disciples in a convincing manner that 'without Him we can do nothing,' but that with Him, and when we simply do what He tells

THE KALI BABOO'S WIFE.

us because He tells us, we can do everything. Night is the natural time for catching fish in the sea, but the disciples caught none, though toiling all night. In the broad daylight, at the command of Jesus, they caught a multitude. We must, therefore, work in season and out of season, labouring to win souls—in other words, 'to catch men,' and not become weary in well-doing, for 'in due time we shall reap, if we faint not.' Let us tell Christ Himself of our non-success, and having first sat at His feet, and eaten the living bread, as the disciples did on this occasion, let us go forth at His command to catch men ourselves in the gospel net. How encouraging is this narrative to all who feel anxious about the supply of their bodily wants. The disciples of Christ have the Lord of heaven and earth as their Provider. The cattle on a thousand hills are His, and He who has said, 'Fear not, little flock,' also says, 'Your Father knoweth,' and 'Seek ye,' etc."

One matter which greatly exercised her mind was the condition of the soldiers, of whom there were a great many (both European and native) in the neighbourhood, both at Seetabaldi, and also at Kampthi, ten miles to the east of the native city of Nagpoor. Her heart was greatly stirred by the ravages of drink among the poor fellows. She saw that they are allowed to imbibe as much intoxicating liquor as they please, and how unable they are to resist the temptation to do so. Moreover, this great crime lies at the door of the British Government. The sad example is a great hindrance to missionary effort among the natives, as they argue that our religion can be no better than their own. Their Vedas teach them that people can only worship devoutly when they are intoxicated; so, at all the great festivals both men and women consider it their duty to become very drunk!

"Can nothing be done? Yes, by the grace of God, as slavery went, as opium is going, intoxicating drink can go. How? Christ is yet amongst us to move our hearts to pity, to move our hands to help. Of His Church, in view of just such organized systems of sin, He says, 'Ye are the salt of the earth, . . . the light of the world.' . . . To us He commits the evangelisation of the heathen; to us the rolling away of the stone from the mouth of the grave wherein they lie." [1]

The following extracts from her letters regarding the welfare of her countrymen are interesting:—

"You will scarcely guess my new sphere of labour. Well, it is amongst the soldiers, up at the Fort! The thought crossed me, one day, that I would get Mr.

[1] See "Slave Shackles of To-day," by Miss Lucy E. Guinness, in *Regions Beyond*, Sept., Oct., 1892.

Douglas to pay them a special visit (he had visited them before), that he might distribute a lot of nicely illustrated magazines, etc., I had picked up when in Bombay. Well, it was suggested that I myself should visit them! as a young lady, whose name I may have mentioned to you, a Miss Mallon, resident in the Zenana Mission House, in Bombay, does; only that it is at the close of evangelistic meetings, or by the wayside, she keeps a look-out for soldiers and sailors. Would it do for me to go amongst them, I inquired? No objection being made, the suggestion took root, and I engaged Mrs. Douglas to accompany me some evening. Meantime, the end of the month was approaching, at which time the relays of soldiers are changed, a new lot coming in from Kampthi, and I was anxious the present lot should be got hold of, and some of them prevailed on to come to our prayer meeting, always so earnestly addressed. I asked God to give me an opportunity of introducing myself to the poor young fellows before the only remaining meeting to be held ere the month closed, but up till ten minutes before the meeting my prayer was unanswered—a somewhat discouraging fact, though I felt that I did not deserve a striking reply on account of my felt inconsistencies of life. But, listen! Just as Mrs. Cooper and I were about to turn in at the gate of the Mission Church, I caught sight of two red coats, and I was after them like a shot! Their little dog snarled (Satan-like) at me and tugged my skirt snappishly, which led the two men to turn round and call it off, so that I had an opportunity of calling out, 'Good evening, I want to speak to you,' etc., etc. Result—one, a Roman Catholic, said he could not come, while his companion such a fine, ingenuous-looking one, did not like to leave his friend, as he always paid! I had, therefore, to excuse them, after going the length of telling the Papist that he could tell his priest what he had done. And gently pulling the sleeve of the other, I told them that Mrs. Douglas and I would be up next evening to see them all, as we wished to make their acquaintance, and the announcement was very politely received. We accordingly went and sang hymns, etc., with three invalided ones, and a few who joined us, and departed quite cheered, promising to return. I have been up twice since, alone, and last night a group of twenty dear bright youths gathered round me of their own accord, joining in the hymn-singing, listening besides to a nice piece from the 'Pilgrim's Progress.' Then two of them escorted me down the hill, one volunteering a good deal of information respecting his former experiences. But more of this anon.

"I have had the honour bestowed upon me this

week, too, of being invited to dine at the house of Mr. Neil, the Commissioner—the 'biggest' house in the station—in the absence of 'the chief,' or 'chief commissioner,' as his title is in full. Mr. Fraser is secretary to the latter, and next in rank, I suppose, to the former. I am the only member of the Mission invited on this occasion, so Mrs. Whitton thinks a party for 'young' (in the sense of unmarried) people is probably being given. I think I must promise to tell you how it comes off, but really, if my stiff back does not recover itself, I will hardly be able to go either to Paldi or there, or up to the Fort to-night, to see the soldiers, some of whom will be looking out for me. Only think, two of the first company of soldiers I visited were cut off by sunstroke on one day, or with one day's interval between, in Kampthi, the week before last. It seems they used to join us in singing the hymns, though they were Roman Catholics. They were nineteen and twenty years of age, respectively, if I remember. One, Burns, from near Belfast, who, with his companion, one of my present chief partisans, enlisted just through drink and folly—the other, Stuart, son of a widow in Dundee! They used to be very regular in their attendance at the chapel, morning and evening, my friend tells me. Poor fellows! I trust it is well with them.

"On my way home yesterday evening I came upon Mrs. Douglas's ayah carrying the darling baby, so I ordered Ram Chun to stop, and 'puckerrowed,' that is, seized the infant immediately, and forthwith set to refresh myself by kissing his soft wee cheeks, while I requested ayah to take a seat behind, that she might not be separated from her charge. On carrying the babe up the garden walk, and reaching my own door, I found three red coats, who had been waiting for me at least two hours! The babe took alarm, and had to be soothed and handed over to ayah; but *I*, nothing daunted, began an easy conversation with the three patriots. 'I came to return your book, as we are ordered back to Kampthi in two days,' quoth one of the party, in reference to the volume of the 'Family Treasury' I had lent him.

"In connection with the drunken scenes which he has to witness in the barrack room from time to time, whenever pay day comes round, he says he would not repeat his experience for a fortune. Two of them bought a small hymn-book from us, and with a bundle of interesting tracts to be distributed, as opportunity occurs, they at last bade us good-night. Dear lads! one's heart draws to them. In connection with dreadful sights such as they are called to witness in the course of their life, one of them, who has as gentle a face as you could wish to see, remarked that these come before him when he is acting sentry and feeling lonely. They were greatly pleased with the little instrument—our harmonium. We let them hear a Marathi hymn or two to its accompaniment, and then we had several hymns together.

"Mr. Douglas accompanied me to the Fort the other evening, as it is not thought proper that I should go alone. Now good-bye for a week, says your attached, though detached, member of the family."

"What prospect have I this evening, do you think? Nothing less than the holding of a meeting with some of the soldiers from the Fort in the church. It was themselves who suggested this, because they felt so disappointed on account of my having discontinued visiting them in their own quarters, owing to the fact that the boisterous behaviour of the rougher lot amongst them, as they sat over their beer, or made a clamour outside, was so unfavourable to the business on hand. Once or twice, on my having gone to visit at the Fort, as usual, I was advised to retire on account of this, to the great chagrin, as it turns out, of those who appreciated the efforts I had been making for their good. As you may suppose, I rather shrink from conducting a formal meeting in the Mission Church, but the prevailing feeling is one of thankfulness for the privilege extended to unworthy *me*. I think that it was while reading that touching account of Miss Cotton's experiences, as she sought to shield the boys of the labouring class from temptation by the erection of Coffee Rooms, provided with all manner of innocent attractions, and in which she met with them for Bible reading, conversation, hymn-singing, and prayer from time to time, that the wish to do something for the soldiers sprang up in my mind. One sweet-looking young fellow, since prostrated with severe illness, though now restored, professes to have undergone a saving change, the result of the few gatherings at the Fort, followed up by my personal appeals.

"No fewer than eight of the soldiers in Kampthi died within a fortnight from exposure to the sun! Four sank down under a tree while being marched in here one morning, but of these only one died. They are allowed to drink *ad libitum*, or something like it, which I think is a crying disgrace to the British Government.

"We all attended such an interesting Temperance Meeting held in the Museum last night. We were addressed by a Mr. Gregson, a well-known man, it seems, though *I* didn't know his name before. He is a real philanthropist, not to say a noble Christian man. He was a Baptist minister, I believe, but he became deeply interested in the case of British soldiers out in this country, and finding that his efforts to stem the tide of intemperance amongst them, were singularly successful, he gave himself up to the work of labouring for their welfare in this particular. His barbed words came home with such power to both Maggie's and my heart last night, that when an opportunity of inserting our names in the pledge book was afforded, at the close of the meeting, we took our stand with the soldiers, who were grouping round the table to be enlisted in the army of abstainers, and gave in our names along with them. By this act we merely promise to abstain (by God's help) from all intoxicating liquors, unless prescribed medically, so long as we retain 'this pledge,' that is, the scrap of paper on which we have signed our names. It was pleasing to find some of my old acquaintances amongst the soldiers rallying round me as a point of strength, in connection with the good cause. One of them would have had me on the platform if he could. And, do you know, mother, I look upon the coming of this good, devoted man to the place as an answer to *prayer*, for I had longed for some power to be brought to bear on the poor soldiers here, some of whom, I see, from time to time, hanging about these low native drinking-shops in the very heat of the day. I had also longed for an opportunity of once more *taking my stand* as an abstainer, for I allowed myself to trifle with former pledge signatures, on the plea that I had not signed them with sufficient heartiness, etc. I felt as if I had unadvisedly compromised my 'liberty,' and I used to feel a desire to regain it.

"The lecturer (who told us of a meeting he had had in Aberdeen lately), closed his appeal by repeating that fine poem :—

> " ' Courage, brother, do not stumble,
> Though thy path be dark as night ;
> There's a star to guide the humble ;
> Trust in God, and do the right.
>
> Though the road be long and dreary,
> And its ending out of sight ;
> Foot it bravely—strong or weary,
> Trust in God, and do the right.' " etc.

CHAPTER X.

ALONE.

*O Sister! Sister! hath the memory
Of other years no power upon thy soul?
Hast thou forgot the early, innocent joys
Of our remotest childhood: when our lives
Were linked in one, and our young hearts bloomed out
Like violet bells upon the self-same stem,
Pouring the dewy odours of life's spring
Into each other's bosom?*

* * * * *

*Nay, do not weep, my sister!—Do not speak;
Now know I, by the tone, and by the eye
Of tenderness, with many tears bedimmed,
Thou hast remembered all. Thou measurest well
The work that is before thee, and the joys
That are behind."*

NAGPOOR is a city full of darkness and superstition, and "wholly given to idolatry," and day by day Alexina seems to have become more and more alive to the responsibility and opportunity which was given her to proclaim the glad tidings.

In India the matured saint of God is frequently met with, especially among English officers, yet the apathy with which many professing Christians among the European community regard the heathen lying at their very doors is most appalling. She was much struck at discovering that one gentleman of her acquaintance, who had resided for twelve years in Nagpoor, had never been in the city proper! and yet he considered himself a Christian, and thanked God that he was not a poor deluded idolater!

Very different were the ways of the members of the little mission circle, and remarking on the departure to England, on furlough, of some of these dear friends, she says:—" The Lord never lets *me* see too much of such. They are removed one by one, so that I may lean closer to Himself. 'Blessed be His holy name,' I do thank Him for it, and desire to look to Jesus only."

Alone in her little bungalow she frequently recalled the days of her childhood, and heard again the stir of the falling leaves from the trees, and the far-off murmur of the village brook. Then her thoughts would wander to one in the heart of Africa, still more lonely than herself, enduring all sorts of privations, if indeed he were still alive, and with her usual habit of expressing her feelings in verse, she found herself singing:—

> "We twa hae run aboot the braes,
>   And pu'd the gowans fine,
> But we've wander'd mony a weary fit,
>   Sin' auld lang syne.
>
> We twa ha'e paidelt i' the burn,
>   Frae mornin' sun till dine,
> But seas atween us braid ha'e roared
>   Sin' auld lang syne."

Then, by means of pen and paper, a few words of encouragement and comfort would be despatched to her fellow worker, hoping they would reach him sometime, and cheer him in his exile. The following letter is the reply to one of these much-appreciated communications.

> UYUI, NEAR UNYANYEMBE,
>   CENTRAL AFRICA,
>   *25th June*, 1880.

MY DEAREST COUSIN,—

It was indeed a most unexpected pleasure to me to receive your kind letter of 16th December, 1879. I had just crossed the Nyanza from Uganda, and found our letter-carriers at Kagei in the beginning of May. Before opening the envelope, I did make repeated guesses at the author of the unfamiliar handwriting, for you can well imagine that a "poor missionary" in such an out-of-the-way place as this runs little risk of receiving much fine writing from the fair sex.

Far away, you are not out either of sight or mind with me. I cannot say what joy it gave me when I first heard of your going abroad on mission work. Among other missionary publications, I regularly receive the *Monthly Record of the Free Church of Scotland*, and there I have repeatedly seen letters from yourself, and news of your work.

Long ago, some two or three years since, I remember sending you a note from the coast, at which time I was far from well acquainted with either what the word Zenana meant, or what means of usefulness you enjoyed in engaging in such work. Now I am fairly well informed on these points, partly from news of you which I receive occasionally from my folks in Ventnor, and partly from accounts of work in the zenanas, as recorded in the *Christian Record*.

I fear it is little likely that I shall come across your friend Dr. Peters, as my sphere of work is more than a walk of a thousand miles from Zanzibar. We have not a railway by which to run down to our port, as you have from Nagpoor to Bombay. Legs are our only locomotive, and what is more, the roads in this part of the world are particularly unsafe.

Probably no greater contrast could exist between two mission fields than exists between India and Africa. We have heathen to work among in both spheres, but you are every day in contact with a civilization and a refined idolatry—ages old, while here all is savagedom, and the only religion a wretched combination of witchcraft and devil-worship.

But when I say that I am fairly acquainted with your work from having read your letters, yet less than five minutes' conversation would convince you that I am deplorably ignorant of your work and your whereabouts. I must therefore beg you to write me a clear account of all your surroundings, just taking for granted that my knowledge is less than nothing. I promise you in return a short story of our new mission in Central Africa.

My dear Alexina, I cannot say how glad I am that more than one of our family has ventured on this greatest of all occupations, viz., the teaching of the ignorant heathen. I am also glad to find that our cousin, H—— I——, has joined us in the same good work. Nagpoor is far enough from Bombay, yet you have means of seeing each other frequently, which we do not know in Africa, and I hope that Mrs. Scott and yourself will have much loving intercourse with each other, and much success in your work. If one thing more than another strikes me in mission work —and I am sure it will strike you every day in the same light—it is this, the awful odds that we have to contend against, and the feebleness of our forces and of our efforts. But we know who is our Master, and we know the work is His, and therefore must succeed. He was able to multiply a few loaves and fishes so as to satisfy thousands, and in our day He can and will multiply our feeble efforts, so as to evangelize the mighty masses amongst which we are placed.

I read recently a remarkable paper in the *Catholic Presbyterian*. I forget the heading of the article, but it was by an "Elder," and showed most plainly how low is the interest taken in mission work even by people of God at home. Everything is done by "deputy." People obey Christ's command by proxy. On the other hand, it is not for a moment to be questioned that Christ's command to us all is to give our costliest offerings for His work abroad, and personal service for His work at home.

29th June. Since commencing this note, I have had the pleasure of receiving a mail from the coast. My last home letters (of April 8th) tell me that my cousin Maggie is intending devoting herself to India. May she indeed do so. She will be a great help to you if stationed in Nagpoor, and a great encouragement to you wherever she will be stationed.

I came here from Uganda merely to return at once with a caravan of supplies for our use there. In a week or so I hope to be on the march back to the lake. Many difficulties there are, both on the way and in Uganda itself. My porters are natives, and very self-willed whenever they choose to show their savage nature. The road is beset with danger at every point, every petty chief whose cattle-pen one has to pass using his every endeavour to extort as much blackmail from the white man as he can, and resorting to force when words fail. Highway robberies are also common. One of our number was murdered by a gang of robbers, only a few days from this place. His name was Penrose, and the caravan he was bringing us, of several thousand dollars' worth of goods, was all lost. Only a few months ago a band of Roman Catholic missionaries was passing from here to the Victoria Nyanza, when one of them was speared as he was quietly riding on his donkey. The poor fellow (he was a Bavarian) died immediately.

By the tender mercy and care of our loving Father in heaven I have till now escaped a thousand dangers in my four years' work in East Central Africa. We do not know the future, but we do know that it will bring us nothing except what His all-seeing eye will allow, and what He knows to be best for us.

Now, my dear Alexina, good-bye. May our Lord and Saviour give you much blessing every day. And above all, give you many saved souls.

Your affectionate cousin,
A. M. MACKAY.

For almost three years she had been without companionship in the little bungalow which she called "her home," and when she returned from her daily rounds of house-to-house visitation in the city, wearied and oft-whiles much discouraged, she longed for the society of some of her dear ones, and realised to the full the loving thoughtfulness which at the beginning sent the disciples "forth by two and two."

Unlike some families who appear to get on better with aliens than with those whom God has given them as kindred, she and her sisters each "esteemed the other better than herself," and "in honour preferred one another." Therefore it is not to be wondered at, that although she had forsaken all her loved ones, the ties of affection kept pulling her heart, and in the very first letter written from India (see p. 53) she yearns for the assistance of one dear to her as moonlight is to starlight. How her desire was granted will be seen below.

My Little Bungalow, Nagpoor,
April 8th, 1880.

My own darling Maggie,—

I will write direct to yourself this time, on the subject on hand. Could I only have transferred to paper the glowing thoughts that took possession of me as I lay in a very wakeful state, all alone, under the starlight last night, the enthusiasm would have been catching; but now I will just speak what comes to my mind. As to how long "the hot winds" blow I have forgotten to ask. It is only now and then we have a regular hot *wind*, but the hot *season* runs a course of three months, I suppose, not including the toning down time, and the making ready for the rain time. I would get up comforts about myself, were you here, which I have heretofore foregone, content to bake slowly in my little oven, like a species of salamander, to the utter astonishment of all around me. This season the heat is considered to be more intense, and to have set in more suddenly than usual. My thermometer at present (the doors having been shut since sunrise, I suppose) stands at 91°.

Now, Maggie, how are we to find out the will of God in this matter? It will not be revealed to us direct from heaven, that is certain. The present state of the case is this. The need has arisen for a companion to be provided for me in my labours, and, true to nature, I turn to *a sister*, peculiarly adapted to the work, as I feel convinced, and ask if she will be that companion. If there is another in the field, clamouring, or even quietly thirsting to be engaged in the—oh, so vacant field at Nagpoor!—of whose existence you become aware, on putting in an application, I press for my choice, no more!

"Fields are white, and harvest waving ;
　Who will go and work to-day ?
Loud and long the Master calleth,
　Rich reward He offers thee ;
Who will answer, gladly saying,
　'Here am *I, send me, send me*'?"

P.S.—Of course I will mention you in my official announcement to Mrs. Young, but I will handle the matter delicately. "If any man lack wisdom, let him ask of God." "It is *I*: be not afraid." "When He putteth forth His own sheep, He goeth *before* them." "Follow Me, and I will *make* you fishers of men." "I can do *all* things through Christ which strengtheneth me." Look up!

Thursday, June 10th, 1880.

And *now* I will address myself to dearest mother, beloved father, and the family generally—darling Maggie particularly—for I have had my home letters, and about their wonderful contents I must now speak.

Well, my dear ones, you have gone as far in your trustful and generous acquiescence in connection with the proposal that our dear Maggie should join me here, as you were called on in God's providence to go ; so that now the whole "disposal of the matter rests with the Lord." The proof you have all given me of your self-sacrificing love for me, apart from all higher considerations, is very affecting to me; and should the Saviour graciously deign to accept of the gift that has been presented to Him (even though your loving arm, dear, clinging mother, is still round it), I'm sure He'll make you feel that it is more blessed to give to Him a dear child than even to receive one from Him; and, moreover, He'll be quite willing to say to you, as He looks at Maggie, and then into your and father's tearful eyes: *Mine* and *thine*. Remember, darling ones, in giving *her*, you are giving a corn of wheat, which, though it may become, as it were, dead to you, in as far as feasting yourselves upon it is concerned, is destined, by God's blessing, to bring forth much fruit in the wide, waste field into which you allow the Master's hand to drop it. And in the day when *He* sees of the travail of His soul and is *satisfied*, my precious mother will be satisfied too, and the words, in as far as the gift was given to *me*, may also have a meaning, "Inasmuch as ye did it unto one of the least of *these*, ye did it unto *Me*."

Now, whether Maggie comes or not, I thank you all, my own beloved ones, from the depths of my heart. Let God send me help by the hand of him whom He will send, according to the saying of Moses of old, who occupied a mental position in regard to his being the messenger, pretty much like what Maggie occupies,

I think. Oh, we don't know what a blessing for our family may be wrapped up in this letter, but,

> " God is His own interpreter,
> And He will make it plain."

My letter of doubt and fear in regard to climatic influences on Maggie's health will have unhinged you sadly again, I fear; but such shakes are often sent to test an apparently newly rooted plant's stability, and I hope the faith and hope of all of you will continue to be in God. Maggie's life is precious in His sight, and with our simple habits in the mission circle, and with the arrangements of our movements so entirely (in as far as the zenana department of the work is concerned) in our hands, Maggie has very fair prospects in this respect, too. Well, it is now for me, at least, to wait and see how the matter will turn, giving thanks in the meantime for the inclination manifested to accede to my request. Do not let the thought of what is to be done at my furlough time trouble you. " Take no thought for the morrow," and Mrs. Whitton said, some time ago, that during such a period she would try to make it as comfortable for Maggie as possible.

Do offer to Dr. Laidlaw my heartfelt thanks for all his loving sympathy. The text he wrote in my little book has often been a comfort to me—" Why art thou cast down, O my soul?" etc.

I must just throw in here, that for a great part of the year the climate of Nagpoor is charming, and the hot season is slightly over three months' duration.

One of our girls is in a dying state, I fear, from congestion of the brain. It came about quite suddenly. She merely remarked, on awaking yesterday morning, that she had a bad headache, but very soon she became insensible, and slightly convulsed. She has parents, but her step-mother has treated her and her younger sister most disgracefully, scarcely clothing them. It is very touching to see the poor little dark-faced, suffering child lying moaning, with her hair all shaved off. She looks like what one would imagine Topsy might have looked. To the top of her head and the calves of her legs mustard has been applied. This has roused her a good deal, and she may be brought round.

(*To her Mother.*)

NAGPOOR,
October 7th, 1880.

Ere this reaches you, it may have been settled as to whether Maggie is to join me, or not!

Well, if it has been arranged that she is to come, "Sook roop raha," that means in Marathi, Remain happy; and if she is to remain with you, " Burray," *i.e. Well*, for we read: "He doeth *all* things *well*," and even if we believe *not*, "*He* abideth faithful."

> "Only, O Lord, in Thy dear love,
> Fit us for perfect rest above;
> And help us this and every day,
> To live more nearly as we pray."

My mother has been a grand prayer ever since I knew her, and now, methinks, she is going to be taught to be a grand praiser!

Yes, my mother must learn to *holler* in the praise line (see Frankie or some such curious body in "Daniel Quorm," the book dear J—— is so fond of). I don't know the book well, but I can *imagine* Frankie, if he is the bedridden, simple-minded, child-like Christian introduced to us there, saying to *you*, mother, if you were going to see him:

"Eh, missus! Haller-loo-yer's the chorus o' that 'ere moanin' song o' your'n! Twir-r-r! don't Frankie feel like singin' like a bird this evenin'? 'Tain't no wonder to hear larks an' them birds carrolin' i' the mornin', but Frankie's goin' to sing a dooet wi' maister nightingale. Them's the crack singers that sings whin t'other birds is sleepin' snug i' their beds, an' it's *them* folks takes most notice on, 'cause there's somethin' partikler in the natur o' a bird 'at sings when the sun's no' shinin', bit only the stars a glintin' an' a glimmerin', fearfu' like, o'erhead, like the lynx een o' a devoorin' hoolit (owl). Nae doot it's a mighty mistak' the brave bird's makin', whin he likens the sparklin' orbs o' heevin til a wild beast's een, bit sik mees'rable, miscalkerlatin' craters we be's, that the bonniest objecks o' creation are misshapin' an' mis-ca'ed by our ain misbelievin' een! Ech, missis, bit ye're a braw 'ooman the day, gin ye bit kent it. *Twa* o' yer bairns ta'en into yer dear Lord's service, did ye say? Dance, 'ooman, dance! Frankie 'ud show you how, but his sinfu' legs is stiff, an' canna do the thing they wud! But he's a-praisin' in's heart sae lood that the angels aiblins is hearin', lat alane the Maister Hissel'."

* * * * *

Did J—— enjoy the above attempt at imitating dear Frankie, or whoever it is that speaks that way in the book?

I hope it has not been to *you*, dear mother, like singing songs to one that has a heavy heart? I would not mock your grief, my own dear mother. I would be inclined, rather, to put my arms round your neck and soothe you, if I were near you. If you could have listened to Mr. Whitton's discourse in the prayer meeting last night, on the sympathy of Jesus, as expressed in His mode of dealing with the grief of the poor widow of Nain, whose son He restored to life, you would have felt your very heart drawn out in longing to *know aright* that sympathetic Saviour. I confess *I* don't know Him. May He reveal Himself to us all. "Then *shall we know*, if we follow on to know the Lord."

Paul's one desire was, that he might know Him, and the power of His resurrection, and the fellowship of His sufferings, being made conformable unto His death, and he was able *afterwards* to say: "I know whom I have believed, and am persuaded," etc.

My Little Bungalow, Nagpoor,
November 11th, 1880.

My Beloved Father and Mother, and all the Family,—

You may guess what is filling my heart! While I was on my way down to the city, sitting all alone in my tonga (for Cheenie could not come with me to-day, and I had no companion till I picked up Karoona in the city), I met the postman, and he good-naturedly undid his bundle on the back seat of the tonga, and gave me my treasure—a pearl (by the bye, Maggie's name *means* pearl) set in emeralds, in the shape of two other delightful letters; one from Miss Gimson, and one from Mrs. Langford, of Kampthi.

I had been praying in my heart for some token of loving favour from the hand of Jesus, whose side I so often forsake, looking for this in the shape of some words of Scripture applied unmistakably to my heart, when lo! the news of an invaluable gift, direct from Himself, just bestowed upon *me*, shamefully unworthy as I now, in some measure, feel myself to be, reached my heart, through the medium of my eyes! And I reasoned in this way :—

"Seeing that this dearest desire of my heart has been bestowed upon me (in these last days), and that He gave Himself for me long before, independently of my foreseen character, may I not trust Him in my present heart's trouble?"

In my little birthday text-book for to-day occur this text and verse:—"Though He slay me, yet will I trust Him."

> "Through waves, and clouds, and storms,
>   He gently clears thy way;
> Wait thou His time, thy darkest night
>   Shall end in brightest day."

Let us all seek to occupy the waiting attitude, for we read that it hath not been perceived, except by God Himself, what He hath prepared for *him that* waiteth for Him.

The words of Mary in the Magnificat have occurred to my mind in connection with my present position :—" My soul doth magnify the Lord, and my spirit hath rejoiced in God, my Saviour ; *for* He that is mighty hath done to me great things," etc.

May "the desire granted" be indeed "a tree of life" to my soul ! God bless us both ; and doubly bless you all, my darlings.

"There is that scattereth, and yet increaseth."

If you had seen how the face of my gharree-man (tonga driver) *shone* the other evening, when he ascertained, after questioning me (in Marathi) on the subject, that my sister was likely to come. He expressed himself as overjoyed on account of the news ; and a like feeling prevails amongst all my friends here. As to the feeling of kindest sympathy cherished by the circle of home friends, it is very sweet to my heart to think of it. Do tell dear Dr. Laidlaw and all how cheered I am by their unmerited kindness.

I shall write a little account of my work, along with this, that my warm-hearted friends in Aberdeen may be able to follow my movements a little.

There will shortly, God willing, be *a couple* of little horses in harness, instead of one faint yet pursuing animal, and you know how Solomon explains that "two are better than one." In regard to this, "my cup runneth over." For the rest, let me be silent unto the Lord, remembering the short direction: "Wait on the Lord, and He will save thee."

Goodbye, darlings.

Your loving
ALEXINA.

P.S. (An hour or two after.)

Kindly thank the Misses Fettes most heartily for the beautiful gift they sent me. It was immensely admired. Tell them I'll be sure to wear it on the day I become the Rajah's wife! but should he keep me waiting too long, I may venture to don it on some even less illustrious occasion.

I have a miniature painted likeness of an Indian lady, with all her feast day finery upon her, which I shall take an early opportunity of forwarding to them as a small acknowledgment of their kindness.

Ameer Khan rejoices with me over Maggie's expected arrival. He has been here, giving me a Hindustani lesson, after a two days' absence from fever. He told me, on my announcing the glad tidings to him, that he had meant to make it his first question (as to whether it was settled or not). Mr. Whitton and I mutually, and with one consent, stopped our respective conveyances in meeting each other this morning, in reference to "the news." He did not know, of course, that I had met the postman.

Dear Dr. Fraser, of Punah, *our* Mr. Fraser's father,

who is in this quarter just now, expressed his great joy on hearing of the likelihood of M—— coming (though his own loved wife has just been taken *from* him—he will meet her soon above, most likely). Thus unselfish are the lovers of the Lord, and those supposed to be His people.

This morning, as we sat delivering our God-given message, first by song and then by sermon, of the truly evangelistic type, in a certain verandah, to which " a little child had led us," the thought passed through my mind that not M—— only, but J—— too, might come!—for that two labourers to the perishing thousands might well be made three, since the bite that serves two would serve three, were I to offer to keep her! and she to volunteer.

Mother, darling! I'm speaking lightly now, in as far as practical results are concerned, but not so lightly from the point of view of reasonable service, and from *God's* point of view. Of course, my mother, I take your feelings into consideration, and may I never rob you of your treasures, or deal ruthlessly with you. Still, lying there in the quiet night, the *reality* of the work lying before the Christian world (and laid in great measure at the door of our family, to all appearance, in connection with Nagpoor—for I may—) ; well, I'll finish my sentence. I may say that though —— is an excellent Christian girl, she is no born missionary, [lacking the aggressive spirit so necessary to the prosecution of this work, as well as the smiling, free-and-easy manner so reassuring to the timid, self-ignoring women of India.

Now, dear mother, some of your children have that; and they have it from *you*, under God; and I may tell you further, that this in itself draws the natives. They look on me, as a rule, with such favour, real pleasure lighting up every feature. They feel at home with me, even the little children. To-day I sat singing away, with a sweet wee babe nestling in my lap, with its " rings on its fingers, and bells on its toes," so to speak, the mother sitting a little way off, the father standing near, and a number of neighbours, many of them children, grouped around. I almost think the father would have *given* it to me! I asked him with a quiet playfulness to let me have it, and his answer was, " Gya ! " *i.e.* Take !

Now, Maggie dear, your patronizing manner will at last find its true use. *It is* wanted here, coupled with love.

(*To her Sister J——.*)

NAGPOOR,
December 15*th*, 1880.

Just at present all things are propitious, and, while others are having the usual cold weather holiday, I am going on with my visiting, day after day, rising at five o'clock, setting off at six, and not returning till eleven or later, as a general rule.

I have had much encouragement lately, efforts to secure a hearing proving very successful, and invitations being given us spontaneously from unexpected quarters. I hope, with a new year, to supply the home friends with many accounts of my experiences from day to day, and Maggie's first impressions will be like new kindling both to me and them. As I drove along the street to-day, casting an observant eye around, I was much struck with the general appearance of "dirt and desolation," for these words fitly describe the picture presented to the view. Here, on a damp doorstep, sits a shivering woman, as like a human frog as you can imagine (I wish I could sketch like some of the members of the Fallon family); there, a street-sweeper in rags is causing the dust to fly into your nostrils in a dense cloud, only suffered to subside a little, as you pass, if you call out, "Kudder ow," in good time. Yonder, a man trudges along, bearing aloft on his head a basket, containing, doubtless, something precious to him, but strangely unattractive to the unintelligent beholder, who would be certain to mistake it for a contribution to the dust heap! But immortal spirits are inhabiting these sadly abused mortal bodies, and many a beautiful face peeps out from its dusty chudder, bearing the impress of the Divine hand that originally stamped upon it the image of glory and virtue, lingering still, so loath to disappear.

May our darling Maggie and myself be the privileged pearl divers in the surrounding sea of sin—gold-diggers employed by the King, destined to sit one day at His table, to be fed by His own royal hand, the warfare and work of "this present time" over and gone for ever.

Meantime, with me, it is like this,

> "But now we watch and struggle,
> And now we live in hope," etc.

But oh, *then* may it be:

> "The morning shall awaken,
> The shadows flee away."

I've got my desire; I'm in the missionary field (as I'll call it), surrounded by foreign, heathen faces, just as it seems to me I pictured it, years ago, when I sat in the little parlour schoolroom at B——, surrounded by the B—— children. But—oh! I need something yet—a heart satisfied with Jesus.

> "Content to let the world go by,
> To know nor gain nor loss."

(See beautiful hymn: "Beneath the Cross of Jesus, I fain would take my stand"). Well, I trust I'll get even this. Ask it for me, my darlings. It is the temptation Jesus experienced in the wilderness: "If Thou be the Son of God, command these stones," etc., that vexes my soul, and to which I yield. Enough! I'll not analyse myself more. "Thou understandest my thought afar off." "Though I walk in the midst of trouble, Thou wilt revive me."

I have much more cause to give thanks than complain, even in connection with this trouble; and in other things what indulgence has been shown me—friends ready to be pleased, Maggie coming, my loved ones all spared to me, and the prospect held out of seeing them once more (I don't mean only once), ere very long.

Soon after the arrival of her sister, Alexina addressed the following lines to her mother:—

AN ECHO FROM THE LITTLE BUNGALOW.

Look at your two dear lassies here,
   Within their Indian nest,
And tell me, is their present life
   Not spent in what is best?

Their dusky sisters live around,
   To whom it must be told,
That Jesus Christ more precious is
   Than all their gems and gold.

Oh! if you saw the thoughtful mien,
   And mark'd the up-turn'd eye,
When one dear child proclaims Christ's love,
   And one is sitting by,

Would you not say, " How glad I am,
   My Saviour honour'd me,
By asking twice in pleading tones,
   'Wilt lend this child to Me?'"

The tears which first in sorrow flow'd,
   When came the parting hour,
May well grow bright with rainbow hues,
   Beneath His touch of power!

Our present work is but to sow
   The seed with patient hand;
But one day, through the Spirit's power,
   Ripe sheaves shall fill the land.

And when the cry is "Harvest Home,"
   And Christ is "satisfied,"
Won't you rejoice you let us go
   To tell of Him who died?

List to that voice of tender love,
   "She hath done what she could;
Well done! thou good and faithful one,
   The test of love hath stood."

(*To her Mother.*)

February 15*th*, 1881.

You would like to hear us speaking away to each other in the old home style, imitating the cadences of certain voices that used to strike our youthful fancy, and then breaking out into a merry laugh, etc. Then, when I feel downcast, it is sure to come out sooner or later to Maggie, and she acts like a ventilator, admitting fresh air to the fainting spirit. So true is it that if one fall, another will help him up. May we indeed be increasingly useful in strengthening each other's hands, and may a double portion be given into your bosoms for that you have lent out on such a philanthropic mission.

> "Oh, Christ! He is the fountain,
> The deep sweet well of love."

Let us seek to be ever, with joy, drawing water out of this well of salvation, remembering hour by hour that all our well-springs are in Him, and that the water that He gives becomes, in those who drink it, "a well of living water springing up into everlasting life."

We have a quiet, monotonous life of it, taking it as a whole; but it is the steady grind of the work-a-day machinery that produces the most striking results in the end, after all, and the old inscription: "Line upon line; line upon line; precept upon precept," etc., writes and re-writes itself on *most* of the pilgrim paths of this world! I find the quietude and confinement irksome *to my imagination*, now and again, but by doing "the next thing," the machinery generally rights itself.

"Tick, tick, tick," went the old clock on the stair, but it was refreshed every now and then by the visit of some kind friend, inquiring with upturned face as to the time, and periodically by the return of the winding-up occasions, when, not only would "father" look in upon it, with a kindly "How d'ye do?" and a firm but friendly shake of the hand, but dainty little feet would patter up, and laughing dimpled faces would gaze in awful wonder to see the liberties "father" was taking with the imperious old inmate of the well-known niche in the wall. But a truce to day-dreams!

CHAPTER XI.

OPEN DOORS.

*" Alas! I still see something to be done,
And what I do falls short of what I see,
Though I waste myself on doing."*

IN the autumn of 1880 a few of the zenana agents in connection with the Free Church of Scotland, in India, started a little monthly magazine, entitled *Jottings by Busy People,* having as its motto, "I am among you as he that doth serve." Miss Paterson, of the Boarding School, Bombay, was editor, and Miss Annie Small, of Punah, author of "Light and Shade in Zenana Missionary Life," the publisher; for there is a printing press at Punah, worked by the Orphanage boys, in connection with the Mission there. The object of the little paper was to stimulate interest in each other, as fellow workers in the mission field. Under the signature of "Phœbe," Alexina sent frequent contributions to its pages, some of which are given below.

LIFE.

"What is your life? It is even a vapour, that appeareth for a little while, and then vanisheth away."

"This is life *eternal*, to know Thee, the only true God, and Jesus Christ, whom Thou hast sent." So many thoughts spring up in the mind when we give ourselves to contemplation on the subject of life, that all one can do is to jot down a few of them, in the hope that answering chords in the hearts of friendly readers will vibrate in sympathy, and that responsive notes will, in due time, be echoed back.

With what interest life, to each of us, is invested! Were we to look deep down into the heart of each human being, I think we would find an impression there that his or her life is *the life* being lived in the world! And, after all, each individual's life is the one life he is wholly responsible for.

"Every one of us must give account of *himself* to God." We must earnestly seek, however, to mould our lives after the one perfect pattern held up before our eyes in the Word of Truth, not looking every one on his own things, but also on the things of others. The noble character is ever the self-forgetful one; rather, the one that keeps self in the background, and looks out on the great world around in the attitude of one who considers himself the *servant* of all. What a glorious motto for any life: "I am among you as he that doth serve"! I think the figure Jesus used in explaining the meaning of His own life is very remarkable—the corn of wheat, which must fall into the ground, that it may not abide alone.

We, too, must *decrease*, if the kingdom of God is to increase by our means; but "he that loseth his life in this world shall keep it unto life eternal."

"WE ARE HIS WORKMANSHIP."
(EPH. ii. 10.)

I think it is a very comforting thought in connection with the discipline of life, that we are God's workmanship, and that God, as our Heavenly Father in Christ Jesus, knows and will do exactly what is best for us.

There are several figures used in Scripture to illustrate God's present manner of dealing with us. We are spoken of, for example, as "lively stones," and we know that stones need to be prepared for the place they are to occupy in a building. More especially do we see ourselves represented in the stones of Solomon's Temple, each of which was accurately shaped and prepared far away, beyond the precincts of the holy building, so that no sound of tools jarred on the ear in its immediate neighbourhood.

How sweet is it to find a human spirit so made meet for the inheritance of the saints in light that only calmness and beauty pervade the face of the departing one! Is anything more fitted to stimulate the onlooker to submit himself to the Father of Spirits, that he, too, may live, than the sight presented by some death-bed scenes? The luminous countenance and kindling eye speak volumes concerning the skill and success of the wise Master Builder, under whose guidance every living stone is being prepared.

But not only are believers destined to occupy a place in the heavenly Temple, but the Master is to adorn Himself with them as the jewels He has so dearly purchased. He is spoken of as "making up" His jewels. But what jewel ever displayed its beauty before the graving tool did its apparently cruel work upon it!

"All things work together for good to them that love God," the filing process of long-continued, weary waiting, reminding of the words, "Let patience have her perfect work"—the sharp blows, severing away parts of our very selves—the final polishing, only produced by subjection to what we had considered as very rough handling, indeed—all have worked together for good, and the tried saint is enabled to testify, "He hath done all things well."

Many other figures we are furnished with, both in

God's Word and in the book of Nature, beautifully illustrating to us God's mode of working in relation to His children down here. Are we heirs to a Kingdom? We must be under tutors and governors until the time appointed of the Father.

Are we plants of the Father's planting? The Husbandman must subject us to pruning.

Are we precious metal? We are sure to be chosen in the furnace of affliction. But—"We *are His* workmanship," therefore, God grant that we may never fear. The hand that moulds us is a pierced hand—the heart that plans all for us was *broken* for our sakes. He says: "I will do you no hurt."

HOPE.

"We are saved by Hope."—ROM. viii. 24.

Have we ever sufficiently thought of the precious gift of Hope bestowed on every one of us by the Giver of every good and perfect gift? I scarcely think we have, and yet how mentally and morally helpless we would be, were we to sink into a hopeless state! Hope, like a rainbow, lights up the dark cloud of sorrow; like a star, it twinkles in the midnight of grief; like a strong anchor, it steadies the trembling soul amid the billows of adversity. It is, in fact, to the human spirit what blood is to the natural body; the possession of it nerves us to action and sustains us in it, enabling us to accomplish much hard work of various kinds, from which we would shrink and turn away without such a stimulus.

How different is this natural hope, however, from the hope full of immortality, which animates the breast of every child of God! "If in this life only we have hope, we are of all men most miserable:" so writes the apostle; but the hope of the Christian enters into "that within the veil, whither the Forerunner is for us entered," and the promise has been given, that where He is, there shall also His servants be.

The hope of the Christian is closely linked with faith and love: "Now abideth these three," and they cannot be dissociated. *Love* is the fulfilling of the law, and we read that it *believeth* all things, and *hopeth* all things. The Divine plant of grace has faith as its root, drawing nourishment from the Saviour Himself; hope as its stem, vigorous and healthy; and love as its golden, soul-satisfying fruit—a fruit so attractive, that hungry and thirsty souls can enjoy it as they enjoy none other.

Jesus Himself is spoken of as "a plant of renown," and even His enemies were constrained to testify of Him that "He trusted in God." As to hope, it may surely be said of our great Exemplar that His helmet in the day of battle was "the hope of salvation," the salvation He was working out for His people, while the record left us of His life of loving self-sacrifice is, that "He went about doing good, and healing all manner of sickness and disease." Hope looks up. David says: "I will lift mine eyes unto the hills, from whence cometh my aid;" and elsewhere, "Mine eyes do fail with looking upward." Fear looks down, and sees the yawning wave; and destruction would certainly follow, were it not that *He* sends from above the succour we so sorely need.

Let us frequent the throne of grace more than we do, as an antidote to every kind of soul-discouragement. The more we bask in the rays of the Sun of Righteousness, the less will the damps of depression rest upon our spirits, and the stronger we shall be for the Lord's work. Of the Captain of our salvation we read:—"He shall not fail, nor be discouraged, until He have brought forth judgment unto truth." May we continually encourage ourselves in the Lord, so shall we be enabled to "do exploits" like David. "Hope thou in God" was the rallying cry of the great monarch himself, when he found his soul disquieted within him, and can we adopt a better? What more beautiful title does the Bible afford than "the God of Hope"?

Would we be like our Father in heaven, we must

seek to abound in hope. What a useful companion Hopeful was to Christian, as portrayed in Bunyan's allegory! All through the pilgrim-journey of Christian, and even in the river of death, his soul was refreshed by the words of cheer spoken by his friend. "A word spoken in season," how good is it! He who "spake as never man spake," knew how to speak a word to the weary, and He will teach us how to do it, if we sit at His feet as learners. How sweet the promise: "They shall be all taught of God," for "who teacheth like Him?"

Zenana Mission Work at Nagpoor.

I think those of my friends who are engaged in zenana mission work in what we may call the more fashionable cities of India would be surprised to find how commonplace is the work carried on in this connection in Nagpoor.

The houses visited are, for the most part, of the humblest sort, though we have access to some of the better class as well. An imaginary morning's visitation along with me will furnish the best idea of the nature of our work here.

Before I speak of the houses in detail, I must remark that my native helpers and I give ourselves to general evangelistic work, in addition to the regular visiting, so that our day's programme is often interfered with when we find opportunity of occupying new ground.

At this season of the year we set off for the city, or the less distant town of Seetabaldi, as soon after six o'clock in the morning as we can, and return between ten and eleven o'clock ; but we must start a good deal earlier as the heat increases, and come home sooner.

A tonga, drawn by bullocks, is our mode of conveyance, and we have quite a long drive of, say, two miles to the entrance of the city, along a very pretty country road. We always walk for at least a quarter of a mile, for the sake of exercise, and on certain days we have a good deal of walking in the city as well, when the streets are too narrow for the tonga. Part of the road leading to the first house we visit on Monday morning is swamped with water, and part is cut into such deep ruts that it is difficult for any conveyance to keep from upsetting. At the end of the journey, however, we reach a nice house, the owner of which at one time, many years ago, all but embraced Christianity, but failing in courage to make an open profession of his faith, he has fallen back into heathenism.

He is sensible enough, however, to value a measure of education for his two wives and the other members of his family, and he does not at all stand in the way of our imparting Christian instruction to his household. He has even come to our Mission Church now and again lately, but he goes no further.

One of his wives is such a gentle, affectionate woman. She listens attentively and prepares her reading lesson carefully. She wrote a very nice letter to me one day, in response to my suggestion, and in that letter she thanked me so lovingly for taking an interest in her, and expressed a prayerful desire that God might bless me.

This woman's daughter, after having been one of my pupils for some time, died of consumption last year, leaving behind her a little girl of, perhaps, a year old. The child pined sadly for a time, and I scarcely expected her to survive; but her sense of loss has now passed away, and she was looking very well when I last saw her. Since then, however, she has taken smallpox, I hear, and I am prevented on this account from paying my usual visit.

The first thing we do, on sitting down in any house, is to sing a hymn in Marathi and explain its contents, following this up, at times, by reading a little from one of the Gospels, or some nice little book published by the Tract Society. After this we sing another hymn, and then give lessons to any who wish to learn. As a general rule, I decline to teach fancy work to those who will not take the trouble to learn to read; but an exception is made in the case of a woman advanced in life, or when our friend happens to be a Mussulman, caring only to know her own language.

Near to the above-mentioned house is a Hindu temple, into which we are generally invited as we pass. We introduced ourselves there first of all, and were soon surrounded by a goodly gathering of people, curious to see what we were about, and now we are expected to look in when we are in the quarter.

The poor old man in charge of the idols sits poring over the Shastras, half unconscious of what is going on around him, or even lies on the floor asleep, while the words of life are falling on the ears of the others, until his attention is gained by some words addressed to him personally. Even then, however, he has nothing to advance in reply, good or bad. His dotish appearance, indeed, suggests the thought that he has become painfully assimilated to his helpless charge!

There are two houses a little farther on, where we are made welcome, in one of which I had a pupil for *one day*, if I remember; but her father prohibited her from learning, on the score that she would be too proud to work if she knew how to read. The little girl's brother is allowed to go to school, but he constantly plays truant. His sister, on the contrary, was quite eager to learn, and bade fair to become a good scholar.

In another house in this vicinity, my former pupil has been sent to a girls' school conducted by a young woman educated at the Free Church Boarding School, Bombay. Her daily attendance there will give her an opportunity of making much more rapid progress than she could have made, had she continued to receive only occasional lessons from me.

We have visited this school a few times, hoping to win the hearts of the children attending it; for there is no religious instruction given there, as it is under Government.

We are now and then called into native *boys'* schools by the Hindu teachers, and not long ago I was dignified to the office of Inspector, and requested to write a report of the state of the school in the visitors' book. I did not feel prepared to do this, however, the examination having been wanting in thoroughness!

One day we observed a number of gaily dressed women gathered together on the street near the home of a pupil. We asked them if they would like to hear a hymn, and, immediately seating ourselves on the protruding base of the mud house opposite to which they stood, we began to sing. A good many passers-by swelled the number of listeners, and after our little open-air meeting was over, a most respectable-looking man invited us into his house. This man has one of the sweetest little girls I ever saw, and I proposed teaching her to read. The father acquiesced smilingly, but on our calling again the other day, we found that the little maid was away on some expedition connected with her marriage!

This seems to be the auspicious season for weddings, and I like to take by surprise a large party assembled to do honour to the bride and bridegroom.

About ten days ago we had a splendid opportunity of singing gospel hymns, and telling the story of Jesus' love to one of the most motley throngs I ever saw. We became the central objects of attraction as soon as we had entered the large pavilion, and the attention bestowed was wonderful. The youthful bridegroom could not read, so there was no use of giving him a book; but several little fellows present carried off small prizes gained on the spot, by a public exhibition of their proficiency in the art. One of the women present carried the bride down from a raised platform in the far end of the tent, that I might inspect her more closely.

When we rose to go, we were presented with " pan," and we parted on the best of terms.

I have been very much encouraged by the welcome I have received in the homes of two native medical men. The wife of the first of these Baboos is a nice woman, and her home is a model of neatness. She takes great delight in hearing us sing our gospel hymns, and she likes to practise reading English. Both she and her friend, the Kali Baboo's wife, are adepts in fancy work, so that there is no need of instruction in this department. Her husband is the head native doctor of the hospital, in the compound of which his house stands, and this gives us an opportunity of looking in on the poor sufferers there. It was affecting to hear that one poor man I had twice visited for a few minutes had been longing for my return shortly before his death. He said that what I had been telling him made him feel well.

Here there are no little children to enliven the home, but an air of cheerfulness is imparted to the otherwise silent homestead by the presence of a number of live pets. A flock of beautiful pigeons, a deer, and some singing-birds are conspicuous amongst these. Our friend has long ago attained great proficiency in various kinds of fancy work, and it is now her ambition to become a good reader of English. This desire on her part gives us an errand to the house, and an opportunity of imparting to her, day after day, the truths of the gospel as they are embodied in the sweet hymns contained in the *Bul Bul* and *Gayan-amrit*. She is very fond of these, only, as they are written in Marathi, they have to be translated into Hindustani ere she can appreciate their meaning, the aid of my young companion from the Orphanage being called into requisition at this point. I may remark here that I am more and more convinced of the necessity of a knowledge of colloquial Hindustani to any one hoping to be *universally* useful as a missionary in this country! It is pleasing to see the friendly familiarity existing between the mistress and servants in many of the houses we visit. Only this morning I was quite struck with the freedom with which a poor, meanly-attired woman, employed as a cook to this household, seated herself in the doorway to enjoy the singing, while she succeeded by her humble, earnest appeal for one more hymn in getting us to open our books again, and do as she desired!

But we must hurry on to our second house, the home of another medical Baboo and his wife, one of the nicest couples I have met in India. It is believed by those who know this Baboo well, that he is a true Christian, although he has not yet made an open profession of his faith. His wife is a gentle, retiring woman, of great sweetness of disposition, and his three fine sons, who are being educated in our Institution, bid fair to turn out manly, and, as I would hope, *Christian* youths. On one occasion, when one of our missionaries put the question to his class:— "Supposing you were all convinced of the truth of Christianity, how many of you are prepared to make a stand for it?" one of these immediately rose to his feet. But to return to the mother. She also is an accomplished needle-woman, and, in addition to being able to read Bengali, her native language, she has acquired English very well. She reads a lesson to me, carefully prepared beforehand, twice a week, and has it explained in Hindustani. She was so much delighted with the harmonium kindly sent to us lately from home, as a help in our work, by the ladies of the Committee in Aberdeen, that she requested me to teach her to play on some such instrument. Her husband entered most kindly into her wishes, and ere long a very nice little harmonium was got for her, and she is getting on well with her new study. My sister and I had the pleasure of entertaining her in our own bungalow one day, not long ago, her husband having brought her to see us in a covered conveyance. She was arrayed in a rich purple sarree, embroidered with gold, and there was no lack of handsome jewellery, though she is by no means a vain woman, her dress when in her own home being of the simplest kind. She thoroughly appreciated seeing all the little novelties connected with our English mode of living, and it was a real pleasure to show her everything likely to interest her.

A Brahman family, a little lower in the social scale, lives not far off from this Baboo's house, and here we have two pupils, orphans on the mother's side. The elder of these has a refined, sensitive-looking face, suggestive of quick feelings, and her relatives complain of her that, when offended, she refuses to eat, and remains fasting for a long time. I have informed them that the book she is now reading will give her good advice as to how she ought to behave, and I hope she will improve ere long. The punishment of continued wilfulness is to be that no nice hymn will be sung on the occasion of my next visit, and as this would be a disappointment affecting all round, it is possible that more conciliatory measures may be adopted with the poor child.

We look in, as we find opportunity, on some other houses in this quarter. In one of these I lighted on a poor woman suffering from a terrible sore on her forehead. I persuaded her to come with me to the hospital to receive proper treatment for it; but nothing would induce her to remain there, as this would involve the breaking of her caste! It was strange to hear such an excuse urged in the circumstances, for the poor creature was destitute of relatives, at a distance from her own part of the country, and dependent upon strangers for her daily bread. All that could be done was to give her some medicine in her hand, with some wholesome directions as to how to apply it. A promise that she would return every day for inspection was easily extracted from her; but, alas! as I could not but predict, she very soon gave up doing so, and settled down amid her pain as before.

On Wednesday it is hard to decide to which quarter we should turn our steps, so many houses requiring to be visited suggest themselves to the mind. We have just to take one set of them one week, and another the week following. In one of these directions we generally visit, first a mere hut, closely adjoining a very tiny temple, tenanted by an unsightly little dirt-begrimed idol, whose guardian the neighbouring family seem to be. The head of the house is, apparently, very near death. He was, at one time, a very wild man, I understand, but of late he has been quite subdued, listening earnestly to the gospel story, and declaring that, if restored to health, he will profess Christianity. His father, before him, seemed near the Kingdom at one time, I am told, but I am afraid he became hardened afterwards, his courage having failed when the duty of *confessing* Christ was urged upon him. Our good Bible-woman associated with me in the work knows the history of the family well, and it has fallen to her lot to minister at the death-beds of both the father and son.

In another house, not far off, a very interesting family lives. The burly Brahman at the head of it receives us very graciously, but he is a very bigoted idolater. His five sons are being educated at our Institution, which is much in their favour, for they can scarcely grow up so bigoted as their father. Their mother is a quiet, sensible woman, possessed of a good deal of perseverance, judging from the steadiness with which she pursued the working of a topee she had attempted, till it was brought to a successful conclusion. The only fault was, that it turned out to be rather small, the child's head having possibly grown while the operation was going on! By dint of coaxing, accompanied by the promised reward of an English doll, one of the little girls was secured as a pupil in reading. The mother attempted to learn to read, but gave it up as hopeless, her mind not lying so much to it as to the topee-making. I could mention many other houses visited on Wednesdays and Thursdays, but I refrain, preferring to give a sketch of to-day, Saturday's, visitation, in conclusion. (The Tuesday's round is repeated on Friday.)

We set out at mid-day for Seetabaldi, instead of Nagpoor, intending to visit several houses where we are duly expected on a Saturday; but after paying our first visit, we got amongst a new set of houses while in quest of a certain influential one to which we had been called, so that we were unable to complete the day's programme. Such a hearty little woman lives in the first house! She leads me forward by the hand, almost *places* me in my chair, and then, drawing her own one near, she joins with all her might in singing the hymns, which have a great charm for her. Her husband is a very enlightened, liberal-minded man, and he has taught her to read well, so that she is content to be a listener. A very appreciative one she is, so ready to respond to what strikes her as being particularly forcible, her face meanwhile glowing with pleasure at hearing her own language rendered by a stranger, for we have but recently made each other's acquaintance. When I asked her the other day if she really worships images, she assured me that she does not, and that she believes in only *one* God. It was pleasing to hear this, but it remained for me to tell her of the necessity of the God-appointed *Mediator*, even His own dear Son.

On leaving this dear friend, we made our way, under the guidance of a little girl, who moved on before us, to quite a new house, the owner of which I had encountered on the street on a former day, when he promised to make us welcome on our return. Our interview with him was by no means satisfactory, however, though it was nice to get access to his household. He seemed disposed to make light of us and of our message, pretending all the time to be very simple and illiterate. Notwithstanding this, he bore with me while I read a chapter from "Summary of Scripture Doctrine," besides listening quietly to the hymns, in this way allowing *others* an opportunity of profiting, if *he* did not feel inclined to do so. A young man, doing some work as accountant, as he sat in the verandah surrounded by his papers, was very glad to have a little book bestowed upon him too, so that I hope our visit was not altogether in vain.

On leaving this house we turned by mistake into a courtyard leading to a house we had never been "called to," but as the intrusion did not seem to be taken amiss, I proposed singing a hymn ere turning away. No objection was offered, and we had a capital audience, consisting of fair-complexioned Brahman women and girls, some of whom were engaged in cleaning rice for the evening meal.

In the next house we found a young girl who had been under instruction in a town forty miles distant from this, where Christian influences have been at work for many years back. The sister of her former instructress told me about her, and it was an unexpected pleasure to make her acquaintance. A pundit was engaged in helping a little boy with his lessons, as we sought to make friends with our new acquaintances, and it was very evident that his sympathies were with us. He had overheard some of our conversation in the former house, and had become interested, it would appear. He most gratefully accepted a copy of the *Bul Bul*, from which we were singing, and assured me he would make a study of its contents. This highly intelligent man is in charge of a school attended by two hundred boys, and if his influence over them is for good, much will have been gained in the cause of Christianity.

But I must hasten to a conclusion. This is but the sowing time. Be it ours to "sow beside all waters," remembering that the Lord of the harvest has declared that those who do this are "blessed."

About this time Alexina talks much of open doors multiplying on her, and of grateful receptions given her, not only in the better-class houses, but even in the Poorhouse, in the suburbs of the city, where one forlorn old woman assured her that "its inmates were all *her children;*" so she felt it her duty to return frequently and attend to them. "Our field of labour is very wide," she says; "may we have grace and wisdom to occupy it well."

Talking of the principal gods worshipped in Nagpoor (for Hinduism has diverse aspects), she mentions Vishnu (*i.e.* the Preserver). There are nine manifestations of this divinity. Many consider Krishna one form. Then there is the bestial god Shiva (the great destroyer), the husband of the horrible Kali, who is greatly feared, being supposed to be the originator of all trouble. Even the Gónds "do *pujah*" to Kali. Besides these popular gods, the Hindus in Nagpoor do homage to the cobra, while in the villages bordering the jungles there are many representations of the wagha or tiger.

Alexina always, as far as practicable, took advantage of the holy festivals to collect an audience. On these occasions her hymn-singing was very valuable, as it tended to disarm prejudice, and afforded an excellent opportunity for directing the listeners to the Saviour. She writes :—

"One day Amundibai, our valuable Bible-woman, told me that she wished to conduct me to a part of the city I did not know, where a large temple dedicated to Yagoba rears its head. There was to be special honour done to this god on that day, and large crowds would assemble, giving us an opportunity of usefulness not to be had every day. On our reaching the spot, and attracting the attention of a number of the worshippers by beginning to sing, a seat in a very novel position was assigned to us, the pedestal of the temple being selected, and in a few minutes we were hemmed in by a motley throng, eager to see and hear. Hymn after hymn was sung, with some simple explanatory remarks accompanying each, till hoarseness compelled us to desist and retire to our gharree. This day's visit opened up the way for further visiting in that quarter, and several private houses are now added to our list."

And again :—

"Well, Monday was a holiday in the city. It was the day for doing honour to *bullocks*, by way of redressing the grievances they are subjected to throughout the year (every driver poking at and pulling the tails of his animals continually, by way of urging them forward). I went out visiting as usual, however, as I had regretted on one or two such former occasions having remained at home. On the way we met the usual complement of country carts and tongas, only the horns of the weary beasts were finely gilded up and surmounted, in some cases, with a handsome pair of silk tassels. I think they ought to have been provided with looking-glasses, that they might at least have had the pleasure of admiring themselves, and seeing what honour had been put upon them!

"We had capital opportunities of sowing the seed that Monday morning, so many of the men and boys in the city being disengaged. We were called from one house to another in rapid succession, the hymns being the great attraction, and when at last we called a halt (our proceedings evidently being looked on as affording a species of 'tomasha,' or popular entertainment), I found that, slow as I had supposed my watch to be, it was one o'clock, and I had had no breakfast!"

The Rev. John Douglas, late of Bandhara, also relates an account of an interesting service on one of the feast-days, in which the Rev. Narayan Sheshadri took part. The visit of this man of God to Nagpoor was greatly enjoyed by Alexina. He thoroughly tested her in her knowledge of Marathi, and expressed himself as well satisfied with the result. He also initiated her, in three lessons, into Hindustani, drilling her in that language during the course of his visit.

Mr. Douglas says :—

"Not the least interesting service that Mr. Sheshadri held while with us was the large open-air meeting he addressed in the bazaar on Thursday morning. It happened to be a Hindu feast-day in honour of Gunputti. The Institution was therefore closed, and all business in the city was suspended. The image of this divinity represents him as a man possessing four hands and an elephant's head. Like all other objects of Hindu worship, he has anything but a prepossessing appearance. Immense numbers of these images, made of clay, and varying in size and price to suit the

A HINDU FEAST-DAY.

taste and purse of the purchaser, are sold on the first day of the feast. While it lasts they are objects of divine homage, and at its close are thrown into the river. Early in the morning Mr. Sheshadri, Miss Mackay, Mr. Nordfors and myself started for the scene of our labours. On the way we secured the help of some of our native Christians, who gladly accompanied us. As we approached the city we could easily perceive that something unusual was going on. Strains of not very melodious music greeted our ears from every side. Processions in honour of the god passed hither and thither at frequent intervals. These were generally headed by musicians, who caused the discordant noise of which I have just spoken, and standard-bearers holding aloft banners on which were emblazoned many strange devices. These were but the heralds of the god himself, who followed immediately after, seated in a palanquin, which was borne on the shoulders of four men, and looking as attractive as paint and tinsel finery could make him. Behind him, and closing up the rear of the procession, were the members of the family to whom the god belonged, seated on horseback or mounted on elephants, which were richly ornamented with gold and silver trappings in honour of the occasion. Through the busy streets we slowly threaded our way until we reached the market-place, a large square situated in the very centre of the city. Along each side of this square the merchants squatted upon the ground, with their goods spread out before them. The articles most in demand seemed to be grain and vegetables and Gunputtis. We selected an open space under the shade of a tree, and commenced our meeting by singing one or two Marathi hymns, which Miss Mackay led, being supported by the lusty voices of our native Christian friends. Soon a considerable crowd gathered round us, and listened most respectfully to what was said. Mr. Sheshadri made the parable of the Prodigal Son the basis of his remarks, from which he spoke at some length with great fluency and ease. It was interesting to watch the different expressions upon the countenance while the address was proceeding. Many seemed to look on with idle curiosity, treating the whole affair as if it were a part of the holiday entertainment provided for their express benefit. One man, who held an image of Gunputti in his hand, listened most attentively, and at more frequent intervals than was agreeable, loudly re-echoed the sentiments that pleased him, accompanying the remarks with numerous approving nods and smiles. At the back of the crowd was one whose fantastic dress and emaciated appearance pointed him out as a religious devotee. Although less demonstrative than his neighbour, the word seemed to be sinking deeper into his heart. Who can tell but that it was the first time in his life he had heard that the God he had been so long trying to propitiate by a life of privation and suffering was a loving Father who wanted to welcome him to his heart and home, and yearned to supply those cravings which the unsatisfying husks of heathenism failed to meet.

"Two of our Christian teachers followed Mr. Sheshadri with short addresses, one in Marathi and another in Hindi. Hymns were interspersed between each address. As a goodly number of English-speaking young men were in the crowd, it was suggested that I should address them a few words in that language. This I did, prefacing my remarks with one or two sentences of Marathi, which, whatever intelligent ideas they conveyed to the minds of the audience, had the effect of causing their faces to relax into a good-humoured smile.

"With the singing of another hymn our meeting came to an end. Doubtless, many in the crowd wondered to see a European lady standing with us, seeing that it is contrary to the Hindu ideas of propriety that the two sexes should mingle so freely together as is the habit in our country. Mr. Sheshadri therefore took the opportunity to advertise Miss Mackay's work by explaining that she had left her friends and home in order to teach their wives and sisters, and that she would be only too glad to visit the houses of those who would be willing to receive her. Before we left, a number of copies of the Gospels and other religious books were distributed to those who were able to read ; but the eagerness of the crowd to receive a book was so great, and the jostling became so violent, that we found it necessary to beat a retreat into our conveyance, and to stipulate that no more books would be given unless we received coppers for them.

"We returned home, thanking God for the high privilege of spreading abroad the knowledge of His name in a city which is so entirely given up to idolatry. Whatever be the visible fruits of such efforts, this we know, that not one of the Lord's words "shall return to Him void." Frequently it is the experience of those engaged in the Lord's work in India, that the bread which is cast upon the water is found, even though it should be after many days. Especially is this true of those who come more systematically under the teaching of God's Word than is possible for those who hear it only occasionally preached. An instance of this came under my own observation a few months ago. One day a young man called upon me to have some conversation about religion. Formerly he had been a student at our Institution, and had read the Bible there. He prosecuted his studies until he obtained the degree of F.A.; and now he has a good appointment as teacher in an Anglo-vernacular school in the Central Provinces. Although he had ceased to read the Bible he had not forgotten its teaching, and the deep unrest of his soul compelled him to seek help from those who he thought would be able to assist him. The result of a long conversation I had with him that day was that I presented him with a copy of the Bible, which he promised to study anew. I encouraged him to communicate with me whenever he met with any difficulties in the course of his reading, and from time to time I have received letters from him, asking explanation of important texts connected with the person of Christ, the necessity and nature of regeneration, and other subjects bearing upon the plan of salvation. In one letter he says: 'Write me by return of post—just by return—because there is a deep-seated excitement in me which leads me on to study the Bible with all the eagerness necessary for a pursuit of this kind.' Surely the Good Shepherd is going after this lost one, and will yet bring him in with rejoicing."

Invitations from many homes, and the removal of prejudice where it formerly existed, together with permanent friendships continually being formed, gave Alexina hope and encouragement.

> "The best men, doing their best
> Know, peradventure, least of what they do;
> Men usefullest in the world are simply used;
> The nail that holds the wood must pierce it first,
> And He alone who wields the hammer sees
> The work advanced by the earliest blow. Take heart."

She sighed and groaned and longed for more conversions; but there are many results—often the best and most enduring—which do not appear in missionary reports. The Rev. W. Grey,[1] in connection with this, states:—"Numbers and figures give us but a very inadequate view of missionary progress and prospects in a country like India. We are thankful for them, but our view of progress may well be a brighter and more hopeful one than even the brightest and most hopeful which the statistics furnish. In estimating progress, we must notice the various indications there are of the inward working towards Christianity of the people's minds. The springing into existence of every new Somaj may be regarded as a new form of uttering the words, 'Sir, we would see Jesus.' The inert mass of Hindu thought is being more and more moved."

The Rev. James Johnson, author of "A Century of Missions," also declares that "India's millions are passing through a crucial transition stage. The old

[1] See "Nine Years' Missionary Progress in India," *C.M.S. Intelligencer*, May, 1893.

faiths have lost credence, the new has not yet been accepted. Fermentation of mind prevails everywhere, and is the strongest evidence of the progress of Christianity."

> "'Upward and onward' in faith, then, we sow,
> Depending on God to cause it to grow;
> And though we may not behold it take root,
> May those who succeed us rejoice in the fruit."

How the sowing progressed will be seen below.

Notes in Connection with my Visiting in the City.

Feb. 10*th*, 1880.

Reached our first house, and found only my pupil Peesabai and her mother at hand. My chair was set, however, and the piece of cotton carpet spread for Amundibai and Cheenie to sit on, and very soon the neighbours were called, and the company swelled in magnitude, as we went on. "Christ, the Nectar of Life," was the hymn we began with, after explanation of which, I read a little from the Gospel by John about Jesus being the Bread of life. After Peesabai and a friend who can already read had done with their lesson, treating of the Commandments and the Lord's Prayer, Peesabai asked me to sing "Jesus of Nazareth," and this formed a beautiful basis for the narration of the gospel story. I sometimes think how pleased Dr. Bonar and other hymn-composers would be could they overhear us rendering their hymns in Marathi to these simple-minded heathen. A curious picture we presented at that first gathering. I had slipped off my chair, to get out of the way of the sun (we were sitting outside), and taken a seat on the ledge of the small door leading into a tiny room in the gable-end of the house. In this room Peesabai's mother and some male relatives were sitting on the floor, forming part of the audience. Peesabai sat close beside me, her arms resting upon me confidingly, occasionally whispering into my ear a question in Marathi, such as, "Why didn't you come last Thursday?"

On the earthen bank surrounding the little courtyard several women and boys were "perched," for their sitting posture is not unlike that of fowls in a roost! and, crowding upon each other's shoulders were a number of the passers-by, who had turned in to see what we were about.

As we drove to our next house a little boy ran after us, to ask us to follow him to a house where they wished to see us. I alighted most cheerfully, and in a few seconds we found ourselves in a little centre of domestic life.

A middle-aged man in thick brass (perhaps *gold*, by the bye!) spectacles was the presiding genius in the scene. He is an artist of some kind, probably a painter of the portraits of the gods and goddesses! and he aspires to having certain members of his household taught to read. At first a boy was brought forward, for whom instruction in English was desired, but, upon our mission to the women and girls being explained, some four or five little maids became candidates for the proposed instruction, as well as one grown woman, and anon, these were told off to their three respective teachers, not, however, till after the head of the establishment and all in the verandah had been regaled, and in some measure edified, by the singing of two nice hymns. The first began like this:—"Teerta, yatra, juppa, suana, dana, tuppa—kālëanay hay pápādzata nahee," *i.e.*—"By pilgrimages, bathing, giving of alms, etc., sin is not removed." "Wah!" was the appreciative interjection made use of by our friend in spectacles, when we had finished, and he gave a most attentive hearing to the explanatory remarks made by Amundibai, when we had done.

Saturday, Feb. 15*th.* Yesterday we had such a pleasant morning's visiting—different from that of the day before, when no one seemed particularly interested.

Our women at the first house turned out in full force, and we gave a lesson in reading to about half a dozen of them. It was arranged, at the same time, that the little boy, my favourite, with the thoughtful face and large, mild eyes, should present himself at once for admission into the Free Church Institution, his mother at last having acquiesced in the matter of the trifling monthly fee necessary to the carrying on of his education. On leaving this house and turning our faces towards the large Brahman domicile to which we were lately called, we observed all the little girls on the outlook for us, from the flat roof! It was pleasant to see that they were eagerly "watching our path," or "looking at our path"—the literal translation of the Marathi expression for "to expect." We found quite a row of seats placed for us in the upstairs verandah—a spacious, but tumble-down-looking erection (in this country, literally, "change and decay in all around I see"); for Mrs. Stothert and Nellie, who accompanied me last day, were evidently expected again. Well, we sat down, sang and explained our hymn—a very beautiful, swinging one (I'll sing it to you, D.V., when I get home, and you will see that the adjective is not misapplied), entitled, "Life is Fleeting." Then I read the two parables about the man having an hundred sheep, who lost one, and the woman who swept the house diligently, to find her lost piece of silver, finishing off with the hymn, "Come to Jesus." Meantime a servant arrived, bearing in his hand a small parcel done up in green leaves (paper they never use), and in a minute a perfectly lovely necklace of roses, threaded together as thickly as they could lie on the string (a pendant of the same, varied with white snowdrop-like blossoms, being attached in front), was thrown round my neck by "Tanibai," the little woman I teach, while a packet of home-made, wee, white sweets was put into my hand. These had been brought upstairs by the mother of my pupil, a stout, very fair-complexioned, youthful-looking woman, in whose eyes I was very much pleased to have found favour, because at first she seemed to look suspiciously upon me, and moreover, there is a certain haughtiness of bearing about her, as well as a good degree of temper within, which led her one morning to give quite a sore pinch to one of the little girls sitting too near her (after she had taken her bath, I suppose). I bestowed unbounded praises on the roses, pronouncing them "phar soonder," and asking if any man could bring such beauty out of the dark, ugly earth. They confessed that it was Dāw who made them; and I told them that we should worship the great Creator, and not His works (as they do, walking round a tree ever so many times, etc.). In addition to the little girls present, we had eight or ten of the grown members of the household, and some of the school-boys. A crazy woman has taken to following us, here and there, reminding me of the demon-possessed maiden we read of in Acts, who called out: "These men are the servants of the most high God, who show unto us the way of salvation." She began smoking a rude pipe in our midst, the other day, but when the woman of the house got up to tell her to leave off, she darted out like a scared hare! She has a strong voice like a man, but she hushes it down when she joins us, as if she understood what we are about. Wild creature as she is, she does not neglect to touch her forehead well up with the idolatrous marks worn by her neighbours. Who knows but, like Mat, the idiot boy, she may be so influenced by the Spirit of God as to be led to love and trust Jesus, of whom we tell?

I had a novel bit of experience a morning or two ago, in the appearance amongst us of a youth, who craved my assistance with his English lesson. He was required to give the meaning, in plain English, of Cowper's humorous piece: "Between nose and eyes a strange contest arose" (as to which the spectacles belonged). It gave me great pleasure to help him, but, when he remarked complacently, when we had done, that he thought he would often get help from me in the same way, I felt it my duty to tell him that, unless he were to come to my house, I could not help him again, as I devoted my mornings to the women! He said nothing particular in reply.

So much regarding my work, as at present carried on! I like to write a little about it, when I have got some cheering incidents to narrate; and lately, new openings and hearty receptions have encouraged me.

I am going to have a rest for a few days in Kampthi just now, as suggested by Mrs. Cooper. I go there to keep Mrs. Stothert company, she again taking a motherly oversight of Dr. Theobald's little orphans, in his absence from home. Mr. Stothert is away on a little missionary tour. I never met any one with more of the missionary spirit than dear Mrs. Stothert has. She is in full sympathy with the native women.

A. MACKAY.

(*To the Children of Holborn Free Church Sunday School, Aberdeen.*)

MY LITTLE BUNGALOW, NAGPOOR,
May 10*th*, 1880.

I have been thinking that the Sunday School children of Holborn Free Church, Aberdeen, might like to hear something about the missionary work I am engaged in here; and for this reason I propose to send them a letter, containing a little account of what I am seeing from day to day. But the better way will be for me to suppose that I am speaking face to face with you, so I will just begin my talk with you at once, leaving you to ask through your teachers any questions you would like me to answer next time I write.

This morning, Amundibai, the native Bible-woman, and I had a very long way to drive in our bullock-gharree before we arrived at the first house we visit on Monday morning, but at last we reached it, and found six women, a young girl (who is a *widow!*) and a little boy, eager to be sung to and taught.

How much you would like to hear a Marathi hymn! The strange sounds are so interesting, but the beauty of it is that the meaning of the words is as clear to the people we are singing to as *our* language is to us. We sang a hymn about the folly of thinking that the mere use of words in prayer will please God, and Amundibai explained all about it. Then I listened to four of the women as they read out of such a nice book called, "Stree Kunt Bhooshun," which means in English, "Ornament for the neck of females," while two of the others were being taught the Marathi alphabet by Amundibai. One or two other women and the boy merely listened, and a little baby boy tumbled about on the floor, playing with my boot, which must have been a curiosity to it! The lesson for to-day was about the necessity of teaching children the truths of God's Word, and after we had finished reading, I talked with the women about the sinfulness of worshipping idols. One elderly woman, seated quite near me, on the floor, opened her eyes very wide when she heard that it was her duty to give this up, and, to convince her of the truth of what I was saying, I told her that this is God's command, and I added that I never worship idols though I pray to the true God every day before going to the city. I was then asked if God speaks to me when I pray to Him, all alone, in my room!

Before we left, I asked Amundibai to offer up a short prayer, hoping this would show them what I meant, better than a great deal of explanation, but though most of the listeners behaved remarkably well, one laughed out loud, so strange did it seem to her to hear a prayer offered to *Nobody*, as she supposed. The one who behaved badly was rebuked immediately by one of the women at the other side of the room, and a little conversation began, so that I had to turn round and ask them to keep still. We cannot wonder at this way of behaving, when we consider that the heathen do not understand what spiritual worship is at all. I am glad to tell you, however, that at least two of those present seemed to like the thought of praying in this way, and agreed to follow it.

No more, at present, my dear young friends. Pray for me very often, that I may be greatly blessed by God, and made a great blessing. It is exactly two and a half years to-day since I reached India, and my earnest hope is, that if God spare me for just as long again, I will have the great joy of seeing all my loved friends at home again, and *you* amongst them. Good-bye.

Yours very affectionately,
A. MACKAY.

P.S.—The following lines I composed while lying awake the other night.

"FOR JESU'S SAKE, AMEN."

How many thousand little lips
  Each day these words are saying,
Come, children, tell me what they mean,
  And in whose name you're praying.

"For Jesu's sake." What has He done?
  Why is His name so sweet,
That saints in heaven and saints on earth
  Are gathered at His feet?

"He died for us," I hear you say,
  And you have answered right,
The Lamb was slain, and, oh! His blood
  Is precious in God's sight.

"For Jesu's sake." His lovely robe
  Of spotless righteousness,
When put upon my sinful soul,
  I'm clothed in heaven's own dress.

> To meet the pure and holy God,
>   Who cannot look on sin,
> I'll ready be; "for Jesu's sake"
>   He'll bid me Welcome in.
>
> "For Jesu's sake." This golden key
>   Can open heaven's gate ;
> The angels know His name so well,
>   They will not bid me wait.
>
> I thank Thee, Jesus, Saviour dear,
>   For all Thy love to me.
> Oh, may I, when this life is done,
>   Go Home to be with Thee !

(*To the Home Committee.*)

NAGPOOR,

June 2nd, 1880.

I had an interesting experience this morning, and I would like to tell you about it.

Amundibai and I were guided to a new house by Cornelius, one of our native Christian teachers in the city, a very large house, towards which, I believe, I used to cast longing eyes, being anxious to gain admission. Things did not promise very well, from an outside point of view, the surroundings of the entrance being so neglected and untidy-looking, but on our being introduced to the housekeeper within, we discovered, by the study of her person, that poverty had no place in her circumstances. The amount of jewelry the otherwise sensible-looking woman had on was simply marvellous, her fingers alone *exempted*, strange to say! for a couple of silver rings on one finger was all they had to boast of. In her nose was an immense brooch, rather than ring, solidly made up of pearls, varied by a few blue stone beads! In her ears were such pendants—regular suspended bells of pearls! On her neck a necklace of common beads, of about the thickness of an infant's wrist, to which was attached an ornament that reminded one of the breastplate we read of as being worn by Aaron! It was somewhat square in shape, studded thickly with emeralds and rubies alternately. Above the elbow she wore a gold armlet of about an inch and a half in width, while on her wrist, extending upwards, was a succession of tinsel-looking bracelets, confined at each end by a massive gold-knopped one. On her toes were a number of richly-wrought silver ornaments, with chains linking them together. Her cholee (inner little tight-fitting jacket) and sarree were of broidered silk, corresponding in richness with her ornaments. Excuse my going into detail like this. You see, the sight was an unusual one to me, too, seeing that it is amongst a humbler class of people, generally speaking, I have been, as yet, privileged to labour. I took special notice of the above to-day, while Amundibai was explaining the hymn we had sung, in Hindi, a language I am a stranger to. As you will readily believe, I felt the force of the caution given by the apostle in reference to female attire, as I took an inventory of the scene before me.

The strange contrast is that the tables, etc., in the room occupied by this elaborately adorned housekeeper were allowed to stand covered with a shameful coating of dust.[1]

After sitting for a little while, a tumbler of scaldingly hot milk and weak tea was put into my hand, an act of really *considerate* kindness, my European taste being deferred to!

So much for the *external* view of things. As to the rest, we made good friends, first of all imparting what instruction we could, through the medium of a pretty hymn sung; and last, though by no means least, in our friend's estimation, a rather lengthy lesson in topee-making was given to a very apt pupil, who can already handle a needle and thread very skilfully, as the many rich patterns for the ornamentation of cholees she showed me can testify. Of

---

[1] Probably the mistress of the house was afraid of having the cobwebs removed, as spiders are religiously protected by Hindus. Every product of the cow is also considered sacred, and in many parts of India, the crockery is washed, and the floors sprinkled with sârri, which is not pure water, but a fluid having a savour suggestive of the cowshed!

these patterns I was permitted to keep one, to show my friends at home.

Our friend has a daughter, a girl of sixteen or seventeen, whose husband's home is in Calcutta. We will try to get her to consent to learn to read while she is here. It would have made you very sad, could you have peeped, as I did, into a side verandah, where the father of the family was performing his devotions. There he sat, like a child amidst its toys, tiny, shell-like dishes, etc., etc., containing flowers, paste, etc., his eyes shut, and his lips moving as fast as possible, as he counted off, on a concealed rosary, how many prayers he had given utterance to, or, more likely, how many times he had repeated the name of his god. He took no notice of us, but I *insinuated* a "salaam" upon him, as he passed through the room when he had finished. He did respond, but not pleasantly.

A dear little schoolboy joined us, before we left, who could speak a little English. He looked so glad to see us. A representation of the Saviour hung on one of the walls, unknown to our friends!

Good-bye, dear friends,

Yours affectionately,

A. MACKAY.

(*To an Uncle in Nova Scotia.*)

NAGPOOR,
October 7th, 1880.

MY DEAR UNCLE,—

I am going to give you a little sketch of my everyday work here, in connection with my calling as a missionary. Well, you must imagine me as taking a seat in some verandah, or outer room, belonging to a very humble style of house, and presently being surrounded by a motley gathering of passers-by, in addition to the inmates of the house itself. A native Bible-woman and one of our elder girls from the Orphanage accompany me, and we three peregrinate from house to house all the morning, now in our covered conveyance, drawn by bullocks, now on foot, in every house singing and explaining gospel hymns in the native language, or reading a little aloud, as the case may be, and in addition to this, giving lessons in reading and fancy work to those who desire to be taught. The little boys in the streets, wherever we go, are our *special* adherents, and many a little hand becomes the medium of conveying the gospel message into idolatrous homes into which we have no access, it being a favourite habit of mine to distribute little books, gratis, to those who can read. I had a nice little sum of money sent me, not long ago, by the Sunday School children belonging to the church I used to attend in Alva, and with that I got a fresh supply of such gospel publications.

Dear Uncle, I feel that I have been called to angelic work, but the enemy of souls seeks to hinder me by harassing my own spirit. I am sure you will grant my request, when I ask you to remember me in your prayers. I doubt not you do so already. May we be enabled to "continue instant in prayer," remembering that "greater is He that is *for* us than all they that be against us."

Adieu! beloved Uncle,

Your affectionate niece,
ALEXINA.

My Experiences in the City this Morning,
April 14*th*, 1881.

Cheenie, my companion from the Orphanage, and I started at about six o'clock this morning, on our usual round of visiting. In little more than half an hour we were in the city, and soon had reached our first house—that of a Marwadi, or member of a certain mercantile class of people, from another part of India. My pupil here is a childish, good-natured girl of perhaps fifteen years of age. She has been trying to do a little fancy work, but she is far from clever, and finds difficulties where there appear to be none! It is pleasant, however, to be welcomed to the house, on whatever pretext, as an opportunity is given us of delivering our message. The girl's mother and her little lame brother usually join us, and occasional listeners besides.

On our way to the second house I purposed visiting, we turned down a wrong street by mistake, and as I recognised by my surroundings that we were near a certain new house I had failed to find my way back to, on a preceding day, I resolved to renew my inquiries after it. A kind woman we occasionally visit undertook to be our guide, but we found ourselves amongst strangers, on entering the house she conducted us to. So much the better, I thought, for we were well received, and a First Book was solicited for a young woman who was disposed to become a learner.

We have gained access to a new house by this mistake, for we were invited to return, and the hope was expressed that we would teach our friend to *make a scarf,* as well as to read !

We were successful, at length, in finding out the house that was the real object of our search, and our re-appearance gave great satisfaction. Including my pupil, a young widow, whose father is very anxious that she should be taught to read, we had six interesting women as listeners, one of whom, in particular, was most attentive.

On leaving this little company, I invited myself into a neighbouring house on observing a number of people in the verandah and courtyard, busily engaged in conversation. My companion and I were allowed to take a seat, but there was little sympathy evoked by the singing of the sweet hymn with which we introduced our subject, the Lord Jesus Christ Himself, and on the mention of *His* name a spirit of opposition was aroused in the breast of a man sitting near me, and he, somewhat rudely, urged on his companions to resume with him the copying work they were engaged in before we looked in upon them. I felt quite repulsed, but simply remarked that he seemed to be in a great hurry, adding that at the time of death we would have to leave all our earthly concerns behind.

"What do you say?" he inquired. "Will there be no *second birth?*" (referring to their transmigration theory).

The day before yesterday I was so cheered by having an invitation into another house. It was given by a girl with a very nice face, who had joined us in a house recently opened to us, about which I told Mrs. Anderson in my letter to her. There we found a middle-aged, nice-looking woman, with grey, shining curls clustering on the forepart of her well-shaped head. She was taught to read when a girl, but she has lost the art, though she remembers her letters a little! She is eager to recover it, however, and I had the pleasure of putting her in the way of doing so once more. It was pleasant, while engaged in singing a hymn, to *feel* her exchanging looks of great satisfaction with the other women present. The girl who conducted us to the house was simply a *help* in domestic work. Was it not like the "little maid" we read of in the story of Naaman? Mrs. Fraser, energetic little creature, is going to accompany me to the city to-morrow morning, if all is well. I had been asking her husband, in her presence, if he was not curious to know how I got on amongst the women, and this led to Mrs. Fraser expressing a wish to go with me, some day, to see for herself. She is to be ready for me at six o'clock. I have not been going out so early lately; the mornings are darker, and Pikoo, my man, in his eagerness to get me up in time, had roused me several times at such unearthly hours as a quarter and half-past three! So I told him rather to be a little late than make such mistakes. On certain days of the week, indeed, my women are not ready for me, even when I arrive at half-past six, sometimes. Twice a week we have, *at least*, a drive of three-quarters of an hour, ere we reach the first house! So that we would need to start early, especially as I like to walk the first part of the way for exercise. It is such a good thing they consent to have me in the early morning, for it is good for the health to be out then.

I have had some most interesting experiences within the past few days. One morning, when Amundibai, Cheenie and I were on our way to the house to which Bulwunt Rao (for I had been *coining* a name for him, I find!) introduced me, our tonga was besieged by a company of schoolboys, one of whom used to come and listen in the house we were going to. He now begged of me to go to his house; so the gharree had to be turned, and caused to proceed up a lane anterior to that we had been making for. By-and-by we had to alight, as we had come opposite to the house, which is removed off the lane a little. Following the boys, I found myself ushered into a little verandah, well peopled with spectators, and conducted to an arm-chair ready for me, in front of which stood a tiny covered table, with a coloured wineglass filled with flowers, standing on each side of a brass plate containing a heap of white chrysanthemums, which speedily resolved themselves in a long necklace and bracelets for "Mem sahib!" The latter, the fine bright boy put on me with his own hands. "Oh, I am really too grand!" I said, for several of the boys understood English, and I really felt it; the pure, freshly-gathered flowers so decidedly contrasted with the winter garb I had donned, in consideration of the cold morning in which I had set out, while it was still twilight. I had on my shepherd tartan morning-gown and my thick cloth jacket. Of course we sang a hymn and explained something about the true God before we passed on to another also new house, in which an old friend, however, lives, who used to be seen in the Brahman house I have often spoken of. It is she whose baby goes by the name of Johnnie (Jannie, as they call it), as suggested by me! Said infant is duly put into my arms each time, and on that morning, as I sat on a swinging seat in the verandah, dandling the almost naked little object, speaking baby talk to it (such as, " Where are your teeth?" in Marathi, sounding like this: " Toomtsay dánt kot-hay áhait?" " Do you love me?" *i.e.* "Toom-he muz-wur predë kurëta?") and bestowing an occasional kiss on it (Mooka) in the presence of all assembled, I wondered what you would all think, if you saw me!!!

NAGPOOR,
June 18*th*, 1881.

WELL, MOTHER DARLING!

I will just plunge into the subject-matter of Maggie's and my revealable thoughts this morning, connected as they are with the unlooked-for experience of the last few hours of our existence! I think I told you before that Mrs. Blake, the doctor's wife, had kindly asked us to be present as guests in Church on the occasion of " Lily's " wedding to-day; but last night the doctor's carriage and pair was observed by me to drive up to the door of the big bungalow, four persons being seated in it. Maggie and I were just about to take a little walk before the usual hymn practising, when, lo! the gentleman who had alighted from the carriage was seen making for our small abode! " Can any of our relations have arrived unexpectedly?" I inquired mentally. It was Mr. Browning, Inspector-General of Schools in the Central Provinces, sent by Mrs. Blake to invite us to the wedding breakfast! Two gentlemen had been obliged to decline at the last moment, and "it would give so much pleasure if we would come instead." We had been much wished before, but there was no room. We saw that a kindly feeling towards us prompted the invitation, and accepted it, remarking at the same time, that we could not be so suitably got up as we would like to be. All this was waived, however, and much satisfaction expressed that we were not too proud to accept.

Well, as you may imagine, the question as to how we could get ourselves up pressed on us somewhat imperatively. Maggie's blue dress, I knew, would be very suitable, but my white alpaca has seen better days. However, on retiring to our little bungalow for the night, we set our wits to work, and I manufactured a kind of feather trimming for its adornment out of the material of a bonnet! We went to bed very tired (at least I was), but awoke refreshed, and before I was half dressed, I heard a noise at the outer door, and a voice intimating that there was a letter for me. I threw on my dressing-gown and hurried to the door, to find Mrs. Whitton's burly cook bearing "a chit" from his mistress. The contents ran as follows:—

"DEAR MISS MACKAY,—

"I have been thinking could you not get your bonnet touched up a bit for the wedding? I have got half a yard of white satin, I would make over to you, and I can lend you some white feather tips, if the straw is not too soiled for such an attention. Mr. Whitton is off to school, so I am visible, if you like to come over.

"Yours, in the early morning,
"H. WHITTON."

I said, "Bot salaam," and was over in a shot, bag and baggage. In a twinkling the old trimming was off my bonnet, and we had set to work. . . . In short, ere the time had arrived for us to step into the carriage, "a love of a bonnet" was turned out, the cost of which might be two guineas, at least, in a Parisian or Bombay fancy warehouse! In the end I looked awfu' nice! Smairt sheen wi' buckles! Queen Anne-like fine black stockin's! Elá-borately trimmed goon o' a rich creamy hue! Neck, terrible swell! Heed, awfu' bonnie! Hauns, nicely glived! An' fat mair? *Tout-en-semble*, Alexina! An' Maggie? Oh, she was richt nice tee. I did up her neck for her in a *recherché* lace front, and in her pretty bonnet and canary-coloured gloves, she looked exceedingly well."

After this, the wedding and guests are described, and she concludes by saying, " Love to all my dear ones. Have I entertained you? It is not selfishness exactly that has made me speak so much of self.

Your loving daughter,
ALEXINA."

(*To her Father.*)

NAGPOOR,
September 27th, 1881.

Now may I tell you a little about my morning's visiting?

We first reached the clean house of which I speak in "Jottings," the house of the "Big Baboo," and I may truly add, his big wife. Her husband asked me, in her name, if I would excuse her if she did not prepare a new lesson (English) for next week, as the feast "Dussera" is at hand! I said it was for *her* pleasure I came, and that I wanted her to do as she felt inclined. I asked, moreover, "Shall I not come, then?" in reply to which her husband said, "Oh, yes; you may come. My wife likes to hear your singing." I might have added that her female attendants like to hear, too, for a more touchingly sweet face I have seldom seen than that of the humble woman who does the cooking, but is actually *sent for*, now-a-days, by her mistress, that she, too, may hear. The familiarity between mistresses of households and their servants is beautifully primitive in many cases. To-day, for instance, a stupid-looking man, who had come into the room of his own accord, tried to make my meaning *plain* to his imposing-looking mistress, as she had failed to catch the sense of my attempted

Hindustani! The Big Baboo is greatly given to flattering, and he will say to me on the rare occasions I see him: "Oh, ma'am, I never saw such a good lady as you," etc., etc. In reply, I say, "That's a *pity*," etc. Do you think the reason that we enjoy even flattery to some extent is, that it is *suggestive* of our possessing the good qualities attributed to us, just as a beautifully executed paper rose (like those in the fancy basket to my right) suggests the living fragrance of the real one?

In one house we were in to-day, a man was lying sleeping on the floor, with a "chudder" drawn over him from top to toe! (They all sleep with their faces covered!) He had been working all night in the Parsee Cotton Mills, which are now lit up at night by the electric light! On more than one occasion, when remarking on the ghastly appearance of some young man listening to the hymn-singing, I have found that he was one of the night workers! One poor fellow said he had got up from his sleep to hear us sing! I am glad to say that one relay of night-workers relieves another at the end of a fortnight, otherwise their lives would be greatly shortened, no doubt; but even on Sunday the mills are open. Yes, and Government roads are mended, etc., so that the Sabbath is not much of a sign amongst the heathen!

How the children in this country rally round us

zenana visitors! To-day, a little fellow, on catching sight of me in a neighbour's house, ran to his own, shouting, "Alee! alee!" (She's come! she's come!) I never met with such loving respect from the young as I have done since coming to Nagpoor. It makes it easier to work amongst the people when our path is thus strewn with roses.

THE LITTLE BUNGALOW,
August 12th, 1882.

MY DEAR MOTHER,—

I had some interesting experiences in the course of my round yesterday. My dear little Brahman girl turned up, as she generally does, in Trimbuk Rao's house, and stood close to me most of the time, being joined by two loving wee boys, who, with herself, followed me into the next house as well. She asked me in her musical little voice if I was coming to her school to give an examination. "The master has not called me," I said. "If he calls me, I'll come." "Toomcheekhooshe" (It's your good pleasure), she said. The little darling helps me to sing the hymns, having committed one or two to memory from a small collection of them I gave her as "baksheesh," and she chats away with me as much at her ease as if I were her little companion. I wish I could remember her name.

An old acquaintance in another house did not receive me nearly so warmly as usual, and I was afraid I had offended her by staying away too long. Her depressed spirits she immediately accounted for, however, when she gave me the sad, sad news that her eldest son was dead. How? He had been drowned in the tank, and, saddest of all, *by his own act.* The reason of the mad act seemed to be quite unknown to his mother. He was a married man, twenty-five years of age, but had no children. He had at one time attended our Mission School, I learned, and his younger brother, whom we saw, is still a pupil there. We sang the hymn, "O Lord, give me Thy true peace," and Dnyanapoo dwelt so nicely on the sweet thoughts it contained, with special reference to the case of the bereaved widow before her. Another bright intelligent woman was present, with her four-year-old girl seated at her side—a veritable *baby*, still dependent on her mother, and on her alone, for sustenance. The woman in another house had quite an enraged expression on her face as we entered, encouraged by the welcome given us by other members of the household. On inquiring as to the cause, Dnyanapoo told me that she was terrified lest I had touched her "kupperas, sarrees," etc., which were stretched on a line to dry in the little yard through which we had passed. I took occasion to remark a

ANGER DEFILES THE HEART. 217

little afterwards to a girl, across whose face an angry look flitted, that anger in the heart defiled it, but that a cloth got no defilement by being touched. A beaming smile and an assurance that she was not angry was the reply. (I think some children had been annoying her by making a noise). Fancy my borrowing a shawl from the Baboo's wife, to whom I paid my last visit, to protect me from the damp, as it had been raining heavily. I got it at once; her youthful-looking husband bringing it out to me himself; a beautiful white one, like a Ramport chudder. This Baboo, "Bebin Bhose" his name is, belongs to the Brahmo Somaj persuasion. His wife reads to me in English, from the Gospel by Luke, and gets anything she does not understand explained in Hindustani. Her own language is Bengali, but she understands the other. She dresses her children in old-fashioned English style, like the pictures you see in Sunday School books. She came to our Bazaar, and laid out a good many rupees in adding to their wardrobe.

A Mussulman came to the door yesterday, selling fancy goods of various descriptions, and I had some talk with him on the subject of fasting, etc. He told me that his people fast [1] (religiously) for a month at a time, by the commandment of God. I told him

[1] This does not hinder them from eating sweetmeats, etc.

that he made a great mistake by so doing, that the Koran, Vedas, etc., did *not* come from God, only the Holy Scriptures, and that we would have to give an account, one day, as to how we had treated our *bodies* (which are God's gift) as well as our souls. The poor tired young woman carrying his basket declined my offer of a cup of tea.

CHAPTER XII.

ON AND AFTER FURLOUGH.

"*Five years have passed: five summers, with the length
Of five long winters! and again I hear
These waters, rolling from their mountain springs
With a soft inland murmur.*"

IN the end of 1882 the Rev. J. G. Cooper of Nagpoor writes :—

"The Misses Mackay, with their native assistants, Amundibai, Cheenie, Dnyanapoo, and Karoona, have diligently prosecuted their important labours during the year, but I leave the details of their efforts or work to be given by themselves. It is evident that they occupy a wide field among the women of the city, and have no lack of excellent opportunities of sowing the good seed of the Word among them. Miss Mackay, after finishing her five years' engagement, left this on the 14th November to return to Scotland, but after a little rest, hopes to come back with renewed energies, to resume her efforts among the women in this part of the Lord's vineyard. In the meantime, she carries with her the high esteem and Christian affection of all the Mission circle, as well as many, both native and European, outside of it. To supply Miss Mackay's place, we have happily secured the services of Miss Jane Small, daughter of our missionary brother at Punah. She is well qualified to carry on the work by her Christian character, experience in zenana labour, and ability in speaking the Marathi language. We have had great pleasure in welcoming her to take part with us in this branch of our mission work."

At a conversazione held on the 18th January, 1883, in the large hall of the Christian Institute, Aberdeen, a numerous audience met to welcome Alexina, and heard her explain how she and her fellow labourers endeavoured to convey a knowledge of the gospel to those who are, by the customs of their country, precluded from entering mission schools and churches. In the course of her remarks she gave interesting details regarding the religious habits of the people of Nagpoor, and referred to the great success which was attending the work there. She also rendered, in illustration of the language, several native airs in a highly tasteful manner, accompanying herself more than once on a peculiar musical instrument, which is used by the inhabitants of India.

Under arrangements made by the Edinburgh committee, she met many friends in that city and neighbourhood, and during her furlough she held altogether about a hundred meetings, which she thoroughly enjoyed; but they were a great strain on her strength, and deprived her of much of the benefit of her greatly needed rest.

On one of these occasions she visited Ventnor, in the Isle of Wight, and was invited by a ministerial friend to address his congregation at a neighbouring village Baptist Church. Thinking there would only be a few people at the ordinary week-night service, she consented, but when the time came, she was surprised to see groups arriving from all directions, and ascending the steps to the pretty stone edifice, beautifully situated on an eminence, and surrounded by its own burying-ground. The place was crowded, and she seemed nervous for a moment, but immediately regained her composure by taking refuge in singing a Marathi hymn, to the great delight of the audience.

She then dwelt on the wide door of entrance that had been granted to her in India; on the wonderful freedom with which she had been permitted to go in and out, daily, among the heathen; and on the great affection which many of the Hindu ladies manifested towards her. "It seems, indeed," she said, "as if the invisible yet omnipresent Saviour had gone before me, breaking up the way for the spread of His own gospel."

Many incidents were related, one of which was the following:—" Amongst the women expressing regret on account of my going away for a time, was one feeble old widow, who finds her way into the little gathering we have in a certain house, supporting herself by means of a long stick, reminding me of the 'rod' Eastern shepherds are said to make use of. This poor body is a real representative of the forlorn Brahman widow, dressed as she is in her thin sarree, (underneath which she is not permitted to wear the tight-fitting cholee others indulge in), having her head shaved, and being devoid of ornaments. She certainly has one ornament, however, 'the meek and quiet spirit, which, in the sight of God, is of great price.' Old as she is, her faculties remain wonderfully unimpaired, and so much does what she hears come home to her desolate heart, that ever and anon some ejaculation expressive of her emotions escapes her thin lips. One day, after hearing a hymn the word 'Maharaj!' broke forth. Literally, that means, 'Oh, king!' I believe, but she just meant, 'How wonderful!' As she stood listening sympathetically to the plaints of the other women on the subject of my going away, I asked Joanna, my native Bible-woman, to tell her that Jesus Christ, called in their language, 'Yāshoo Kreest,' or as one old friend pronounces it, 'Āsoo Keest!' had a peculiar regard for widows and fatherless children, and that even when He was suffering so much on the cross for our sakes, He thought about His mother going to be left alone, and, in the midst of His pain, gave her in charge to a friend of His. As soon as she had heard this, she burst out crying, and vehemently uttered something I did not understand, but which Joanna explained to be: 'Why should we not love Him, when He suffered so much for our sakes!' I thought I observed the sympathetic tear spring into Joanna's eyes as she listened, and on hearing the translation I felt affected myself, as I turned away. On observing the poor body wending her way home at a little distance behind our gharree, I remembered that I had some *pice* (coppers) in my handbag, and calling out 'Bai! Eekerie Ya,' *i.e.* 'Woman (in the respectful Eastern sense), come here,' I put them in her hand, telling her to buy something nice to eat with them. Well, she again burst out crying, quite overcome by the kindness bestowed on an 'outcast' like her, and piteously expressed her desire to do something for me in return! The last I saw of her was a figure standing motionless in the distance, watching our gharree, a hand raised to wipe off a tear with the corner of her sarree, and finally, a purpose-like setting of her face homeward. How different her conduct from that of the host of beggars we encounter in the streets, some of whom are quite well-to-do-looking."

In contrast to this poor outcast she next described getting access to the home of a high caste lady: "Such a pretty woman with large, lustrous eyes. It really did me good to look at her, and she kept her finger-nails, etc., with as much nicety as an English gentlewoman would. She was sparkling with lovely ornaments. Her nose-ring, a large, graceful hoop, richly set with a profusion of tiny pearls, her elegant necklets and necklaces, bracelets and anklets, finger and toe rings, were very gratifying to the eye, especially as I believed that she had donned them in honour of her visitor. Having made 'salaam' to her, I immediately occupied the arm-chair, evidently intended for my use. And now, what was to come next? I had been previously warned by Amundibai (one of my native Bible-women) 'not to speak many religious words' in this house, in case of giving offence, and shutting the door against future visits, so I felt a little embarrassed. However, I asked if she (the lady) wished to learn to read and sew. She replied that she was very anxious about learning to read, but did not care about work. 'All the better,' perhaps, you will be inclined to say, but one's opinion is modified by the recognition of the fact that work is considered undignified and unnecessary by many of the better class. However, I explained that I thoroughly agreed with her in considering reading, etc., more valuable than fancy work, but I suggested that when she got tired over books, it would be nice to turn her attention to a little piece of work. I entertained her by singing some hymns and giving her a lesson in the 'First Book,' the first sentence of which is, 'God is always near you!' By request of the husband, who sat outside in the yard, listening, we sang an English hymn, choosing for this purpose, 'Safe in the arms of Jesus.' Before we left, we were presented with 'pán,' composed of a small bunch of leaves, with cardamoms, broken small, betel nuts, etc., made up into a neat packet, like an ounce of tea in shape, also delicious little oranges and plantains. On the back of this a brass dish containing wreaths of flowers was brought forward, and our hostess proceeded to hang floral necklaces round my neck and those of my assistants, and to provide us with bracelets of strung roses, adorned with which we afterwards drove through the city to visit some other houses, thinking it well to show the attention bestowed upon us! I was very gratified to hear my benefactress express her gratitude for my kindness in going to see her, and she was most anxious that I should return soon."

Alexina also explained many of the strange customs, superstitions, and religious beliefs of the Hindus, and gave an account of the holy days and festivals, more especially those observed in Central India, dwelling especially on the fact that the real undermining of the citadel of Hinduism must be done by women, as now that the boys are being educated in the Government Schools, they are fast learning to see the absurdity of their own religion; but the great hindrance to their reception of Christianity is the bigotry of the mothers; for it must be remembered that Hindu youths and even old men, have great veneration for their mothers, and are most unwilling to displease them. Some one has said that "no nation ever rises higher than its mothers. As are the mothers of a nation, so is the nation." It is therefore clear that the key to the evangelization of our vast Indian empire is in the hands of the gentle sex, for they alone have access to their deeply religious Indian sisters, who are quite half a century behind the male portion of the community in light and civilization.

At this time she might have made what the world would call a good marriage, but ease and comfort would not tempt her. When a mutual friend ventured to point out the advantages of such a step, and the influence that money would give for the cause she had so much at heart, she feelingly replied in the strong Doric of her native county, "Na! na! lassie! dinna speak o' sic a thing. I'd a hunnerd times raither gang back to my dusky leddies." And so she did, reaching Nagpoor on the 20th February, 1884, with what feelings the annexed report to the Home Committee will testify.

"It was my privilege to resume zenana mission work here some nine months ago, after a year's absence at home—a year ever memorable, bringing with it abundant opportunities of usefulness, and much refreshment of spirit, apart altogether from the great benefit derived by a renewed measure of health and strength. Never before did I enjoy so much delightful intercourse with Christian friends. After seeking to water dry and thirsty places here for five years, I 'was watered also myself,' and, oh! how refreshing the showers were felt to be! Never shall I forget last year's memories.

"Arriving once more in Nagpoor towards the end of February, I found my sister's approaching marriage being busily prepared for, and it was difficult for me to settle down to work till the event took place, on March 18th. I am afraid, indeed, that I did not sufficiently rejoice with them that did rejoice, for in a foreign land we are specially reluctant to give up any vestige of a home-tie that may remain to us. Once in harness, however, there was little time for sentimental brooding over bygone days, and the accession of Miss Bella Small to our number gave something of the family feeling to our little household. Whilst at home I used to beg for a *third* worker, on the principle that 'a threefold cord is not easily broken,' and now that the request has been granted, I trust that much blessing will rest upon our united labours.

"It fell to my lot to take up the work my sister had been called to leave, part of which had originally been my own, and as, in addition to this regular visiting, I had to look up a great many old friends, my hands were soon full enough. Several of the Parsee families mentioned by my sister are no longer on my list, as the pupils have either got married, gone to school, or discontinued learning through prejudice. The Bengali and other houses open to instruction, however, are on the increase, while the length and breadth of the city has to be traversed with a view to bringing the gospel to as many of its teeming inhabitants as we can reach. It is interesting to find fresh welcomes from old friends, and more willingness to learn on the part of some formerly too indifferent; but I like, best of all, to be called to some new house, since we never know where 'the gems for His kingdom' may be hidden away, and the hope stimulates one that we may be led to where there are such. The fact that the native Christian workers accompanying us generally in our wanderings can command more than one language is a great help. The other day, for instance, we were begged to visit a large household of Hindi-speaking people, newly arrived from a great distance. Without Karoona I could have been of little use there, as Marathi is quite unintelligible to them. With her as my interpreter, however, I shall get on nicely, and we hope to be successful ere long in breaking down the strong antipathy to Christianity felt by the head of the house, whose only object in calling us was that we might impart the knowledge of *fancy work* to the numerous ladies composing his household. There are four daughters-in-law here, and a kind-looking mother-in-law, in whose presence etiquette demands that they should cover up their faces entirely, with the exception of one eye. Before beginning to teach sewing, we told a Bible story,—it was the raising of Lazarus from the dead,—the mother-in-law remarking that there was nothing like that in *their* sacred books. After this and a hymn she thought it best to retire to the verandah, as it was impossible for much sewing to be done so long as the ladies' hands were engaged in covering up their faces !

"If spared to another year, I shall hope to be able to report progress in connection with several new houses opened up. Meantime, I am very glad to be at my loved work once more."

In November, 1885, she reports:—

"In moving about in the city during the past year the question has very often been put to me, 'Where is your companion?' My answer has been, 'She is teaching in one of our new girls' schools.' In this way I have been able widely to advertise these schools, and to explain satisfactorily the non-appearance of Amundibai, Dnyanapoo, Cheenie, and Karoona, all of whom have been more or less associated with us in our zenana visiting.

"Almost without exception the houses opened in former years continue friendly; but in certain cases the pupil has been forbidden to learn any longer, on account of her approaching marriage, in case of giving offence to the future mother-in-law. One nice girl, already married, was eager to learn during the few days she was on a visit to her own mother's house; but when I proposed to follow her to her own home, I was told that she would be beaten if she were to be seen with a book!

"Some sudden deaths have occurred in families long visited; other friends have removed to different stations; and the system of early marriage always deprives us of a certain proportion of our pupils. It sometimes happens, however, that pupils lost to us are taken up by missionary ladies in the places they go to. I was interested to hear that an old pupil of mine is being visited in Bilaspûr by a friend I met at the Hills last hot season. Another turned up, some time ago, in Calcutta. We read that to those who have, more shall be given, and I often see this verified in connection with the work of Missions. We frequently find that in the houses where we are received as visitors, some member of the family is, or has been, attending our Institution, and is favourably disposed to the truths of Christianity. In one such house, on asking to see the husband of my pupil, he came into the verandah with a book in his hand. 'What is this?' I inquired. 'The Psalms of David,' was his reply. I glanced at the open page, and my eye lighted on the words, 'I said, I will take heed to my ways, that I sin not with my tongue.' I felt very much interested in the circumstance.

"Another day I was impressing on a young man, who was pushing some children aside, the duty of being kind to children, and letting *them* hear God's word too. 'That is a saying of Scripture, is it not?' was his answer. He must have remembered the words read in school: 'Suffer the little children to come unto Me, and forbid them not.'

"There is something very sweet in the way the little ones come about us. In one haughty Brahman's house three lovely little girls quite hang upon me all the time I am seated in the house, although only one of them is actually learning. Bheemi, the youngest of the three, committed a sad mistake the other day, in the eyes of her elders, by leaning upon me after she had been bathed! I informed them that I had bathed also; but this did not seem to mend matters. The religion of this country resembles very much that of the Pharisees of old, and the old truth has to be insisted on, that defilement comes from *within*, not from without.

"I may mention here that a Jewish family from Punah has recently settled in Nagpoor. The head of this family, Reuben Benjamin, is brother of Bundoji, the convert to Christianity. Rutenbai (or Ruth, as I suppose), one of the children in the family, attends Miss Janie Small's Budhwari School, and Rachel, the daughter-in-law, has become my pupil. I like to look at the little brothers, Isaac and Moses, and to think of them as representatives of their great ancestors. Rachel is reading John's Gospel with me in Marathi, and both she and her father-in-law join with me in singing the praises of Jesus, not a dissenting word being uttered by any member of the household. One would fain hope that the head of the house, at least, is not far from the Kingdom of God.

"Much could be added in connection with the

FALSE RUMOURS AND SUSPICIONS.

many under gospel instruction, but at present the leaven is working so secretly that only faith in the promises enables us to go forward. Many are the 'hearers' of the Word. May God grant that, in due time, the 'doers' of it will appear."

The following interesting letter[1] and report are addressed to the late Mrs. Colonel Young, Edinburgh :—

I left home, yesterday, at six a.m. in my tonga, reaching the city in little more than half an hour. I was there joined by Karoona, one of our native assistants, and together we pursued our way to a distant quarter of the city, known as Eitwarree. In the first house we visited we have two little girls as pupils, Mainabai and Tannabai. Their mother did not call us to her house, but she consented to receive a visit. We sat on a swing seat, suspended from the ceiling of the verandah, the children taking up their position on the mud floor at our feet. The relatives looking on asked us many questions as to our ultimate intentions, as it had been told them that after teaching our pupils for a certain time, we would force them to leave their homes, and make them useful in our work ! We assured them that ours was a labour of love, and that no such result would follow.

[1] Unfortunately the first part, with date, is missing.

A little child of about five years of age was carried to us from a neighbouring house, with the request that we should teach her; but, as we get no satisfaction from such infant pupils, we explained that we do not care to teach children under seven! When we had finished giving the lessons, we sang a hymn, and talked over its contents. In the next house we would not consent to sit in the large verandah downstairs, as the head of the house was there, and we would have had no privacy. This man has frequently heard the gospel, but he does not act up to its precepts. He has lately been slighting his own wife, and giving his attention to a woman of low character. After saying firmly that I would not sit down unless a private room were given me, where I could give instruction to the lady of the house, I was conducted upstairs, into a pleasant room, hung round with pictures, English and native. Here we were joined by three other women, one of them a widow from her childhood, who told me frankly that she can only join us when her father is out, as he is very bigoted against Christianity! We had a very nice time together in that upper room. A few boys listened, along with the women, one of them the child of the house. Great curiosity was displayed, in the middle of our earnest talk, as to whether my *cuffs* were made of paper or cotton. And much surprise was expressed when, in explaining our English fashions, I remarked that nose-rings are only used by us in the case of wild bulls (the women enjoy a little humour)! In the third house visited lives a silversmith's family. The daughter-in-law can read very well, and a number of women gather round us to hear the hymns. One day lately we were asked to sit in the verandah, used as a workshop, before leaving, and sing to the men assembled there. We were glad to do this, and we had a good opportunity of gaining a hearing from an intelligent old man from an outlying village, who read to us, at my request, from a Christian book I had by me. He was asked to carry the books along with him to his village, etc.

Another young widow I have been accustomed to visit has disappeared from the house, all interest in her having ceased, apparently, with her young husband's demise. I hope she is happy in her own home, and that now that her earthly father and mother-in-law have forsaken her, the Lord will take her up. It is affecting to me, in moving about amongst my old friends, to find that death has been busy during my short absence, and that one and another of those I was interested in have passed away, very prematurely, as *we* would say, in some cases. The face of one dear boy, who always used to hang about me when we were visiting his relatives, haunts me now. I sometimes wonder whether it is because "some good thing toward the Lord" has been found in the hearts of such that they have been removed. The young widow I used to tell you about, whose mother-in-law died soon after performing a pilgrimage to the Ganges, is still a pupil, but great patience is required with her. I do not think she touches her book in our absence, and we can only give her a weekly visit. Still, the fact that she continues under Christian influence is something to be thankful for. I don't think you would like to come into the compound in which her house stands without having the colonel with you! for we are greeted, on every occasion, by an angry chorus of barking of dogs, some seven or eight of which gather to resist our onward progress. There must surely be a prize worth winning in the "Hazaratsa Wardha," since it is thus guarded!

This is now Tuesday, and I am writing about the events of yesterday, one of which was that I became so hungry while teaching, that, waiving ceremony, I asked if I might have a mouthful of food of some kind—a bit of native *scone*, or "chapatti," I proposed! There was positively nothing in the house, "from hand to mouth" being the order of the day in a Hindoo home, but a mixture of baked flour, sugar and water was made up for me, with the hand with much goodwill, and this I had to drink out of a brass vessel! On finishing my potion I asked if my friends would act in the same confiding way with *me*, should they feel hungry in my house! I think one of them said she would. A visit in any case is looked forward to as a first step in the way of friendliness!

And now, dear Mrs. Young, I will draw to a close. Letter writing is formidable in this hot weather, and my letter ought to be re-written and pruned, but I will trust it to your tender mercies.

Affectionately yours,
ALEXINA MACKAY.

(*Missionary Notes from Nagpoor.*)

March 17*th*, 1885.

Yesterday, Monday, I paid my third visit to a Mahommedan household newly opened. Sheik Ahmed, the head of this house, is an enlightened, very gentlemanly man, speaking English very nicely. He was educated, as a boy, in our Mission School at Kampthi, and he was taught his profession by a Christian officer, Col. Tripe, who was a great friend of Mr. and Mrs. Cooper. My Mahommedan friend cherishes the memory of this officer, now retired from the service, with lively affection, and he is very anxious to get his home address, that he may write to him.

Sheik Ahmed's wife and oldest daughter have been taught to read Urdu, their own language, but the little girl is anxious to acquire *Marathi*, too, and this gives me an errand to the house. She promises to be an apt pupil in reading, but she does not take so much to sewing. Her father has allowed me to put a Gospel in Urdu into her hands, and the other day she read to me from it, while I read along with her from the Roman Version. One cannot but feel a little nervous as to the effect such words as these will have upon a Mahommedan, " The beginning of the Gospel of Jesus Christ, the *Son of God*," for we know well how repugnant such language is to a true Mahommedan. In the present case no opposition was offered.

On the occasion of my first visit I was presented with a cup of tea, and a saucer of nuts and almonds, and I would be equally well treated every Monday morning, were I sufficiently appreciative, but having just finished chota hazri (little breakfast) at home I have asked to be excused for the future. A basket of roses and vegetables was packed into my tonga yesterday instead.

On leaving this house I visit a sweet Telugu woman, who can read and understand Marathi very well. My sister, now Mrs. Danielsson, of the Swedish Mission, Narsingpûr, has all the credit of teaching her. She handed her pupil over to me when she left. This friend has almost no ear for music, but she is, nevertheless, very fond of our hymns, and having bought from us a hymn-book, is not at all shy to perform to the best of her ability. She has a dear little boy, who attends a native school in the neighbourhood. One of the neighbours, who frequently assemble to listen, asked me one day what was the difference between my religion and that of the gentleman (a Roman Catholic priest) who visits the opposite house. "Well," I said, "the difference is that I teach *only* what is in the Bible, while he adds thoughts of his own." Was this an orthodox reply?

Some of the friends at home must have heard of the Kali-Baboo's wife, who has been a pupil for a long time. She has lately begun to read the Old Testament in private (in her own language) for the first time in her life. It seemed to be a revelation to her that there was such a book, though she has long been familiar with portions of the *New Testament*. I had to send for a copy of the former to Calcutta. She has finished reading the Gospel by John, lately, in English (compared with Bengali on her part, and Romanized Hindustani on mine), and she is now going through the Acts of the Apostles, in which, as we know, there are many accounts of converts being baptised, the vexed subject in the case of the Baboo, who professes to be a believer in Christ, and yet declines to confess his faith according to the Saviour's own appointment.

Mrs. Baboo still receives lessons in music on her little American organ, "Home, Sweet Home," and "The Blue Bells of Scotland," being favourite airs. I hope to have the young daughter-in-law as a pupil immediately. She is even now on her way here from Calcutta, under her mother-in-law's escort. Another Baboo's [1] wife (also visited on Monday) lives in the same compound. She is a dark-complexioned, commonplace-looking little woman, of some fifteen summers, with considerable force of character. It amuses me to see her the bearer of the keys in her mother-in-law's house. She is learning to read

[1] My poor Baboo's wife (of whom I told you) "departed this life" two days after I wrote my letter, and her kindly disposed but non-decided husband asked me to "pray for her soul," after her death. He had a notion that I, as a "righteous person," would be listened to by God on her behalf!
Is it not strange that this Roman Catbolic delusion should have found a lodgment in his mind? Of course I told him what the Bible teaches on this and kindred subjects—such as the question regarding degrees of punishment, which he wished me to answer for him. I had regarded the Baboo as a much more enlightened man than he turns out to be. He read the "Pilgrim's Progress" through quite lately, I lending him a very handsome copy of my own, and yet !

English with me, her husband being well versed in our language, and she is expected to prepare a portion of Matthew's Gospel to be read also in her own language, in which she is making progress, week by week. In the sewing department she is making a pair of slippers for her husband. I am always very kindly received in this house, and made welcome to a drink of milk. On one or two occasions a fish has been sent all the way to the bungalow, and some pets, in the shape of white rabbits, were offered to me one day. Such tokens of goodwill are always cheering. As I looked at my basket of vegetables yesterday, and thought of them as given to one engaged in the service of Christ, the beautiful words of Psalm lxxii. occurred to me,—

> "The kings of Tarshish, and the isles,
> To Him shall presents bring;
> And unto Him shall offer gifts
> Sheba's and Seba's king."

And the prophetic meaning was faintly realized.

To-day I visited a pupil living in the precincts of a temple reached by a steep flight of steps. She is a very willing but dull pupil. A friend of hers undertook to help her, if I would bestow a book upon her too, and as may be supposed, the request did not need to be repeated. Both women listened, one especially, with intense interest to the story of the raising of Lazarus from the dead, as introduced in the hymn sung, and I was begged to come without fail next week. I have an enthusiastic little partisan in this quarter, in the shape of a little boy who joins me the moment my tonga appears. He is a scholar in the Eitwarree School, where the native Christian Mark teaches, and he was able to tell me to-day the meaning of the difficult Marathi word for repentance. "Ask him," one of the women said, when she could not answer a certain question herself!

In the next house I visited to-day there is one of the dearest little girls I ever saw. She is a very tiny specimen of womanhood, not having yet completed her fourth year; but she is got up in complete sarree costume, just like her mother. She prattles away in the presence of her elders, to the entertainment of all present, and the no small admiration of her father, who will be quite pleased to have her learn to read by-and-by, I hope. She bears the name of the sacred plant to be found in every Hindu courtyard—Toolesie. A cousin of her mother, a former pupil, is on a visit to the house just now, and as I was engaged teaching her to sew, some neighbours of the other sex seated themselves in front of the little verandah, to see and hear what was going on. The good-natured woman to whom the house belonged made no objection to this intrusion, but remarking that I had now a good congregation to listen, she retired into the shadow of the inner doorway, where she could hear without being seen. One of the audience had been formerly a pupil in our Institution, and he was very glad to receive a copy of Luke's Gospel. He was requested by his friends to show, there and then, how he could read, and he was not slow to comply.

On Wednesdays I visit a very mixed population in Seetabaldi, the larger bazaar adjacent to the cantonment. I have only two Marathi-speaking families there, all the others being Tamil, Telugu, or Bengali. All know some Hindustani, and so do I, so we get on. Rambaje Rao, the head of one of the first-mentioned houses, knows enough about Christianity to enable him to emerge from Hinduism, but it seems to be his *will* to remain a heathen. The walls of his house are covered with portraits and pictures, some of the latter being very hideous. One picture of a different type has found its way into this motley group—a small coloured engraving, representing Dr. Judson at the deathbed of the King of Burmah on one hand, and Schwartz amid his heathen surroundings on the other. Taking advantage of this love of pictures, I provided myself the other day with a beautiful Scripture scene entitled, "Our Saviour Healing the Sick," and I was not disappointed in the reception it got. Perhaps friends at home, anxious to help in the good work here, would like to send us some of these Scripture scenes, issued by the Religious Tract Society, London. A roll of them could be sent out easily by post, and we can have them mounted upon cardboard here. We might leave one or two such pictures in the houses we visit, as pleasant reminders of the gospel stories we are seeking to tell from day to day.

On Thursday I resume my visiting in Nagpoor city, my first pupil, Pochee, having been formerly in Maggie Timothy's School. I had to turn away from the door the other day, as her little brother was laid down with smallpox, but in a few seconds I had wended my way past the Rajah's immense granary, with its complement of sepoys on guard, to the house of some very warm friends, whose acquaintance I made in a time of great sickness in the family. I feared at that time that one patient would never rally, but she has been brought round again, partly, I believe, through the use of a bottle of Keating's Cough Lozenges, as recommended and provided by me! It is a wonder they were accepted. The gentle old schoolmaster who teaches a boy's school next door regularly joins us, followed by his pupils, and an opportunity is being given him at last of becoming acquainted with the gospel. Some of the little boys who can read well are very glad to have a tiny book bestowed upon them.

I often think of the words, "A little child shall lead them," in connection with my Indian experiences, for the young people are very much the hope of the country. The number of interesting children one meets is surprising. They are indeed like sweet fresh flowers in the desert.

I must not stay to tell of the other houses visited on Thursdays, but I must mention one interesting Friday house, where an old Brahman widow hails a visit as often as she can secure it. She is a great reader, and very clever. A boy attending the Government School came in one day, while I was seated in her house. "This is a servant of Jesus Christ," she said, "not of Ram," and the dear gentle boy never denied it. I got him to come to the Mission Church, some three miles off, next Sunday, and I mean to give him a Bible first time I see him. I fear he may be unwell, as he promised to come again the following Sunday, but did not, and he had been complaining!

I hope this peep into "City Mission Work" in Nagpoor will stimulate the interest already felt by many dear friends at home.

ALEXINA MACKAY.

The following letters to her family further show how the work grew on her hands.

(*To her Sister J——.*)
THE LITTLE BUNGALOW, NAGPOOR,
March 20*th*, 1885.

I am in a writing mood, as my morning interested me. Let me describe it. It was about 7 a.m. when I found myself on the road leading to the city. I was seated sideways (to get support to my back) in the covered tonga, and I thought to myself, "—— would be touched, were she to see me setting out, all by myself, on my labours, equipped in my simple, becoming, brown, summer serge dress, enlivened by a paler tint of machine lace, an object of interest to many uninitiated native eyes. My thick green shawl was thrown round me, as the morning was damp after the unexpected thunderstorm and fall of rain last night. My sun-topee was on my head; my leather handbag, with its complement of Gospels, First Books, and tracts or booklets of various kinds, lying on the seat beside me; and my "Sarah Gamp" umbrella outspread to keep out the glare!

I very soon met an ayah, bearing in her arms, as usual, a white baby, or rather, a sitting-up baby-girl, who was immediately directed to "make salaam" to me! A little farther on I espied some handsomely caparisoned native equestrians, and I wondered who they were. Anon, our Chief Commissioner and his wife—Mr. and Mrs. Crosthwaite—appeared in sight (they were in front of me). They were walking, while their tonga slowly followed. Their driver looked very tidy, and there was a round Indian basket on the front seat, filled with fresh flowers! "Where can they all be going?" I thought. "To the station? Scarcely, at this hour." I afterwards saw them turn down the road leading to the Hospital! you will guess with what intent when I tell you that Mrs. Crosthwaite is a Christian, seeking to "occupy" well the high station she finds herself in. Gathering myself together, I prepared to say "Good morning" to my superiors, who always meet me as an equal, however. My salutation was brightly responded to by Mrs. Crosthwaite, who called out, "Are you going to the city?" "Yes, I am," I replied. And then I alighted to speak for a minute. "Are you quite well?" I was asked. "Pretty well, thank you; but I'm suffering from rheumatism, so I have to wrap up well." "*Rheumatism!*" with surprise. "Your hand is dreadfully hot!" "*Is* it?" I said, adding, "I often feel a kind of internal fever." Mrs. Crosthwaite then referred to the coming rest at the

Hills, so kindly, and anon I was again in my tonga. In a second, however, her voice broke again upon my ear :—" Will you dine with us on Sunday night, after church, just quietly, and both the Miss Smalls, too?" "Oh, thank you! It will be a great pleasure to us." Response, " Good morning !" Wasn't she kind? She was originally an Edinburgh lady, I believe, brought up amongst Free Church people. She went down to see Janie's Schools yesterday. She wrote to *me*, thinking they were mine. I explained to her that my sphere lies in house-to-house visiting, and she wishes to accompany me some day.

On reaching the city I went first to a large Mussulman house I had not been in for months, as the member of the family I was most helpful to had got married, and had gone away, after nearly crying her eyes out, at having to part with all her loved ones, myself included. As a little comfort to her I gave her that carte of Karoona and me, to take away with her; but she was so overcome with grief that she scarcely took any notice of it at the time.

You may suppose how pleased I was to find her once more at home! Her husband has had to come to Nagpoor for treatment, as he is suffering from a species of jaundice. Again and again I was told how much *yad* or remembrance my friend had had concerning me, and her own expression of face was unmistakable. She referred, this time, to the carte with much appreciation, asked me to sing a favourite hymn; and made up *pan sopari* for me. I have often felt so drawn out to this sweet creature that I could have put my arms round her and kissed her. The former I am sure I did on her marriage day, when I saw her sobbing and crying on a bed, surrounded by her friends, who were loading her arms with native-made bracelets of many strange devices; the latter I did this morning, when we were left alone in the room, after I had had an interview with her nice husband, in whose presence *she would not show her face !* Two other things in the interview touched me—her telling me that she had seen me in her dreams (her friend adding that she had started up in bed, saying that " her Missi Baba " had come!) and her conscientiousness in producing a four anna piece in payment of some wool, etc., she had got from me, some months before! Once before, when I complimented her on remembering a little sum she owed me, she said that "Allah" would be angry with her if she did not! I gave her husband a Gospel to read, and he was quite pleased to take it. He told me, when I asked him, that he *had* such a thing at home, but he could not tell me the name of it. He can read both Urdu and Marathi.

(*To her Sister, Mrs. Danielsson.*)
HINDU WOMEN'S FRIENDLY BUNGALOW,
NAGPOOR,
May 18*th*, 1885.

* * * * *

I don't remember what Purdeshi woman you refer to, but Dnyanapoo or Cheenie may be able to tell me. That dear, round-faced Telugu woman in Seetabaldi has been asking the girls to write out little prayers for her on paper. I always considered her a hopeful case, and she was confiding to Cheenie, the other day, that she likes so much what we tell her, but that the other members of the household do not like it. You should join us in praying for her, dear Maggie, and for the clever woman, a few doors up the street, who is also a very attentive listener. It encourages me to find tokens for good in the very houses that seemed out of our beat, as regards the Marathi language. They are not out of *the Saviour's* beat, evidently. "The Son of Man is come to seek and to save *that which was lost.*" "Preach the gospel to *every creature.*" (Our old Punkah Walla's wife is another I am hopeful about, with her dear, patient, toil-worn face.) "Behold, God despiseth not any," is a text we would do well to remember in this country.

A NATIVE WEDDING PARTY.

That wedding ceremony in Subunna's house was, indeed, a grand affair. Our two pretty, lady-like pupils were exposed to the view of the assembly in a wonderfully public way, for India. They and their respective husbands had to sit in an elegantly ornamented swing cot, the principal object of attraction at the upper end of the immense pavilion in which we assembled, and, as the evening wore on, we were invited to go up and speak to them! There were dancing girls there for our entertainment, and, of course, music; and the European part of the company were regaled with English beverages and viands, to wit, port wine, lime juice, aërated waters, cake, biscuits, etc., and tea. Subunna was politeness itself. He did me the honour to invite me first into an inner room to see his wife, who kept in the background, and she was so hearty. I had furnished myself with a little present for each of the brides, in the shape of that pretty little brown and white basket, and a nice fancy-wood workbox I bought at home. I am sure they would be gratified when, the excitement over, they would be able to notice them! Subunna's fellow-clerks and their families were the other Europeans.

(*To her Sister, Mrs. Danielsson.*)

NAGPOOR,

July 10*th*, 1885.

On Friday I called at the house of Narsing Singh, a Bengali Baboo, whose family are always pleased to have a visit. As I was having a talk with the few members of the household at present at home, one of them opened a side door, ran across the compound, entered an outhouse, and immediately returned bearing something in her arms, carefully wrapped up in her chudder. Could it be *a baby?* I wondered. It was nothing less; but, oh! the tininess of the child! It is just two or three days old, I concluded; but, no, I was informed that it was *two months* old! My surprise was great, and I mourned over the little starveling, as it appeared to be. At this point the remark was made, "There's another." "Another?" I said; "let me see it;" and once more my friend ran to the barn, returning this time with a much smaller parcel! Never in my life did I see such a specimen of babyhood as was now presented to me! Can you believe it? the thickest part of the child's arm was barely as thick as my finger, while the limbs would contrast unfavourably with the wrist of an ordinary individual! The size of the head, lengthways, was quite out of proportion, while the face was that of an old man, the eyes rolling about and directed upwards, while a hungry look pervaded the whole face! The infant I am now describing is a girl, the other is a boy. The mother presently came in, and was quite delighted at finding the smaller morsel in my lap, vigorously sucking my finger, while *the superior being* occupied the attention of the Bengali girl at my side. "Oh, Bai!" I said to the mother, "why are the children so thin?" "I have not enough nourishment to give them," she replied quite calmly, adding, "They scream all night." I was quite distressed. "Give one of them the bottle," I suggested ; but such a thing had apparently never been seen by the mother. One of the others present was more intelligent, however, and explained the mystery. To make a long story short, I hurried to a Parsee shop in the neighbourhood, procured the article in question, and returned anon to be eulogised as is no patron saint I know of! My lesson that day was on the Law of Love, and it came home.

I called on your Sudder Bazaar woman, who reads Marathi so capitally, to-day. It is the first time I have seen her. What a nice house she lives in! The steps up make it look quite imposing. She asked after you, wishing to know where your new home is. What a willing pupil she is. She sent for us by Mark's mother. I am quite pleased at having such a house to add to my list (thanks to your legacy). She will do well in English, too, I see. Her topee is still unfinished, as she had no pattern for the crown, but I will let her have one anon. I mean to visit her first, on a Wednesday, at about eleven o'clock; so you can think of us (Dnyanapoo and me) then. It is nice, though touching somewhat, to see your little marks on the books of your different old pupils. This little woman must have gone on reading to herself, I fancy, for she is far beyond the last marks. To-day, I think it was in the ninth of John she read, about the blind man who was "cast out of the synagogue." She read the whole chapter, while I made a running commentary upon it? She asks about any expression she does not understand. I have got copies of Telugu, Tamil, Gujerathi and Hindustani Gospels from Bombay, for our mixed population, and I have sent to Calcutta for a few Bengali ones; so the Lamp of Life *may be had* by all who will!!!

ZENANA MISSION, NAGPOOR,
August 8th, 1885.

MY DEAREST MOTHER,—

As I have nothing particular to tell you, except what will come in nicely towards the close of my letter, I will describe my yesterday's visiting.

Well, after our ten o'clock breakfast, I set out in my covered spring-cart affair, called a *tonga* here, as you may remember, and drawn by two bullocks, white in colour, and named respectively, "Doocker" (or pig), and "Brahman," names symbolical of the physique of the animals. (Janie's are called "Rachel" and "Leah" with similar intent). Threading my way through the narrow, rough streets of the Sudder Bazaar, not far distant, the inquiry of the driver after a new house, to which I had been called, was answered by the popping in of two good-looking gaily-dressed little boys into my gharree. They were the children of the house, and would show me the way. A few yards on we were directed to stop, and forthwith a young Sowkar, or money-lender, led the way through his shop into an inner room, on the floor of which sat his wife, a handsome woman, well covered over with her chudder or sarree. She was anxious to learn to knit, and to copy flowers upon canvas— nothing more. I expressed my readiness to gratify this fancy, but explained that the chief object of all my visits was to tell Dāwatshee gosht, *i.e.* the things of God. No objection was made to this condition, and anon, a conversation on the difference between nominal and real Christians followed, several Christians unworthy the name having been quoted to me as included in the circle of the family acquaintance.

After this a bundle of variously coloured wool was produced, and selecting a pleasing, bright colour, I cast on two dozen stitches, and proceeded to initiate my pupil into the mystery of the garter stitch, the chief difficulty being to get her to cast on the thread properly, with the first finger of the right hand. She was left-handed, she informed me, and she was fain to press her left hand finger into the service. As Marathi is not the language of the household, I inquired what *their* term for the right hand was. "The hand with which we eat our food" was one answer, and this is literally a true description, in this country, where knives and forks are not used. There were at least three onlookers (male members of the household, strange to say), as the lesson was being given. The pleasant interview over, I went on to another house, this time a Mohammedan one, speaking Hindustani; in the former house they were most at home in Hindi, Maggie's present language. The head of the house met me in the doorway. He can speak English very well, being an educated man, our Mission School in Kampthi having been his medium of instruction. His wife and children have to be reached through their own language. The young "Bégum," my pupil, shook hands with me, and led me into the side room, where we both seated ourselves on a basket-work couch, with one or two soft

THE LITTLE BUNGALOW.

bed-pillows upon it by way of increasing its comfort. (Very, very tired did I feel, that day [yesterday], far more fit to lie down on the couch and rest, than to sit bolt upright and teach.) On asking the father, who was present for a little, what was the odour pervading the room, he informed me that it was onions and garlic stored away in the roof (the ceiling-cloth holes forming good conductors). A Marathi lesson was first given, and then part of a chapter from Mark's Gospel read in Urdu, while I followed from the Roman copy. As we two were thus engaged, a dear, bright little deaf and dumb boy was flitting about the room beside us, now fingering and enumerating the smooth, round buttons of my alpaca dress, handling my brooch, etc., and again rummaging in a drawer, his little hand pushed through a hole meant for the handle, and finally drawing out a large, cast-off *serpent's* slough. The sister informed me that her father made use of such for medicinal purposes. A younger sister coming in, stroked my hand for the pleasure of it, just as one would do with a piece of satin. I do like these homely touches of comparatively baby fingers. The gentle mother listened for some time, while her daughter read, and then we talked about the sharp turn of illness she had just recovered from, etc., etc. If you, dear mother, could manage to collect a little sum of money that I might expend on English dolls, or get some young people you know (better still) to *send* me some, dressed in clothes to come off and on, by this newly-arranged-for parcel post, I would be very glad, for my money is all done now, except a few *annas*, and I find that the promise of a doll stimulates a little girl to try to learn to read. I could buy plenty from Mrs. Cooper, of those sent out in the Bazaar box, if I had only the money, however. I bought several bullocks for our Zenana Mission work, out of my limited private funds, besides affording treats for the Girls' Schools, buying three little clocks for them, etc. (I refer to the money given me when I was at home), so it has been laid out to good account. Try your luck, dear mother, thus resuming your good work of collecting funds in aid of " Female Education in India " (*minus* Africa for the present).

At the end of 1886 the Rev. J. G. Cooper writes :—

" Miss Mackay is soon to leave us, after nine years of devoted labour, as she has engaged herself to become the wife of a Swedish missionary at Chindwara. We will greatly miss her loving, bright, spirited presence on our staff of workers, but she will carry with her our best wishes and fervent prayers for her happiness and usefulness in the new sphere to which she now looks forward."

Reviewing her long term of service at Nagpoor, she says:—

"Nine years have rolled past since it was my privilege to join the staff of mission workers here, and now that I am about to retire from my present sphere of labour as zenana missionary, and to enter upon another of a more homely nature, at Chindwara, I should like to take a retrospect of the past with a view to finding out what progress has been made in the direction of native female Christian education in the city of Nagpoor.

"It will be remembered that Miss Berrie was one of the first workers here in this department, and the little paper she contributed to the quarterly publication, entitled 'Woman's Work in Heathen Lands,' gives a graphic account of her experience during the brief year she was permitted to spend among the women of Nagpoor. The annual reports of Miss Duncan (now Mrs. Eagles), who succeeded her in the work, give a further peep into the homes open to visitation at that time, while my sister's and my own more recent reports continue the narrative.

The outstanding land-mark in the march of progress, in *my* eyes, is the opening of two new Girls' Schools by Miss Janie Small, a work which could never have been satisfactorily accomplished had not the Ladies' Society seen its way to add a third worker, Miss Isabella Small, to our Zenana Mission staff. The success which has attended these schools is remarkable. A multitude of children hitherto unreached has been gathered into them, and some old pupils of our own attend as well, two of these being engaged as teachers. The existence of the schools reacts very favourably in connection with the house-to-house visitation, as pupils withdrawn from school after marriage can sometimes be followed into their homes, and kept up in the knowledge already received, while access is had at the same time to their mothers-in-law and other members of the household. I shall now give a sketch of a single day's visiting in the city, as affording a glimpse into the nature of the work we are engaged in from day to day, and from year to year.

"Yesterday, Friday, 12th November, I left home at half-past ten in the morning, two of the girls from the Orphanage, Jessie Macdonald and Phulwanti, accompanying me in my tonga as far as the Budhwari School, in which they are teachers. After dropping them at the school door I drove on through a crowded bazaar, till I reached a much-frequented temple, in the neighbourhood of which there are some houses open to visitation. Leaving my tonga behind, I proceeded down a narrow rugged lane, at the end of which stands a humble enough looking

Sunar's, or goldsmith's shop. The only specimens of jewelry to be seen here consist of broken anklets, ear-rings, etc., the property of women occupying the surrounding houses, sent for repair, while a potsherd, supplied with hot ashes, is the furnace into which these are thrown, to be beaten out thereafter on a rude, uneven stone for an anvil.

"The owner of the shop would not allow me to pass without looking in, as I had done on former occasions, and although there was no pupil, I had not the heart to refuse the old man's request, couched as it was in true native idiom, " Have mercy on us poor ones," etc. On this occasion a bundle of old Christian books was produced, the gift, many a year ago, of old Pahat Singh, once an active catechist, now a broken-down old man. Mr. Hislop's name was quite familiar to the owner of the books, and there was no lack of conversation in consequence. Some women, gathered at the door, could not help indulging in a quiet laugh when they heard me question the old man as to when he had last read from the books, and immediately after, as to when he had *eaten* last! "Oh," I said, "you are far more kind to your body than to your soul,"—a fact which he did not attempt to deny. After reading and singing a little to him and his fellow-workmen I passed on to his dwelling-house, where I had a most interesting interview with a large family circle of women and girls. Two tiny children profess to be learning here, but their infantile lips can hardly do justice to certain alphabetic sounds. The promise of an English doll, after a little progress has been made, had a decidedly stimulating effect. None of the older members of the household could be prevailed upon to learn, but a great deal of information as to why I had come to India, etc., was imparted without difficulty in answer to the numerous questions with which I was plied. The reading of a Scripture portion and singing of a sweet hymn brought our little meeting to a close, and I set out for a third house in which I have a dear little pupil. I was again stopped on the street, however, by a panting little fellow of about nine, who was carrying the stool lent me to sit on by the Sunar. He invited me into his own home so eagerly, that the words I have often thought of sprang into my mind once more,—' A little child shall lead them.' His elder sister, who was seated on the floor doing some household work, began, as I had half anticipated, to remonstrate with the child for bringing me in, but a word in praise of her pretty house disarmed her, and very soon the pleasant mother appeared, and was an attentive listener. As a specimen of the good-nature of the people, and their appreciation of a little fun, I may mention that when

I remarked upon the way in which the little boy's face was disfigured by the heathen mark on his forehead, which suggested to me a goat's lick (goats are very common here), they laughed heartily, and sent the little fellow to wash it off, which he readily did!

"Farther up the street I met a boy, of some fifteen or sixteen, an old friend who, when quite a child, used to dart in upon me when I was seated alone in my bungalow, writing letters, or otherwise engaged. He would hang over me, watching with wonder the movement of my pen, until I was free to turn my attention to him and entertain him in some way. He has taken to acting as my pioneer in that crowded district, and I am hopeful that he may find some new pupils for me. The mob that gathered round us on the street yesterday put an end to the attempt he was making to introduce me to some new houses; but we shall try again another day. I was able to pay a visit to his mother's house, as it is in a quieter locality. On at length reaching my pupil's house, found that she had gone off on *pilgrimage* with her aunt, so it was well I had some opportunities on the road. A long drive to another part of the city landed me in another series of lanes, to be threaded successfully only on foot. In the first house I directed my steps to, lives an interesting Brahman family, very unlike heathen, but very much given up to idolatrous rites and ceremonies, nevertheless. This family has been under Christian instruction at Bhandara, as well as here, but the scales have not yet fallen from the eyes of the mother, in particular, who seems to do pujah for all the household. But space fails me, as I have written too much in detail, and I must leave my sketch unfinished. I returned home about four o'clock, glad to rest until the beginning of a new week.

"I don't know who will succeed me in the work here in God's providence, but the 'Lord of the harvest' will 'send forth labourers into His harvest' in answer to prayer."

CHAPTER XIII.

"THE TRUTHFUL GÓNDS."

' Then they rose and followed Lingo,
Followed onwards to the forest,
From the mountain Dhawalgiri.

* * * *

Over mountain, over valley,
To the glens of seven mountains,
To the twelve hills in the valleys,
There remained with holy Lingo."

THE inhabitants of India differ as much among themselves as do the various nations of Europe. The prevalent theory is, that long before the dawn of history, two great hordes from Central Asia entered the country from the north-east and north-west, overrunning the whole peninsula, and meeting and crossing each other in the neighbourhood of Nagpoor, in the heart of the Central Provinces. Centuries afterwards, some say about 1000 B.C., a branch of the

Aryan[1] or Japhetic race swarmed off from the east of the Caspian Sea, and poured through the mountain passes of the Himalayas into the Punjab, crossing the Indus, from which they received the name Hindus, becoming the dominant race in the Indian peninsula, and more or less imbuing the former population with their own language, customs, and religion. In the course of ages, however, these Hindus, although generally spoken of as one people, have come to differ widely from each other in different parts, but like all nations sprung from Japheth, they are naturally highly gifted and intellectual. Corrupt religion and centuries of despotism have, however, had a debasing effect on their minds. In the higher castes they have graceful, agile figures, regular features, and a rich olive complexion; while the gentlewomen are often very beautiful, having exquisitely-moulded hands and feet, and dark gazelle-like eyes.

The influence of the Aryans did not extend far into the table-land of the Dakhan, while the aboriginal tribes inhabiting the thickets and mountain fastnesses of the Central Provinces effectually resisted the tide of conquest and civilisation, retiring still further into their inaccessible retreats.

[1] *Arya*, in Sanscrit, signifies "honourable," and is probably allied to the Greek *ari* (stos), the best.

The Hill tribes are named respectively: Santáls, Gónds, Bheels, Paháris, Kois and Hill Arrians.

Of these the Gónds were to Alexina the most interesting.

Early in 1884 her beloved sister Maggie became the wife of the Rev. Gustaf Danielsson, a Swedish missionary labouring among these people. Two years later the Free Church of Scotland passed over the Chindwara Station, in the heart of the Gónd country, to the Swedish Evangelical National Society, and about the same time the C.M.S. called away the Rev. H. P. Parker from Mandla, in the Satpura Hills, to succeed the lamented Hannington as Bishop of East Equatorial Africa; and of him and his sudden end, ere he reached Uganda, she heard much from Alexander Mackay. Ultimately her own lot was cast at Amarwara (*i.e.* Place of Immortality), a village in the lonely jungle, twenty-six miles from Chindwara, as she had been married to a Swedish missionary, the Rev. Johan Ruthquist, at Bombay, on the 13th October, 1888, the anniversary of the birth of Alexander Mackay, and the day following that never-to-be-forgotten 12th of October, in Uganda, when the Arabs vanquished the Christians. "Chiefs and commons, rich and poor, free and slave, fled before their foes, who hotly pursued them, while the European missionaries were plundered and expelled, and hope for Christianity in Uganda seemed to be at the very lowest ebb."

Dr. H. Grattan Guinness, than whom there is no better authority, says :—

"The missionary spirit exhibited by the Swedish Christians we have met is delightful to witness, and the simplicity and whole-heartedness of their consecration makes them an example to others."

Mr. Ruthquist possessed the same aggressive spirit in ministering to the heathen which consumed Alexina, and they both realised that

> "The world waits
> For help. Beloved, let us love so well,
> Our work shall still be better for our love,
> And still our love be sweeter for our work,
> And both commended, for the sake of each,
> By all true workers and true lovers born."

The name Gónd, or Gund, is from the Telugu word for a mountain, and signifies "hill-men." This simple race believe that they were created by the invisible God on the snowy peak of Dhawalagiri, the third loftiest of the Himalaya Mountains; and their legend of the five "Songs of Lingo" describes how they descended the torrent which sprang from the melting snow on this majestic summit, until they reached and settled in the ravines and jungles among the hills of Central India. Over half a century ago

Sir Donald M'Leod—a Scotchman, who had also the blood of the Huguenots in his veins—created and supported for many years missions to the Gónds and some other aboriginal tribes; but although he spent "his all" in the work, and had the reputation among the native population of India, "that if all Christians were like Sir Donald M'Leod, there would be no Hindus or Mohammedans," yet his efforts were unsuccessful.

It remained for the Scottish missionary Hislop to reduce the Góndi language to writing, and to reveal to the world the folk-lore of the Gónds, and their social and religious condition.[1] Whenever the cold season came round, he itinerated among them, gaining their affection, and unfolding to them the gospel plan of redemption. Since the beginning of Hislop's pioneer work, and the later efforts of the Church Missionary Society, and of the Swedish Evangelical National Society, thousands from this tribe have been drawn into the Christian Church.

To work among this timid, truthful, but superstitious people Alexina gladly settled down with her husband in the lonely jungle. Many of them were

---

[1] For much interesting information regarding the Gónds, see "Life of Stephen Hislop," by George Smith, LL.D. London: John Murray. Also, "The Hill Tribes of India," published by the Church Missionary Society.

bards who could sing and play the drum and other musical instruments, and as they were exceedingly friendly, and very receptive to Christianity, her hymn-singing was greatly appreciated, and she speedily felt herself quite at home among them, and won the hearts of all with whom she came in contact; for, as the Rev. R. Wardlaw Thompson, Secretary of the London Missionary Society, says: "One Christian missionary home, with a Christian wife, does more to humanise, elevate, and evangelise a race of people than twenty celibate men. Christianity has its sweetest fruits and most gracious work in the home; and from the home must radiate its most powerful influence, if any country is to be lastingly influenced by Christianity. Again and again the presence of a missionary's wife has been the first lesson in Christian life and Christian love, and more than that—that has been only the beginning of women's work—a missionary's wife has been the missionary's best helpmate in every part of the mission field."

The Gónds are said to have about fifteen gods, all malevolent, who are regarded as media of communication between the Creator and mankind; but in their homes they have no idols. They are in reality Shamanites, or devil-worshippers; but unlike the Hindus, they have a strong sense of sin, and of their need of a living sacrifice, and of the shedding of blood. Their dense ignorance is very trying, and a great hindrance to the entrance of the gospel ; but at the same time, Alexina considered that, dark and degraded as they are, they are more easily evangelised than the Hindus, as they have less to unlearn.

The Gónd villages are very isolated, and frequently are comprised of only four or five houses, although sometimes there may be double that number; but alas ! however few there may be, one is invariably a brewery! The curse of opium has also fallen upon these simple Hill people.

The Rev. H. D. Williamson, of the Church Missionary Society, who has laboured devotedly for many years among the north-eastern Gónds in the Mandla district, finds also itinerating to be his most engrossing and important work. For six or seven months in the year, right up to the beginning of the rainy season, he is incessantly on the move. The blessed name of Jesus is now daily honoured in hundreds of villages, though not always to the complete exclusion of their old religious worship, and he speaks especially of the wonderful readiness of this primitive million of people to pass on the gospel message to those who have not heard it.

Soon after Alexina's marriage, the Rev. J. Montelins was sent out by the Swedish Society, of which he was director, in order to inquire into and report on the progress of mission work in the Gónd country. The following extracts from his letters to the Evangeliska Fosterlands-Stiftelsens Expedition, Stockholm, afford an interesting glimpse into the darkness which then reigned in Central India, more especially, perhaps, in the rural districts. He formed a very high opinion of Alexina's character, and she, in her turn, was much struck with the depth of his love to Christ, and the delightful communion he enjoyed with his Lord.

NARSINGPÛR,
November 28th, 1888.

*　*　*　*　*

"The Conference has now been at work a whole week, from early in the morning till late in the evening, during which more than fifty different questions have been submitted to serious investigation.

"It has been a real joy to me to meet and become acquainted with our brethren in the midst of their important work, and to wrestle with them in prayer that we might hold fast our hope in spite of the powers of darkness in this heathen land.

"During my stay here I have, as far as possible, visited idol temples, and a so-called holy spring, besides three buildings erected upon places where the dead bodies of kings, together with their widows, have been burnt. One sees with grief how the people walk in darkness, and whilst they think they are serving God, they are degrading themselves in the service of their idols. I have read much of the pursuit of evil lusts to the honour of idols, but never could I have imagined that human uncleanness and worship in idol temples could so blend as they in reality do. We have always been obliged to make our observations through the doorway, as we were forbidden to enter, unless we would draw off our shoes, and such veneration we could not pay to their abominations. Here there is the blowing of trumpets, ringing of bells, and beating of drums for the idols, both when they are to be awakened in the morning, or when they are to sleep in the evening. These idols are dressed and undressed, washed and cared for, whilst the whole time they are being fanned. If there was not under all this the frightful reality of the power of the devil in the world, one might call it the people's play with dolls. This, however, is the state of things among the heathen to whom we should show mercy, and whose eternal welfare we should seek to promote by increased efforts and gifts to our missions.

"We have also been allowed to visit the prison here, and some information I have obtained is very significant. Murder is common among the natives, and the most usual causes are jealousy and theft. It sometimes happens that a man in a fit of jealousy will utterly destroy his wife's nose by biting it. In one of the neighbouring houses lives a young wife whose appearance has been entirely destroyed in this way. In Bombay also I heard of a man attempting to murder his wife in the open street through jealousy. He threatened her first, and she begged him not to hurt her before they reached home, but he would not listen to her. In the prison we found sixty prisoners—more men than women; one being a man who had killed his mother by kicking her. Probably, in a few days that man will be hanged. The prison was extremely clean and well arranged, while rope-making, carpet mending, grinding corn and the making of oil, etc., were extensively carried on. Dr. Mitchel is the governor of the prison. It is impossible for a missionary to obtain entrance there, in order to work among the inmates. A Christian is allowed to visit a Christian, and speak to him of spiritual things; but if a Christian governor should venture to speak to a heathen about Christ, he would, if it were reported, not only be dismissed, but subjected to severe punishment! It is significant of the neutral position the Government of India takes with regard to the religious opinion of the peoples over which, one may almost say, it watches with anxiety.

"To-morrow the Conference breaks up, and I am to accompany Brother Danielsson to Chindwara, and hope to be with Brother Twar in Nimpani over Christmas, and about the middle of January to arrive at Saugor."

"AMARWARA,
"*December 6th*, 1888.

* * * * *

"Now I will tell you something about my journey here from Narsingpûr, where I had days never to be forgotten, with our dear brethren in the mission field.

"A journey lay before me of sixty miles, through large forests, but it signified less to me, as I have come during the best time of the year, and have the experience of our brethren to help me, which they give me in the kindest manner, caring for me in every possible way.

"Brother Lindroth accompanied us part of the road with his spring ox-cart; afterwards I travelled with Brother Danielsson in his gharree, *i.e.* an ox-cart without springs, the only vehicle that can be used when the road begins to be stony and uneven.

"For hours I rode upon a quiet old horse which

Brother Ruthquist had sent with us, to make the journey easier, and two other vehicles followed, to carry the tents, furniture and luggage, etc.

"The natives were greatly interested in me, being a stranger, who could not understand their language, and they laughed heartily when I learned to say something in Hindustani. They were very friendly, however, and gathered flowers and fruit to show me they were amused, when I let them see some drawings which I occasionally made.

"It was a wonderfully beautiful road we had to pass; it went often through uncultivated parks or gardens, and again through wild forests. Higher and higher we climbed. Narsingpûr lies 1,000 feet above the sea, Harai 2,025 feet, Rhapa, which we also passed, nearly 4,000 feet, and Amarwara 2,700 feet.

"Of wild animals we saw many kinds of birds, a number of squirrels, some very large monkeys, and on a steep hill a panther crossed our way, and would gladly have seized a little dog who was with us, if he had not been afraid of our numbers.

"High up on the mountains I saw a snake. It is very dangerous to travel this way at night, for tigers frequent the jungles here. Our brethren have often been afraid of them. Now I understand why they are so anxious to have guns with them when they are sent from Sweden. They are also often obliged on their journeys to shoot game, when they cannot buy necessary food.

"We had three resting-places: Bachai, Usri, and Harai. At the last place we remained quietly over Sunday. We lived in tents, and there was a surprising difference in the temperature between day and night.

"In the middle of the day (the 1st of December) it was like a hot summer day at home, but at five o'clock in the evening one needed warmer clothing, and during the night two blankets and a cloak, to avoid catching cold. The natives make a fire at night, to keep themselves warm. A poor old Gónd had burns on his body, as he had lain too near the fire. They were also very unwilling in the morning to leave the fire to do anything. In Usri and Harai Brother Danielsson showed the people some Scripture pictures through his magic lantern, and preached to them about the prodigal son, and in Harai from some part of the life of Christ. Sometimes they expressed their delight at the pictures and their appreciation of what he said to them, by a peculiar smacking noise.

"The Malgusarin in Usri (within the district of Narsingpûr) was a Gónd, and we saw there the distinctive feature of a Gónd village, viz., that one large street runs through the whole village. Close to our encampment were two old idol temples, but one of them only was in use. The most ancient one was extremely tastefully built, although some of the figures were ugly. The one in use was not in the same style, but was in a measure handsome. It of course influences the people, who do not otherwise see anything of art. On the latter were many curious figures to be seen, among which were painted jugglers, and when I pointed them out to Danielsson, he explained that these figures represented what the gods are supposed to be doing, and according to the people's belief, they do all sorts of things, and even amuse themselves with juggling. It has happened often, and happens even still, that in secret the people here sacrifice human beings, particularly children, to their idols.

"In Harai a native king (see p. 327) governs under the English Government, and his district belongs to that of Chindwara.

"The king was not at home, but his brother, a boy of about fourteen years of age, came immediately on our arrival to our encampment, with four or five other lads in his company, in order to buy some Christian tracts, as he had also done when Danielsson had passed through before, when the king came to see the Bible pictures. The boy looked thoughtful, and although one could scarcely see by his clothes any difference between him and the other boys, he nevertheless seemed accustomed to be waited on, and to take the lead. On his right arm he had two gold bracelets, the value of which must at least have been fifty rupees. Round his neck he had eight or ten amulets, small ornaments which were also intended to preserve him from evil; but, poor boy! he had lost an eye. The king's palace was very large and interesting to see, but opposite the chief entrance there was a platform, on which was a collection of the most disgusting idols I have ever seen. Farther off was a high scaffolding, used at festivals, from which a man is swung on a high pole; formerly he used to be fastened to it by an iron hook stuck into his back, but now, through the interference of the English Government, he is only allowed to be fastened by ropes. In any case it occasions severe pain, and often illness, which ends in death. The king's garden was beautiful, surrounded by a hedge of flowering oleanders, adorned with magnificent flowers of gorgeous colours, and tall flowering acacia trees.

"In the village I saw many handsome men and children, but how the women looked I don't know, for they generally turned their backs to us, or covered themselves, or ran into their houses. The people are, like the country, uncultivated, but they may yet bring forth a wonderful harvest. Oh! that the Lord would soon allow His holy word to be sown among these poor creatures, that they might learn to rejoice in the living God, and serve Him in truth.

"I mentioned before that a panther had crossed our path. It was in Dulha Ghât, a veritable Alpine road; and when we climbed up, we found the idol Dulha under a tree, which, when it flowers, is, I hear, most gorgeous, but now it is leafless, and hung all over with rags. Around the idols, which consisted of three stones, smeared over with some red colour, was a wall of cocoanut shell, which had been offered to the idols. Our poor old Gónd went forward and made a 'salaam' to the idols with great reverence, although another of the servants, who was a Mohammedan, laughed at him. Afterwards Danielsson exhorted him not to make 'salaams' to stones!

"Now I have been three days with Brother Ruthquist. He has just been married to a Scotch lady, a Miss Mackay, who eleven years ago came to India, and laboured as a Zenana missionary in Nagpûr, not far from here.

"God has provided a home for them here, and comforted them in their work by the friendliness of the natives. Our Society has here a good and roomy house for their missionaries at a very low price. The first morning we walked through the neighbouring villages, visited the Government school, and inquired afterwards for a sick woman, to whom Brother Ruthquist had been allowed to give some medicine before he left for the Conference. He scarcely thought she could live, but she was better. He tries to induce the natives to apply for help at the hospital in Chindwara, but generally without success. They have usually a great dislike to it, and will rather die than avail themselves of it.

"The head policeman in one village had, on the contrary, followed the advice to send his sick wife there, and now she is better, after a very severe illness. While we continued our walk two sick persons came out of a house and showed their wounds. Brother Ruthquist does what he can to heal their diseases. In the evening he preached in another village about Zaccheus, who desired to see Jesus, and was found of Him.

"In the village of Amarwara he has been permitted to preach on all three of the Malgusar's verandahs, and besides this, in no less than twenty-eight villages, which lie so near that he could preach in one of them in the morning, and return before the sun had become too hot. Yesterday, with him as interpreter, I preached about Him who loved us, and gave His life as a ransom for all. Among my hearers was a fakir who had just returned from a long pilgrimage. He was very attentive. Mrs. Ruthquist sang a sacred song to a native melody. May the Lord be with them, and uphold them by His grace in joy and sorrow, in prosperity and adversity. To-morrow I hope to proceed on my journey to Chindwara, twenty-four miles distant. Ruthquist accompanies me.

"It is a joy to me if my letters can enable you in a measure to share the blessing I receive from intercourse with our missionaries here."

CHAPTER XIV.

SORROW AND SERVICE.

"I bless thee, God, for past delights—
Thank God!" I am not used to bear
Hard thoughts of death; the earth doth cover
No face from me of friend or lover :
And must the first who teaches me
The form of shrouds and funerals, be
Mine own first-born beloved ?"

IT has been beautifully said :—"Work is but one half of life; suffering is the other. There is a hemisphere of the world in the sunshine of work, but there is another in the shadow of suffering."[1] The traveller's bungalow at Amarwara was speedily transformed into a tasteful and pleasant home, which in itself was an object lesson to the ignorant native women around, for whose improvement, spiritually and morally, Alexina laboured with her characteristic zeal and earnestness.

[1] See "Imago Christi : The Example of Jesus Christ," p. 185.

> "In many a season of sorrow and pain
> Her presence she cheerfully lent,
> No case was so hard that reluctant was she
> For Jesus to spend and be spent."

And wherever she did go, as in the days of her childhood, her presence acted like a sunbeam; but a day came when, in a great measure, the sweetness was taken out of her life. On the 15th November, 1889, her only child—"Mary Juanita," after gladdening the parents' hearts for twelve days, was "transplanted to the garden of the King!" There were very mysterious and painful circumstances in connection with the event, which greatly embittered the cup, yet they bore the sad trial with unwavering Christian fortitude. It was suspected that opium had been administered to the infant, as for twelve hours she was unconscious, and no efforts of the medical man could arouse her.

All night long the poor mother wrestled in prayer, crying:—

> "Oh, take not, Lord, my babe away—
> Oh, take not to Thy songful heaven
> The pretty baby Thou hast given.
>
> *   *   *   *
>
> Thou who art
> So happy in Thy heaven alway,
> Take not mine only bliss away."
>
> *   *   *   *

"But the child spake out to the mother so :—

    'Is your wisdom very wise
    Mother, on the narrow earth,
    Very happy, very worth
    That I should stay to learn?

    *   *   *   *

    Mother, albeit this is so,
    Let me to my heaven go!
      A little harp me waits thereby,
    A harp whose strings are golden all,
    And tuned to music spherical,
    Hanging on the green life-tree
    Where no willows ever be.
    Shall I miss that harp of mine?
    Mother, no!'"

And the little one, without experiencing the toil and sorrow of earth's pilgrimage, found a swifter, safer way to the arms of Jesus.

After this sorrow Alexina realized more and more that Christ was her sanctification; and it was observed by all who came in contact with her that her thoughts were much more in heaven than on earth. No doubt it was the means her Heavenly Father employed to prepare her for her own early translation to the happy land.

About this time she wrote the following lines, which reveal her thoughts more fully than even her letters do.

ON THE DEATH OF "MARY JUANITA," AGED TWELVE DAYS.

Only escaped the narrowness of time—
Only removed from every taint of sin—
Instead of "left without," "received within."

Gone Home before me to that wondrous place,
Where Baby's angel [1] ever saw His face.
Oh! who shall be her Teacher in that sphere of sinless blessedness?
Shall she then hear Thy voice and know it?
Will she hear and see
How Thou dost call the little ones to Thee?

And will she learn in that dear Home above,
All *I* had longed to teach her of Thy love?
And wilt Thou bring her
When Thou com'st again,
And call that little body not to pain,
Such as she knew before,
But raise in power—
(Though sown in weakness)
To that glorious hour?

That little wasted frame—
Oh, shall it bloom—
When Thou shalt beckon her to leave the tomb—
In undecaying health?
Those plaintive eyes,
Shall they be opened to the sweet surprise
Of meeting us again?
And shall we see
Our little loved one very near to Thee?

---

[1] "For I say unto you, that in heaven their angels do always behold the face of My Father which is in heaven."—*Matt* xviii. 10.

The quiet, chastened look—
Oh, shall it cling
To all her little features lingering,
Where pain and sorrow never more shall linger,
Banished for ever by Thy healing finger?

And shall there be the holy, heavenly grace,
Of *Thy* dear likeness
Stamped upon her face?
Sometimes the mother's eye has fondly seen
Some beauty in what *was*,
But oh! I ween,
In that which *shall be*
There shall be a glory
Beyond the reach of any mother's story

Oh! come, Lord Jesus!
Let the days be few
Ere I shall see Thee—
And my Baby too!

Still later on, writing to a dear sister, she says:—

"As I read J——'s letter, and came to the words about 'my dear little one' and her being 'safe in the arms of Jesus,' I began to muse, and musing I looked up at the large picture on the wall which you got mounted for me—'Jesus blessing little children.' They should have put one on His knee, I said to myself, for we read that He 'took them up in His arms.' Do they ever represent the unspeakably comforting scene in such tender, true detail, do you think? I had no idea that Mrs. A—— had passed away! How fast they seem to be 'gathering homeward from every land, one by one!' I have seen three different pictures, lately, of 'Jesus blessing little children,' but in not one of them does a little child appear in His arms! This thought suggested to me the following lines; for a mother bereaved of a little child is always on the look-out for the tenderest representations of the loving Saviour. If a picture can be found of Jesus with an infant in His arms, I should like to possess it."

"HE TOOK THEM UP IN HIS ARMS."
MARK x. 16.

I'VE never seen a picture yet
In which the truth was told
About that story, passing sweet,
In gospel days of old.

The story is that mothers brought
The children they loved much
As near to Jesus as they could,
That they might feel His *touch*.

And *did* He touch them? Yes, He did;
And more than that, we know—
He *took them in His blessed arms*,
His tender love to show.

And on each little head His hands
So lovingly were laid;
The youngest nestled in His arms,
Nor felt the least afraid.

"And blessed them," so the story says,
And blessed they are indeed;
For blessing from the Saviour's hand
Means grace for every need.

* * * *

And has our Jesus ceased to bless?
  And are His hands removed
From little heads of children *now*,
  Tho' children *once* He loved?

Ah, no—thrice no! it cannot be,
  For Jesus is not dead;
He blesses *still*—His hands are *now*
  On many a little head.

And does He *take them in His arms?*
  Ye weeping mothers say.
He does. Why weep? they're safer *there*
  Than were they *ours* to-day.

Yet another sorrow awaited her, for within three months of the loss of her infant, at midnight, on the 8th of February, 1890, the angel of death entered the Mission House on the southern shore of the Victoria Nyanza, and to Alexander Mackay came the royal summons,—

" Lay down the shield and quit the sword,
    The fight of faith is done;
  And quickly towards the glowing east
    Ascends the rising sun.
  Angelic guards wait with the day,
    Thy crown of life to bring.
  O death, where is thy victory?
  O grave, where is thy sting?"

Writing home after she received the news, she says :—

" Few characters have drawn out 'Johan's sympathies so much.' He says, indeed, 'that if A. M. M.

had been still alive, he would have liked to go and help him!' In a case like this the thought of the 'entering into the joy of His Lord' is so linked on to the news of the departure from this world, that his death seems more like a translation than anything else! . . . Heaven seems to be very near earth these days. Little M——'s short step to it seems to have brought it nearer. 'Thither, O Lord, our weary steps are tending.' That is a fine sentence in the little paragraph, noting the death of the Rev. Alexander Cusin, Edinburgh, in *The British Weekly*:—' He has entered the completer service which is followed by no weariness.'

"I was just thinking, as Johan and I were wending our way homewards, on our little horses, from a distant village, where we had a meeting last night, that little babes will be restored to us at the resurrection, just as they were when we parted from them,[1]

---

[1] Her fondly cherished idea that mothers will have their infants restored to them just as they were in this world, does not agree, however, with Longfellow's lines :—

> "Not as a child shall we again behold her :
> For when with raptures wild
> In our embraces we again enfold her,
> She will not be a child ;
>
> But a fair maiden in her Father's mansion,
> Clothed with celestial grace ;
> And beautiful with all the soul's expansion
> Shall we behold her face."

for we cannot imagine that the little body that was laid in the grave will be changed into a big one. The development of mind and body will take place afterwards, I think, but like that of a perfect flower, never to fade again!"

Mrs. Danielsson, of Chindwara, thus describes Alexina setting out with Mr. Ruthquist on an evangelistic tour among the scattered villages of the district. Having few home ties, her main energies were devoted to lifting the simple-hearted Gónds from the low level of their superstitious beliefs, and bearing them upon the wings of sacred song to God and heaven.

"The commodious spring-cart, made by Johan's skilful hands, stands at the door; two little brown ponies, mother and daughter, bearing respectively the names of 'Lady' and 'Lilla' (the Swedish for *little!*) are in readiness, as also the 'thakra,' in which Sewa Ram (the Catechist) and his young wife, Frances, are to travel. The 'Hill tent,' 12 feet by 12 feet, has already been placed on a cart, to be drawn by bullocks; and, in another, the luggage has been stored; while 'Tiger'—the brown striped dog, lies eagerly awaiting the signal for beginning the march. Provisions and a tiny stove are packed away in a box built in front of the spring-cart, so that a cup of tea and some food may be readily partaken of under the shade of a tree, during the heat of the day. 'Lady' and 'Lilla' were the gift of a friend, and were very useful on the rougher parts of the journey, while out on tour; as well as for carrying 'Sahib' and 'Mem Sahib' to villages in the neighbourhood of Amarwara.

"The spring-cart has a roof on it, and can be used either with or without a seat. In the latter case, it is fitted up with a mattress, blankets and pillows, and has often afforded most comfortable night-quarters during journeys performed without a tent.

"The Sunday and week-night services in the neat little church to which the people are summoned by the ringing of a hand-bell, must now cease for a time; medical aid to the daily applicants must be suspended; Alexina's visits to the women in the village, and her Sunday Bible Class, as well as the evening rides to hold meetings in the surrounding villages must all give way to the cold weather campaign, in the shape of a tour in the district. The bungalow and compound are left in charge of two men, who are instructed to water the numerous flower-pots arranged near the house, as well as the rose-bushes and young trees now adorning the once stony soil; and to attend to the poultry and beautiful pigeons, whose circular dove-cot, thatched with grass, forms a pleasing, homely object. The tinkling of the bells so often worn around the necks of bullocks in this country is a-wanting, but the cavalcade moves slowly out at the rustic gate, and the journey has begun! Travelling in the Chindwara district, in common with many other parts of India, is often attended with considerable discomfort, owing to the want of made roads. In the Chindwara Station, however, Government has obviated this difficulty, but up in Amarwara there are only tracks made by country-carts and the conveyances of Government officials on their rounds of inspection, with the exception of a road made by Johan, extending towards Chindwara, on the one side, and to the village of Piperia, in the Narsingpûr direction, on the other. For one so weak as Alexina, it was no light matter to perform journeys under such circumstances, but after the spring-cart was made, she used to enjoy much more comfort, for she could lie down in it, and so escape the effects of many a hard jolt? She used to beguile the tediousness of the way by singing hymns. 'Come, Thou Fount of every blessing'; 'My times are in Thy hand'; 'Oh Thou in whose presence my soul takes delight'; and 'The Lord is My Shepherd,' were special favourites. The latter she used to sing to the fine old melody, 'Auld Lang Syne,' and well did the words and music suit each other!

"Many years before, at a dinner party in Nagpoor, during Alexina's furlough, the host,[1] a Government officer of high position, proposed that 'Miss Mackay's favourite hymn' should be sung. Accordingly, the beautiful hymn, 'O Thou in whose presence my soul takes delight,' was sung to its own sweet and pathetic melody.

"In travelling from place to place, the road sometimes lies over a romantic tract of country, up hill and down dale, and across small rivers, which must be forded; but, fortunately, the danger from tigers and other wild animals is rare! However, on one occasion, while crossing a river on horseback, the terrific roar of a tiger broke ominously on their ears! And they had to hasten from the spot as quickly as the fast-gathering darkness permitted, Alexina meanwhile maintaining a calmness which greatly surprised her husband! (See p. 321.)

But, to return to camp life! Arrived at their destination, Chensa, a Gónd servant, of six years' standing, assisted by the other servants, used to put up the tent in as shady a spot as could be found. Alas! for our travellers when neither mango nor pepul, tamarind nor Indian fig tree spreads its leafy canopy over the canvas roof! If the village were a small

---

[1] Mr. Fraser, now commissioner of Rajpûr.

one, they would only stay four or five days; but if it were a more important place, they might linger as long as ten days or a fortnight.

"My sister's singing of the native melodies was ever a great attraction, and her presence drew many *women*, contrary to Hindu custom, to the services; and frequently these invited her to accompany them to their homes. When Johan visited the southern part of the district, her fluency in Marathi, the language spoken there, was invaluable; and on such occasions, she not only sang, but also addressed the audience."

Regarding these itinerancies, Mr. Ruthquist reports:—

"One encouragement in the work has been, and is still, that the people come to hear. Many say that what we preach is good and true, and that they believe it all, and that they have given up the worship of idols, and serve only the true God. On some occasions the question has been put to them if they will not publicly witness for Christ by receiving baptism, but then they say, 'No! how could we give up and leave the whole world; but if many come, then we will also.'

"Everywhere, by far the greater number listen with attention to the good news; but they retain so little of what they hear, when it is only now and then one can visit the *distant* villages. In one village, after a meeting, some said, 'If you would come here once a week, we should be able to remember what you preach.'

"In Harai, and in several of the neighbouring villages, it appears to me that the soil is partially prepared for the good seed.

"Oh! if we had more labourers in these great fields!"

The following extracts from Alexina's diary, and her letters to the Committee at Stockholm and to her family, give an interesting insight into the work as prosecuted in the years 1891, 1892.

January 15th, 1891.—Came to Sáliwára—a prettily situated village. Johan had to return to Amarwara almost immediately for another cart, as one of ours had broken down on the road. We returned from the village a little while ago, where we had a very nice meeting. One delicate-looking man (the kōtwal, *i.e.* village watchman) listened most intently. He was anxious not to lose a sentence. We sang several hymns.

January 16th.—Went to Benaiki this morning. Found Malguzar affected by drink at the close of the "Panchayat" he had given. This man had much to say in opposition to the gospel message, but the man opposite listened very attentively—his little granddaughter in his arms. There must have been many people from surrounding villages present. We sang "Zara tuka soch" and "Dunyá men dil," and Johan spoke faithfully about the account each one must give of himself to God.

In the evening we had our second meeting in this village, and sang "The Happy Land," etc. We *have* enjoyed this place. It has been so quiet and charming. *N.B.*—Mattaya (the sweeper) has developed in an unexpected way to-night. He has evidently made up his mind that when he is asked any important question, the right answer is, "Yisah Masih," *i.e.* Jesus Christ. Therefore, when he was asked what the great light is that makes the day, this was the answer he gave! Strange to say, unknown to Mattaya, Johan had spoken from the words of Jesus in the village: "*I* am the light of the world."

January 17*th.* Karitee.—A large village of stirring, intelligent people. A religious teacher was inclined to show himself learned and self-confident, but he became quiet when Johan said he might speak afterwards, if he liked. Sewa Ram, our catechist, sang a solo, and spoke very nicely. Then Johan spoke of the follies of the people, and our desire to show them the way back to God. When he declared that although all expect to go to God after death, to many who have lived in sin the words will be addressed, " I know you not," the Malguzar showed that he was struck with the appropriateness of this, for he burst out laughing, and said aloud, " There had been no acquaintance ! " Eight men came to the tent later on to have conversation in regard to what they had heard.

January 18*th.*—Another large gathering in the village. No opposition from " Pundit Zee," (*i.e.* Mr. Teacher) as Johan called him. Large groups of women collected in the two verandahs. Sewa Ram was earnest and hearty. He spoke on the words, " Blessed are the meek, for theirs is the kingdom of God." Johan spoke on " eternal life."

January 19*th.*—Went to Bareilly. Found the Malguzar too much taken up about a theft of twenty-five shillings, committed by a servant, to take notice of the gospel message, or even the messengers ! An elderly man, with a perverted expression of face, interrupted Johan to prove that *God* is the Author of evil, because Satan was created by Him. Of course it was explained to him that Satan was created in a *good* state, like all other creatures of God. A woman seated near me could not rest till her son was called from the field, because he could read ! He at last came, and opened a small bundle of books, in which were two Christian ones he had got either from Mr. Dawson or Mr. Danielsson. I asked him some questions from one of these, but he could not answer them, so he got a little sermon on the subject of his carelessness, and was told to improve! His request for another book was naturally denied, in the circumstances.

Koonda.—We came to this beautiful place on Monday, the 26th (see p. 310), and found a choice site for the tents. Next morning we visited Ságar, and were kindly treated to milk, sugar, and spices by the representative of the Malguzar, who, accompanied by many others, escorted us here in the evening, and we had a very large gathering under a pepul tree in the centre of the village. This morning (the 28th) we rode to Hutnee, and although the people seemed, mostly, unpromising at the beginning, they became good friends before we left them, and escorted us out of the village some way. Two of their number were glad to receive books, one getting G——'s translation of Luther's Catechism, and the other a small hymn-book, by his own request. The last-named man had asked if Jesus Christ is *alive* in a cavilling spirit, little expecting to be told "Yes." He poured out much nonsense, but acknowledged, when asked, that he had got his information from his own heart! Johan told him that the knowledge of the things of God comes from above.

On Thursday, the 29th, Mr. Rensaa (a brother

missionary) joined us, and we went into the village in the evening. We found the people very indifferent and unreceptive. The First Commandment was explained. In Kumsa, in the evening, it was evident that a spirit of disaffection had been roused, for the Malguzar absented himself, and the people were slow to assemble. A faithful message was delivered to them, however, but when they were asked if they would like to hear once more, no one answered. We therefore took another village, Taunri, instead, next evening. On the morning of that day we had a delightful visit to a village called Lukeree, and next day (Saturday, the 31st) we arrived at Măchagora (see p. 313).

On February the 3rd we came *here*, to Jătlapur, on a little branch of the Pénch. Our tent is just opposite the site of the bazaar. Yesterday morning we rode to Cheenia, where there were nice, honest-hearted people. This morning we went to Karaghât, near Dewdar. The people were singularly backward and unreceptive. One man asked if God is *alone* in heaven, or if He has "Bal Bacha" (children); and another if He has a wife, and so on. The darkness was gross. They believed in the old Hindu mythology about Lanka (Ceylon), etc., thinking it had been submerged! The ignorance was great, reminding one of the Scripture words—"Darkness hath covered the earth, and thick darkness the people." In this village (Jătlapur) the people are earnest and thoughtful, but also very ignorant.

February 26th.—We went to Ránikámat last night, and had an interesting meeting. One man made many inquiries as to the resurrection, and wondered how our "kaccha," bodies, could go to be with God for ever. ("Kaccha" has several meanings, *e.g.*, "unripe," as fruit; "unburned," as bricks. Perhaps the best meaning here is "corruptible" or "mortal.") On the way we saw an old hyena ranging about at ease in the jungle. It was a strange sight, with its clearly marked stripes, amid the homely scenery of trees and green grass. Johan loaded, but the animal disappeared mysteriously.

January 7th, 1892. Harai.—We came here yesterday, having broken our journey from Amarwara at a very small village—Moorgutola? I went into the village alone in the evening, but had a good deal of discomfort owing to the boys and women looking upon me as such a novelty. Our camp was enlarged by the arrival of two of the Methodist Christians (native); one, a Robert Hard, an itinerating preacher, the other, a convert from the Mehter (sweeper) caste, his companion and disciple. We gave them a friendly reception (they had really come to see us), and Johan invited them to linger with us a few days if they liked. They are here still. They accompanied Sewa Ram to a village in the morning; Johan going alone to another.

January 8th.—Last night Frances, the catechist's young wife, and I went to some houses quite near this, on the outskirts of the village, and found many people delighted to listen. They belong to such castes as the Chumár. "To the *poor* the gospel is preached." This morning Johan and I went in the chakla to Dheerá, a village some three miles off, and had a nice meeting at the gentle Malguzar's house. We mean to return there some evening. A Brahman beggar was very attentive; he had a very refined face.

This evening we have all been to the Chumár quarter, where we had a very nice meeting. "Robert Hard" was asked to speak first, and he did so very humbly and lovingly. Johan followed, speaking on the Lost Sheep. Sewa Ram concluded. We had nice hymns too, and Robert Hard prayed, by his own wish. May God's blessing attend the preaching of His own Word! I forgot to say that the convert from the Mehter caste added a few very suitable words.

Last night we all went back to the Chumár quarter, but the gathering (especially the children and women) was restless, and it was difficult to go on and not lose patience. We have promised to return there once again.

This morning Johan and I went to the village Amari, and had a meeting with a somewhat strange lot of people. A good many of the villagers had been called out by the Rajah to hunt, however. On Saturday night and Sunday morning we had the doctor with us; and we expect him back to-day from Narsingpûr.

January 16*th.*—We have been to a village far away in the jungle, called Bargee, where the people are in a very sunk condition. The scenery around is lovely. Last night we were in Káhrá village, and Johan pointed out that ignorance of God is *sin*, from the passage:—Out of the heart of man proceedeth foolishness—translated in Hindi into "agyánitá" (ignorance).

(*To the Children of the Free Church Sunday School, Holborn, Aberdeen.*)

AMARWARA, CENTRAL INDIA.
May 24*th*, 1890.

This is the Queen's birthday, and I am going to write to you about one of her little subjects—to give you, indeed, "The Story of Little Benjie." It runs thus :—

A little fellow of eighteen months old has come to live with us up here in Amarwara, from Chindwara.

The little man, when in full dress, wears a little white coat and a small pair of trousers, down to his feet, which are bare! His head is also bare, and as the hair was shaved off lately, and has only begun to grow again, it reminds one of a black, silky ball! But I must tell you about his birth. One day, eighteen months ago, my sister, Mrs. Danielsson, who is the wife of the Chindwara missionary, heard that something had been found in the compound— the piece of ground belonging to the house. What was it, do you think? Some of you have guessed, I daresay. Yes; it was a little baby—no other than little Benjie, who had been left to perish by his own mother, for reasons of her own. If the infant had not been found, the big birds called vultures would have pecked him to death in a very short time and pulled him to pieces, leaving nothing but bones. But our gracious, loving Father in heaven saw the little deserted baby, and would not suffer it to die; so He directed the steps of a little girl near to the spot where it lay, and she brought the news to my sister in the Mission house. Her motherly heart was deeply touched, as you may suppose, and she ordered the child to be brought at once, and had it attended to in every way. She was determined to find out who the cruel mother was, if possible, and would you believe it? she found it was one of her own servants! (native, of course). This servant has now got married, and her husband has come to be our cook, and of course they have brought their little child with them. Will you remember this little child, and pray that he may early learn to love Jesus, who saved him from a cruel death, and died Himself to save his soul, as well as ours, long, long ago—how long can any of you tell? Yes; nearly 1,900 years ago!

And now, dear children, it is more than time to tell you that I have received the money you so kindly sent me lately to help on the mission work. When put into Indian money it came to nearly ten rupees. (A rupee looks just like a "two shilling bit," as we say in Scotland, although *a florin* is the proper name.) I have changed my mind about buying seats for the people to sit on in church. Why? Because only the proud people object to sitting on the nice clean floor! To *them* my husband has said, "If you want a chair, *bring one with you!*" But it would be hard work to *find* one in most of their houses, for the people in villages like this almost all sit on the floor.

Well, what do I mean to do with the money you sent me? First, I have ordered from Bombay a nice Bible picture-book for the children in our compound.

It will be so nice to tell them Bible stories in their own Hindi language, and to show them the pictures at the same time. Do you know two things that children are very fond of? *I* know *one* thing— "sweets!" Yes, but I do not mean anything for eating; I mean pictures and music. Am I right? Oh yes, I am. And the children of India are just as fond of these as Scotch and English children are.

The little Benjie (or Benjamin) of whom I have been telling you, gets into splendid spirits when he hears us singing hymns in our little Sunday gathering. He shows his delight by trotting about amongst us, waving his little hands, and giving a little squeak now and then. Well, I have got the picture-book from Bombay, and now I mean to get from Calcutta a musical box to amuse the children on week-days. I'll tell them about the loving children in Scotland, who wish them to be happy and good, and they will believe in your love when they see *the fruits* of it.

The first thing my husband did when little Benjie arrived was to make a toy-cart for him. In this way he showed his love for the child, and the little one loves him back again.

Before I close I must tell those of you who remember me that six months ago God gave me a darling baby—a little girl; such a sweet little thing, with blue eyes and rosy lips, but she was only allowed to remain in this world twelve days. She fell asleep in Jesus one night to awake in heaven; and I must follow her there, God helping me.

Good-bye, dear children; may God bless you and make you a blessing.

Your loving friend,
ALEXINA RUTHQUIST.

(To Pastor Montelius, Director of Missions at Stockholm.)

AMARWARA,
December 15th, 1890.

DEAR SIR,—

Mr. Danielsson has suggested that I should write to you now and then, telling you a little about what goes on here in connection with our work, and I willingly fall in with his suggestion, hoping that friends in Sweden will become more interested in this little corner of the great vineyard.

Well, to make a beginning. Johan and I have just returned from the village of Piperia, to which you once accompanied us. Colonel Vertue has given me a second little horse (my husband uses the first I had), and I am now strong enough to ride with him to the villages, and I hope we shall have many delightful experiences in the coming cold season, as we tell the gospel message by word and song. We had this afternoon among the audience three *fakirs*, in their customary dress of brick colour, and ashes on their foreheads. They are on their way back to their homes in Northern India, after a long pilgrimage to the sacred Birmán on the Nerbudda river. Johan remarked that their work was a very heavy one, involving, as it does, so much fatigue and hunger, and to this they agreed. He then explained to them that it was also useless, and referred to the teaching of the hymn we had just sung, namely, that all fulness is in God, so that we have only to receive from Him. The three men listened very attentively and politely, calling their instructor Bába (an endearing name for child, though it also means "sir" or "father"), and said they would never forget what they had heard. God grant that it may be so!

I continue on the 17th. Yesterday we rode to Kărăh Dûl, a village beyond Piperia, and were heartily welcomed by the people, even the children coming to say "salaam," when we seated ourselves on the Malguzar's verandah. Very soon some seventy or eighty people assembled, amongst whom was a policeman from Amarwara, who had broken his journey to become a hearer with the rest.

We had a delightful time with these people; their spirit was so friendly, and their attention so good. Johan told once more the wonderful story of the fall of Man and the redemption by Jesus Christ. It seemed to me that he was more than usually helped as he preached. I tried to pray that the message might be brought home to the hearts of the hearers. We finished by singing the beautiful hymn, "Jesus Christ is the Saviour of my soul," and then "Can you believe it?" We were invited to have some food, and after a little delay, the feast was spread on a large plate, made of dried leaves sewed together, in the presence of about a dozen onlookers. We had curry cakes, chapatties, etc., and as we ate we amused the onlookers by remarking on the tingling of eyes, nose, and mouth with the spicy food.

Before we left, Johan said a few salutary words on the subject of *Caste*, pointing out that the great God, who is *above all*, invites all His children *to come near to Him*. Having thanked our kind friends for their hospitality, and sung one more hymn, we rode home in the beautiful moonlight, and being very tired, I went at once to rest; but a most pleasant impression was left on the mind. In the morning sick people poured in, and kept Johan very busy; but we can be engaged in no higher service than in ministering to the bodies and souls of the poor neglected ones of the earth. May God's rich blessing rest on us and our work!

KOONDA,

SOME EIGHTEEN MILES DISTANT FROM AMARWARA,

January 27th, 1891.

DEAR PASTOR MONTELINS,—

Johan and I are out in camp just now, accompanied by our young catechist, "Sewa," who is indeed a great help to us in our work. I was thinking of you as we sat under the large pepul tree in the centre of this village half an hour ago, preaching and singing the gospel to the large crowd that had assembled. You would have been deeply interested if you had been with us; but as this could not be, I shall tell you a little about one meeting, as well as of our present circumstances here. We arrived only last night, but as soon as it was known that we had come, one of the Malguzars, with some of his friends, came to see us, which was very encouraging. He asked us if we had come to his village to tell them about "Yisah Masih" (Jesus Christ), and I need not say what answer he got. I shall tell you, however, what will surprise you—that he came again to our tent this evening, along with a brother Malguzar and a number of the leading men of the village, and, of course, a host of little boys, to conduct us to the raised seat in the centre of the village, under the beautiful tree I mentioned before. A bedstead was placed there, just in front of a hideous idol, and we were allowed to sit with our backs to it, while all the people assembled in front of and around us, to the number of at least a hundred and fifty. We began as usual with a hymn, asking, " Why do you set your affections on this world, in which life is uncertain?" and then Johan read to them from the third chapter of St. John's Gospel the verses about the lifting up of the serpent in the wilderness, dwelling especially on the sixteenth verse: "For God so loved the world," etc. The people listened very attentively, and after Johan had finished, and another hymn had been sung, Sewa took up the same subject. While he was speaking a man interrupted him by asking where Jesus Christ was to be found. "Show Him!" he said. He was told to listen for a few minutes and converse afterwards, and to this he consented. The answer was given to him by Johan, who said, "*I* found Jesus Christ in the gospel, and *you* will find Him if you search for Him there." Our next meeting here is fixed for the night after to-morrow. This morning we visited a village called " Ságár," and were most kindly received. I sang a beautiful hymn about the sufferings of Christ in our stead, which was explained verse by verse, and afterwards Johan had a good deal of conversation with an old Brahman priest seated near him. There are many Brahmans in this place, and they seem to believe in themselves very thoroughly. At the conclusion of the meeting the master of the house refreshed us with milk and spices, and our hearts felt specially refreshed by such unexpected and unusual kindness. Our second meeting in Koonda was somewhat disappointing. It seemed as if some of the people, as in the days of old, had been "offended at the word," and when they were asked if they would like to hear more, not one said "Yes." We have therefore resolved to go to-night to another village instead. I believe, however, that the consciences of some of the people here have been touched, and we trust that the seed already sown will, sooner or later, bear fruit to the glory of God.

January 29th.—Mr. Rensaa has taken a run to see us, and we all three rode to a village this morning, where the gospel message was gladly listened to, and acknowledged to be indeed THE TRUTH. Many of the inhabitants had gone on pilgrimage to a so-called sacred place, and others to a wedding, but a most interesting section of the people had remained behind, and we charged them to tell the good news to their neighbours on their return.

But now, dear Pastor Montelins, I shall draw to a

close. Johan joins me in hearty New Year's greetings.

Sincerely yours,
ALEXINA RUTHQUIST.

(*To her Mother.*)

MĀCHAGORA,
SOME TWENTY-FIVE MILES FROM AMARWARA,
February 1st, 1891.

We were able to return to our tent last Monday and to resume our preaching tour, and this Sunday morning finds us encamped under one of the finest banian trees I have ever seen, while a river is so near to us that we can call for a jug of water from it any time we like! The country round us is very bare, however, compared with the rich district we have just left; but this village is specially interesting because Mr. and Mrs. Dawson are well remembered! The fat Malguzar, in whose verandah we had our meeting last night, told us that the chairs we were sitting on had been his! This rich, kingly man —inasmuch as he owns the village, and rules its inhabitants, in a sense—this important personage seemed much embarrassed by our visit last night, for he has already heard too much to leave him in ignorance of the fact that to accept Christianity

means to leave all and follow Christ; and this he is
not at all prepared to do, apparently. He was
courteous enough, however, to interfere on our behalf,
in his crowded verandah, when a passionate fakir
jumped up on the mud wall surrounding the place
where we were seated—quite near me, and began to
interrupt the proceedings by calling on his followers
to answer us! The Malguzar ordered him away
and said he could speak (as he was very anxious to
do) to-morrow. I do wonder what kind of a meeting
we will have to-night, for this man may be present
to resist, and the Malguzar himself said he would put
some questions to-day! I will resume my letter after
the meeting.

Jātlapur, Feb. 3rd. — The meeting I spoke of
passed off very quietly, but it is too evident that the
Malguzar is a man hardened against the gospel, and
not he alone, but other members of his family circle,
for a brother of his, who is chief man in a neighbouring village, declined to stay for the meeting to be
held in the verandah of one of his own houses, saying
he knew all about what was going to be said, for
that he had been educated in Mr. Dawson's School;
but that in passing through the village he would
send the villagers up to his house to hear! You will
see from the enclosed sheet, that we have both en-
couragements and discouragements in our work; but

what else can we expect? My next letter will probably be written from Chindwara, which we pass through in the course of our round. We intend, however, to live in tent there. Mr. Rensaa left us yesterday forenoon, having enjoyed his visit. Johan had to make up yet another small tent for his accommodation at night, with the help of the village durzee (man who sews). It was made of a verandah, etc., we had, and was needed in any case.

The plan we adopt out in the villages here is this. We visit the village we are stationed near every night, as a rule (Johan, the young catechist, and I), but in the mornings Johan and I ride to a neighbouring village together, taking a different one each morning, while the catechist goes to another by himself. He is a good speaker and singer, and we believe a sincere man. We look upon him as sent to us in answer to prayer, for we really stumbled upon him, so to speak, while in Narsingpûr.

NARSINGPÛR,
March 27th, 1891.

DEAR PASTOR MONTELINS,—

My husband and I had to return home suddenly from our preaching tour among the villages some weeks ago, owing to an unseasonable fall of rain; but I must tell you something about our experience in the last village we visited, as it was exceedingly encouraging and very uncommon.

The name of the village is Jătlapur, and it lies on a branch of the Pénch river, within a distance of eight or nine miles from Chindwara. Our tent was erected just opposite the beautiful shady spot on which the weekly bazaar meets, and as bazaar day occurred while we were there, both my husband and our young catechist had an opportunity of visiting it, and of proclaiming the gospel message. The most effective work, however, as far as man can see, was done in the quietude of two evenings in the village itself. We met as usual in the verandah of the Malguzarin's house, for the poor husband is dead, and a young boy of some twelve or thirteen years of age has succeeded to the title of Malguzar. The boy was away from home the first day, much to his mother's disappointment, but we had a large and attentive audience, two men in particular listening most eagerly. One of these, however, changed his expression, when he heard the worship of idols condemned, and when we paid our second visit to the verandah, he took a back seat and expressed no more interest. Another man, however, whom I had not observed on the former occasion asked, just as the catechist had begun to speak :—" Who *is* Jesus Christ?" and the answer given to this question, embracing as it did the whole gospel story, briefly but thrillingly told, went so to his heart, that his face literally *shone* with delight, and he exclaimed aloud, " Such a story was never told. This is the truth!" Johan spoke shortly afterwards, and warned him as well as the others to beware of the enemies of Jesus Christ, who would doubtless speak against all that they had heard, and try to shake their faith. "I will consider such people to be my enemies," said the man, and then, as we rose to go, he inquired, " Now, what is to be done for our women? for our women have not heard a word of this." "Ask my wife to go to your house, if you like," was Johan's reply, and the request was immediately made and responded to. Not only was I admitted, however, but my husband too, and in a few sentences I told the group of women comprising his household something of the love of Christ in laying down His life for us lost sinners. After singing one or two gospel hymns we rose to go, but first we had to partake of "pan supari," prepared for us there and then, by the vigorous-minded looking mother. I forgot to say that the young Malguzar arrived that evening, and was most polite, making a profound "salaam" by his mother's directions, and then seating himself in the middle of the group of listeners, tired as he was with his journey. We presented him with a copy of

Barth's " Bible Stories " before we left the village, and his mother was so pleased that she sent us milk and fruit in return. We hope to re-visit this village before long.

Sincerely yours,
ALEXINA RUTHQUIST.

P.S.—Mrs. Lindroth managed to leave her sweet little twin babies, the other morning, and to accompany the catechist's wife and myself to see some of the native women. In the first house we visited there is a poor invalid, who has lately had her great toe amputated! She came out of bed, into the verandah, to see us, and to pour out to us the story of her sufferings. What could we do, however, but sympathise with her and try to raise her thoughts to the heavenly home, in which there shall be no more pain. This woman's husband is a man of a very fine disposition. He is assistant to the English doctor here, and apparently a man of great intelligence. His young daughter, being already a widow, is once more an inmate of her father's house.

A spirit of hostility to the gospel pervades the next house we visited, that of a rich man who owns a printing-press. We showed our goodwill, however, by sitting down among the women, and singing a hymn, which was explained beautifully afterwards

ADVANTAGES OF SOCIAL INTERCOURSE.

by the catechist's wife. In this house we were joined by a very nice woman, a Brahman widow who is in charge of the Government Girls' School. Were it not for the fear of man, she would probably become a Christian; but this, I fear, is her stumbling-block. May God help her to overcome this! Mrs. Lindroth invited these women to come to the bungalow to see her babies, and they promised to come; but one of them has had since an attack of fever, which prevented the visit. An old lady, the widow of a Malguzar, who is at present on a visit to Narsingpûr, did come, however, accompanied by two serving women. She brought with her a packet of native sweetmeats, and Mrs. Lindroth treated her and the others to those spices they are so fond of, and which they can partake of from the hand of a Christian without breaking their *caste!* We also sang a sweet hymn to the accompaniment of the harmonium, which they were very anxious to hear, and soon after our friends took leave, not without a hearty invitation from Mrs. Lindroth to return when they might find it possible.

If social intercourse of this sort could be multiplied a hundredfold, the result for good would be incalculable; but it is so difficult to overcome the widespread idea that a woman must not be seen outside her own house. "Common women" may be seen, but those of "high caste" never, unless curtained from public view within an airless gharree of some kind or other!

May He who has come to preach deliverance to the captive, speedily "turn the captivity" of these our sisters!

Sincerely yours,
A. R.

(*To her Father.*)

AMARWARA, CENTRAL PROVINCES,
April 13*th*, 1891.

We left the Mission House on the afternoon of last Monday, just a week ago, in the kind Lindroths' tonga, in which they sent us on the road eight miles, or to the first halting-place. The heat was intense, but the tonga cover and an umbrella helped us much, and it had clouded over before we had to alight and pursue our way on horseback some ten miles. Before we reached our halting-place for the night, we had to cross a large river, the banks of which were instinct with all kinds of life. Johan tried to shoot a splendid peacock, with a tail twice as long as its own body, but it hid away somewhere, to die, we fear, instead of falling at once. Johan was very loath to lose it, and he looked here and there as narrowly as he could. The ravine into which it had disappeared looked so hideous, however, that he dared not descend into it, and it was well he did not, for a tiger might have been lurking there. We got enough of a fright without going out of our way, however; for as we were seated under a tree, having a mouthful of food, we heard a moaning sound, as of some large animal slightly snoring in sleep! Johan felt more uneasy than even I did, for he told me afterwards that the sound was made by wild animals when prowling about in quest of prey, to frighten and rouse up the deer, etc. We made great haste to be off, as you may suppose, for it was the gloaming, just the time when the animals come out of their resting-places to drink. Mr. Thompson, by the by, was rather too sceptical in regard to the likelihood of our ever seeing tigers here! Quite lately, a tiger was going its rounds within less than half a mile of us! and Johan went to see the remains of a horse it had feasted on, in one place! Maggie will be touched to hear that "Matti," the orphan boy with the enlarged spleen, died at Saugor two or three weeks ago! His death was owing to a wound he got on the mouth, while cutting wood, I believe. I think a splinter caught somewhere, and he bled profusely. Miss Rensaa, in writing about it, said, "We trust he has gone to be in his heavenly home for ever." He was a boy of a simple, loving nature as Gustaf and Maggie know.

We had two such different meetings in two separate villages, on the morning of the 6th, after hunting for a certain village Johan had seen on the map, but in vain. It turned out to be so far off, we made for a little one we discovered, of which there was no mention made on the map! A small group of indifferent-looking people were collected to hear, but amongst them there was a refined-looking boy with a very disaffected face! I entered into conversation with him, and found that he had been educated in the Mission School in Seoni, when he was very small, he made out; and he was not ashamed to say that he had forgotten both how to read, and all he had heard about Jesus Christ! both statements being untrue, I fancy. I told him plainly, that I could see by his face that he had hardened his heart, and advised him to begin to read again. He has charge of a jeweller's shop in Chindwara, in the room of his dead father. How different our meeting in the evening was, in the village near which our tent was standing—Jătlapur, by name. Johan, the little catechist and I seated ourselves on the rude bedstead (four bamboos laced together by cords), placed for us on the outer, open verandah, our lantern brightly burning in the midst of the darkness (literally, I mean, for there is almost no light at night in these villages), and soon a large audience gathered to hear, among whom were several little girls, in a group, behind. One intelligent-looking man, with a Jewish face, delicate complexion, and large, lustrous eyes, asked at the outset, in a very purpose-like way, who Jesus Christ is. In reply, our animated little catechist, who is always asked to speak first, gave a beautiful thrilling account of the fall; promise of redemption; coming of Christ; His work and manner of death . . . on and up to His ascension; and the effect produced on the minds of several by this wondrous story brought tears to my eyes.

At least three of the listeners sitting just in front seemed electrified by it, and the suitability of the gospel to the unprejudiced heart of man was fully apparent! One felt as one does at a revival meeting at home, that God is verily and very near. The inquirer before referred to accepted the answer given, and he did not let us go back to our tent until he had conducted us to his home, to tell the good news to his grey-haired mother and other relatives. Please pray for the village of Jătlapur.

AMARWARA,
November 9th, 1891.

MY DEAREST MOTHER,—

Johan and I reached home two days ago, after a toilsome journey on an awful road. With our utmost endeavour we could not finish the journey till three days and three nights had passed over our heads, and yet the distance is only about fifty-four miles! We slept at the close of each day in our nice new cart under some friendly tree, near some river or stream ; for water is a necessity not only to ourselves, but to our servants and animals. Our "train" consisted of a motley throng of beasts of burden, in addition to our own tidy little ponies and bullock-cart; for our luggage had to be strapped on to the little country hack horses and small donkeys. Amongst our luggage were six bundles, carefully packed in straw, containing, you would be long in guessing *what*—the various parts of two little white marble tomb stones we had ordered from Cawnpore, one for our own infant's grave, the other for Maggie's ! We have not unpacked them yet, but later on, when all the preliminary arrangements for getting them erected have been made, I will describe them to you. They are not crosses, but erect tablets, and, in addition to the little names, etc., I divided the text :

"Suffer the little children to come unto Me," . . . so much being engraved on little Gustaf Alexander's, and the remaining words : " Of such is the kingdom of heaven," which had been a comfort to me, on Mary Juanita's. The cost is not *very great*, but the masonry will bring it up."

At this time her sister (Mrs. Danielsson) and her husband were spending their furlough in Sweden, and the tablet on their infant's grave was the surprise gift which awaited their return ! This is just a single instance of the consideration for others which ever animated her. It meant self-denial, for her means were limited, but—

"The least flower, with a brimming cup, may stand
And share its dew-drop with another near"

CHAPTER XV.

IN THE RED SEA.

" Launch thy bark, mariner!
Christian, God speed thee!
Let loose the rudder bands—
Good angels lead thee!
*   *   *   *
Slacken not sail yet
At inlet or island;
Straight for the beacon steer,
Straight for the high land;
Crowd all thy canvas on,
Cut through the foam—
Christian, cast anchor now—
Heaven is thy home!

THE early days of 1892 found Alexina, in the company of her husband, singing the gospel in the palace of a king. Before the third quarter of the year had run its course, her voice mingled in the new song of the redeemed, in the mansions of the King of kings!

The months passed swiftly, and her correspondence

reveals continued self-sacrificing and joyful work in the Master's service. For some years Mr. Ruthquist had not only gone "about all the villages," preaching the gospel of the kingdom, but he had also endeavoured to minister to the bodily ailments of the people. The 20th of June saw the opening of the dispensary, which had been a long-felt want. The people are always ready to show their wounds, and eager for medicine, and Alexina looked forward to having many opportunities of singing and otherwise imparting spiritual instruction, while they waited for admittance to the consulting-room. Further on, we find her ministering to a poor outcast, whom her husband had rescued from a terrible death. It was a most loathsome case, from which even many Christians would have turned in horror; but, as she remarked, the Son of Man came "to seek and to save that which was lost."

(*To Pastor Montelins, Director of Missions, Stockholm.*)

HARAI, CHINDWARA DISTRICT, C.P.
January 10*th*, 1892.

My husband, the catechist and his wife, and I have just returned from the Rajah's palace, where Johan has been preaching to the king and his court by invitation. When we entered the grim old building, and found ourselves surrounded by proud-looking servants of various kinds, a strange feeling of desolation crept over us, for we had entered an atmosphere uncongenial in the extreme to the followers of Christ. No one around us seemed to know either what to say to us, or how to act toward us. After a little, some chairs were brought, and we sat down to await the Rajah's arrival. A simple-looking, smallpox-marked Gónd he is, but his kingly dignity was made conspicuous by the splendour of his gold-broidered head-dress, which reminded me strongly of the oval-shaped Scotch cap, called a "glengarry," worn by school-boys at home. My husband stood up and returned his salutation, but I kept my seat, not knowing that this was the Rajah. After the crowd of residents, as well as outsiders, had settled somewhat into quietness, Johan asked leave to begin the service, promising that it would occupy only half an hour; for we knew that the Rajah meant to go out on some expedition; and a beautiful hymn was sung, entitled "Zara tuka Soch," *i.e.* "Take a little Thought." A short prayer for God's blessing followed, and then Johan read aloud these words: "Like as a father pitieth his children, so the Lord pitieth them that fear Him," and preached from the same, including the words that follow as well: "For He knoweth our frame; *He remembereth that we are dust,*" and emphasizing them. Very close attention was given by nearly all present, very specially by the Rajah, who had to hear, for at least once in his life, that God does not measure the greatness of a man by his learning or riches, but by his humility and fear before Him. He had not a word to object, but a Hindu present, one of His Highness's agents, would have poured out many objections to the truth just proclaimed, had he been allowed. He was invited to choose another time for discussion, however, and we shall see whether he is earnest enough to come to our tent, as proposed, to get his questions answered from the Bible itself. A second hymn and brief prayer concluded the service, and we took farewell, assuring the king of our readiness to return, should he call us.

The calm authority with which the words of life had been spoken had reassured my heart, for have we not the promise to Christ Himself as a foundation on which to stand: "Ask of Me, and I will give Thee the heathen for Thine inheritance"? And we know that "where the word of a king (the King of kings) is, there is power." The Rajah's young brother, with a number of his schoolfellows, had come to say "salaam" in the morning, and Dr. Price, who happened to be with us, and who knew the little fellow, examined him in his reading from "Babuji ke Chele" (the little book translated into Swedish by Mr. Danielsson). As he did very well, he received the book as "baksheesh," and the doctor told him he would examine him as to its contents on the occasion of his next visit. Those of the other little fellows who could read had had a printed text of Scripture on a picture-card presented to them, with which they were quite pleased.

We mean to continue our stay here for at least a week still, and then to encamp somewhere near, so as to reach more out-of-the-way villages. May God bless His own work more and more.

Sincerely yours,
ALEXINA RUTHQUIST.

(To her Mother.)
AMARWARA,
March 8th, 1892.

Just before Maggie wrote her letter this day last week, I had been dressing the little dead infant, if you remember. Well, our care had, after that, to be bestowed entirely on the young mother, who was in a most critical state, as she had to fight against inflammation of the lungs, as it turned out, as well as intense weakness. Johan arrived at about ten o'clock at night, much to our relief, for the infant had to be interred next day, and there was no little coffin ready. He was very tired, for he had ridden fifteen miles in the morning, preached afterwards in the Bazaar, and then he had had to sit for many hours in the little chakla, while the bullocks slowly drove him back the fifteen miles to Amarwara, over an awfully rough road. After he had had something to eat, we both went out to see the poor young mother, and it was most touching to see her husband sunk in slumber, in spite of himself, on the edge of the bed, on which his half-unconscious wife lay (she had no idea that her infant was already gone), while the woman called in to attend to her was also fast asleep on the floor! Well, to make a long story short, in spite of the little we tried to do for the poor woman by having her removed, next day, into the catechist's airy house, and administering suitable medicines and nourishment, she got rapidly worse, and passed away in the afternoon of next day, as I sat at her bedside, along with her distracted husband and the wife of one of the other servants! A hard fight she had, for some hours before her death, with her breathing and the high fever; but she became quite quiet just before her breath ceased, while her husband read, with almost choking utterance, the prayers appointed in his little Roman Catholic Missal, and tried to make himself heard by endearing epithets, interspersed with the name of Jesus in their own Tamil language. A more affecting sight I have never seen. When life was evidently extinct, he broke out in an agony of grief, calling her his *Life*, etc., for his "Paulina" was tenderly loved by him, and they had not been a year married! I trust that there is a glorious reunion for them, for, *up to their light*, they had tried to follow Christ. He used to read the New Testament to her every night before they went to sleep, previous to her illness!

In little more than an hour after, the body was lifted into Gustaf's cart (for ours had not come from the Méla), with a cover on it, and the afflicted young man departed with his dead to have her interred in Chindwara. His father is in charge of the dâk (mail) bungalow down there. We gave him a bottle of tea and loaf of bread with him, and Johan gave him his old overcoat to shield him from the night air; and the young man, in the midst of his grief, held out his hand to shake hands with us, and even returned Maggie's "salaam" from some yards off! His little wages had to be entrusted to the man driving the cart, so confused was the poor fellow himself.

Johan wrote to Mr. Lindroth, asking him to go to see him, and try to say a word of comfort in Chindwara, and Gustaf embraced him when his heart seemed breaking, as if he had been his young brother. As for Johan, he could not refrain from tears.

We are so glad he has made up his mind to return quietly to his work, for we think it is far better for him than to nurse his grief down there, unemployed. A poor, ignorant, but willing Gónd lad has acted as his substitute in the meantime. The little baby was buried here. Not being baptized, it would not have been admitted into the cemetery (the Roman Catholic corner)! But he was admitted into heaven, I doubt not, and that is the great thing.

(*To the Children of Holborn Free Church Sunday School, Aberdeen.*)

AMARWARA, CHINDWARA,
INDIA, C.P.
May 15*th*, 1892.

MY DEAR YOUNG FRIENDS,—

I have to thank you heartily for the sum of 10s. you have lately sent me to help to carry on God's work here. The money has come at a good time, for we have just begun to build a little dispensary— that is, a house for giving out medicine to sick people—and it needed some *windows*. Now your money will help to buy *them!* How nice for you to think that when the poor sick men, women and children come to be cured, your windows will let in the light needed to examine the patients, as well as the sweet air so necessary in such a place! It is a *missionary dispensary* we are going to build, of course; for many people come for medicine for their *bodies* who do not even know that their *souls* are very sick; and before they get any medicine for their bodies, they are going to have the good news of salvation preached to them in the verandah adjoining the house. They need to be told that "sin is the wound, and Christ is the cure" of the *soul*, before they come into the dispensary to explain about their bodies. Will you now pray, dear children, that many souls may be cured by Jesus Himself? You know He is often called "the Good Physician," and the "Great Physician," as in that beautiful 49th hymn in Sankey's collection. Perhaps Mr. Badenoch will let you sing it on the day this letter is read to you. The 6th verse is very encouraging to you, and to me too, for it is a long time now since any of my friends have sent me any money to help on the work here; and I was feeling a little depressed. The verse runs thus:—

"The children, too, both great and small,
Who love the Name of Jesus,
May now accept the gracious call
To work and live for Jesus."

This is what you are trying to do when you save up your pennies and halfpennies for the missionary box. Let us never forget that Jesus gave *Himself* for us.

I have just been reading aloud to my husband a charming little sermon for young people, by the Rev. Dr. Hugh Macmillan. His text is, " First the blade " (St. Mark iv. 28). It is in *The Sunday at Home*, April of this year (1892). All of you who are old enough to understand it should try to get hold of it, and read it. It points out so plainly that childhood is the most important period in our lives! But I do not need to teach you what you are so well taught in your Sunday School. I must tell you, rather, something about India, this beautiful land, still lying, for the most part, in darkness. Can you guess what causes the death of thousands of little children in this land—mere babies? Nothing but the *opium* their mothers give them to quiet them, and make them sleep heavily, when they want to be about some other work than nursing them.

I asked a young mother the other day if she was not very happy because God had given her a little baby girl? " I had a boy first," she said ; " but I suppose he got too much opium one day, and he died." She did not shed a tear, but spoke as if nothing uncommon had happened. I suppose her husband and mother-in-law had blamed her very much, however, although the young mother had only followed the example shown her; for she used to ook painfully sad before the new baby came. I do not need to remind some of you, however, that *a girl* is not nearly so much thought of as *a boy!*

Sometimes, before my husband can give any medicine to a sick infant, he has to let the opium poison work itself out of the system. Some of you know that Christian people in England and Scotland are doing all they can to get the Queen to forbid the sale of opium as an article of daily food. I hope God will prosper their efforts.

"Oh! soon may the heathen of every tribe and nation,
Fulfil Thy blessed word, and cast their idols all away!
Oh! shine upon them from above, and show Thyself a God
ของ love;
Teach the little children to come unto Thee!"

          Your very loving Friend,
              ALEXINA RUTHQUIST.

(*To her Sister K——.*)

          AMARWARA, C.P.,
            May 16*th*, 1892.

You may naturally wonder if the committee is supplying us with the money needed to build the little dispensary! No, for Johan has not even asked it to help. It is so poor. We are managing it with kind Col. and Mrs. Vertue's help of Rs. 100, added to what remains of the Misses Ainslies' gift. We have given up two little outside buildings, erected by Johan long ago, too, that enough of bricks may be available at this season of the year, when only a limited number can be made, before the bursting of the monsoon. Poor Johan had become so tired of being interrupted, at all hours of the day, by applicants for medicine, who come hanging about the bungalow, often coughing to attract attention! And it was very unsatisfactory that no regular evangelistic work could be done among the sick, owing to their coming singly, and, as I say, at all hours. On this account he has resolved to have a little dispensary in the compound, but at a little distance from the bungalow, in a line with the house lately built for our catechist. To this place all applicants for medicine must repair at a given hour, and before they are treated separately, they will be addressed collectively by Johan or me, D.V., while the catechist will remain with the waiters, conversing suitably with them, till one after another has been attended to in Johan's "Consulting Room!" This is very much the plan pursued by others who have taken up medical as well as missionary work, and the necessity of some such method has long been felt by Johan.

Before —— returned to Gustaf, we engaged a Mussulman, but when the time was up for him to come to us, he refused, unless we would give him higher pay. He was therefore allowed to go. He is now in prison, in Chindwara, under suspicion of having helped to murder a fellow-servant. We were at a great loss for a cook, but we tried to cast our care upon Him who careth for us, and to look to Him to supply us with a suitable Christian one.

A Roman Catholic young man most unexpectedly offered himself; a very decent-looking fellow, whose father is in charge of the Chindwara dâk bungalow; and we engaged him to be our cook. He is proving a very satisfactory servant, and the sad experience he has just gone through in losing his infant son and his dearly loved young wife (Paulina) the following day, has drawn us very near to each other in the bonds of Christian sympathy. It is a great advantage, in every way, to have Christian, rather than heathen servants, if they conduct themselves in a way worthy of the name by which they are called. This poor Saliman (or Solomon) has done this to an extent we could scarcely have expected, his daily reading of God's Word, as well as faithful discharge of his daily duties, coupled with a meek and quiet spirit, giving evidence of a wish to please God. It was a pleasure to be able to minister both to himself and his poor young wife in the time of their affliction, for they could eat and drink what was provided for them, which an observer of caste could not do. A blow was aimed at the hateful caste system, when the young man who drives our bullock cart had to choose between driving down the cart in which the dead body had to be conveyed to Chindwara, and leaving our service. He chose to pollute himself rather than starve. The bereaved Saliman has much in common with our catechist, Sewa Ram, who lends him Protestant books, and keeps company with him in his spare hours.

(*To her Sister J——.*)

AMARWARA,
CENTRAL PROVINCES,
June 4th, 1892.

I must tell you how Johan and I were circumstanced the day before yesterday. We had driven in the high gig-like conveyance he made himself, barring the wheels, to a village, some four miles off, to have a meeting, taking with us an umbrella, as there were clouds in the horizon, though we scarcely expected rain. I took a waterproof skirt, too, which

I used to wrap round me on horseback. Well, we sat down amongst a group of people at the entrance to the village, and had a nice little meeting, omitting the last verse of the last Hindi hymn, however, as it had begun to thunder, and rain was nearing. In a trice the bullocks were yoked (there was no cover on the conveyance), and off we started, but Mr. Monsoon has " wings of wind," and he overtook us almost immediately. Then followed a scene the like of which I have never figured in (Johan had something like it last year, when he lost both his hat and umbrella). The wind worked up like a tornado, tremendous rain accompanying it, while vivid flashes of lightning, followed by roars of thunder, kept up an ever-recurring accompaniment. It was very awful, so much so, that at one point of the road the bullocks stood still, and Johan and I could only clutch each other, speechless, not knowing at what moment we would be overturned on the road, and blown bodily across the country. "God help us!" I said aloud, for we were indeed helpless. Well, He who said of old, "Hitherto shalt thou come, and no further," said so then, and we were enabled to fight our way through the storm, home!

Johan had to get out and walk, as he had no protection, to save himself from a deadly chill. My shawls protected me. I could not help thinking, in the midst of it all, "What would the home people think if they could get a peep of us?" You can imagine the violence of the storm when I tell you that the fields and road, which had scarcely tasted rain for the past eight months, were able to contribute as much water to the ditches at the roadside in a few minutes as set them swirling and rushing like so many rapid little rivers. The strength of the wind, too, was such that trees and huge branches strewed the road, one man having been seriously injured by one of them. I always remember K——'s horror of strong wind, and I am not without my own quailings. Johan feels quite breathless on such occasions. His big umbrella, which he held up as long as it was possible to do so, with his hand far up the stem, was squeezed together over his hand, as if with an iron glove. The news we got from some of our own workmen, busy building the little dispensary, was, that the roof of our bungalow had been blown away! So this was what we had to ponder upon as we fought our way home! This proved a false alarm, however, thank God! for only some injury had been done to it, easily reparable. The flying thatch, I suppose, had excited the poor men into believing the worst; for, in spite of their drenched condition, they offered to come back and help us. Well, we will not forget the breaking of the monsoon, June 2nd, 1892, will we? nor our deliverance, I hope; for neither of us got any harm to speak of.

(To her Sister M——.)

AMARWARA,
July 23rd, 1892.

Many thanks for your much-enjoyed letter. The home budget reached us the day after our return from Chindwara. You should have seen the scene at the river Pénch, now flooded. It crosses our path almost exactly midway between Chindwara and this, and as there is no bridge across it, the difficulty of getting over, bag and baggage, is no slight one. On this occasion Johan had to go himself for the rude boat employed to take passengers over, for the boatmen had it away at a spot inconvenient for us, and unsuitable for the piloting across of our large conveyance—a kind of dog-cart, called a chakla. When I saw him stand in the boat, oar in hand, I was reminded of his boating experiences on the little river Luleo, near his home in the north of Sweden, for his mind often reverts to these. The simple fishermen in charge of the boat I speak of must have wondered not a little at the sahib's skill in handling an oar! The luggage and I were first got over, then the bullocks were loosed and made to swim across, a man on the other side encouraging them by calling out, "Ah! ah! ah!" (Come, come, come). Last of all, the chakla itself had to be landed. It was made to sit on the end of the boat, like a gentleman on horseback, the wheels in the water, while the balance was maintained by Johan and some native passengers occupying the other end! The strength of the current drew the boat a little farther down the river than was necessary, which I (seated safe on the bank) did not quite like. But several of the fishermen got out and dragged it, and soon all was right. We were detained two hours at the river, the first part of this time being occupied by attempts made by our young Gónd cook, accompanied by our youthful driver and a friend, to find out the exact depth of the river, as Johan was sure (or wished to be) that it could be crossed *without* the boat, by the bullocks wading through, and dragging the chakla after them. I prevented him from attempting this, however, and it was well. The three lads, with arms interlaced, staggered forward, the foremost having a very long stick in his hand, wherewith to feel his way; but at last we had to call them back.

Thank God we were preserved from accident.

AMARWARA,
August 3rd, 1892.

"The dark places of the earth are full of the habitations of cruelty.—Ps. lxxiv. 20.

MY DEAR PASTOR MONTELINS,—

The other day my husband came in and said, " I cannot understand how people can be less merciful towards each other than towards their horses and dogs." Our sweeper's son-in-law had told him of a girl who was lying in the deserted wayside inn, in the greatest misery. No one gave her anything to eat, or took any care of her. She had "lost caste." Here one could see what it was to be "without caste." Johan hastened to the poor girl, but the smell where she lay was so fearful, in consequence of her illness, that at first he almost fell down backwards. She was being almost eaten alive by worms, which had made large holes in her head, from whence came this dreadful smell. (Be good enough to excuse the plainness with which I describe it.) We called our own servant, and she was carried to the Mission House to be taken care of. I summoned my courage and went to see her. Never shall I forget the sight. Before we could attend to her sores, her hair, which scarcely deserved the name, was obliged to be cut off as closely as possible, and then Johan had more than an hour's work injecting disinfecting fluids, and picking off parasites. The girl was extremely exhausted and began to tremble and complain of hunger before she was cleaned. Our kind old sweeper made as much haste as he could, and comforted the girl, who began to cry, telling her that now she had become quite a new person. Porridge and newly baked bread she ate enormously. How had she come into such misery? and how old was she? She had been turned out of doors by her husband, because she had eaten something which had been offered to an elephant by all the caste, and since that she had wandered about begging, till, in consequence of her wretched condition, every one had driven her away. She had then determined to lay herself down and die alone in the deserted inn, and very soon this would have been her fate, unless some one had rescued her.

She is between fifteen and sixteen years of age, of a slight and womanly appearance. What kind of hearts her husband and her relations who live here, can have, the devil knows best, for he is a murderer from the beginning, and they are like him. Poor "Poosiya," this is her name, begins to smile now. She has recovered quickly, and one day when I went to her, she caught my hand, and asked why I had two rings on my finger. Last Sunday she came to my Bible class together with the other women and children, and tried to sing the song, "Jesus Christ has saved me." I hope that she may one day be able to praise the Saviour's name in truth.[1] Every day her head must be carefully attended to, and now it is getting better. At the same time her strength is also returning.

About four years ago Johan took into his care another girl, under equally wretched circumstances, and she is now a sweet Christian girl (Lydia) in the orphan home at Saugor.

We have just, with deep sorrow, heard of Mrs. Karlsson's death in Saugor. In such a case can He only, who has smitten, heal.

Our united love,
ALEXINA RUTHQUIST.

On the 25th of July, the wife of a brother missionary (Mr. Karlsson, of Saugor) died, leaving an infant a few days old, and another child aged one year and eight months.

With characteristic consideration for others, Alexina offered to go and stay for a time in the desolate home, and mother the children. In the

---

[1] "Poosiya" was very susceptible to kindness, and became much attached to Alexina. It seems the impressions so deepened that on the very day on which Alexina left for Europe (see next page) Poosiya asked for baptism!

meantime, however, Mr. Karlsson had been strongly advised to take the little ones at once to Sweden. So, instead of accepting Alexina's offer, he wrote to ask if her husband could spare her to accompany him to Stockholm, and help, especially with the infant, as it was weakly, and he feared he would have to consign it to a watery grave. The missionary did not wish to return to Europe himself, but felt he perhaps ought not to go against the judgment of the mission circle at Saugor. As there was no time for correspondence by letter, the matter had to be arranged by telegram. At once a man was despatched to the telegraph station at Seoni, with an answer in the affirmative, and now Alexina had to await the messenger's return; for the missionary had written to Bombay to get inquiries made about a suitable person to accompany him home, and failing such, he was to telegraph finally to Amarwara. At length the man returned from his long journey bearing a telegram, " Thankful, come," etc.; and the very next day (August 14th) she started with Mr. Ruthquist for Chindwara, where her relatives did everything in their power to prevent her prosecuting her journey further. They were convinced that she was far too weak for such an undertaking. Indeed, the rapid journey of 102 miles down to Nagpoor, whither her husband accompanied her, was in itself very trying, as it was the rainy season, and consequently the roads were in a frightful condition, and the rivers tremendously swollen; but she merely remarked, "God's biddings are enablings," and beguiled the way by singing one beautiful hymn after another. Her friends hoped that Nagpoor would not be reached in time to catch the train which was to convey the party to the steamer at Bombay. But God over-ruled all, and a fair start was made in an Italian vessel bound for Trieste. Soon, however, she began to realize the seriousness of the undertaking. The disturbed nights with a delicate infant, after the great fatigue of the tedious land journey, combined with the terrible heat, at that season of the year, so reduced her strength that she sometimes wondered if she would require to ask to be put off at Aden! But matters improved—

> ". . . Off at sea north-east winds blow
> Sabean odours from the spicy shore
> Of 'Araby the Blest;' with such delay
> Well pleased they slack their course, and many a league,
> Cheer'd with the grateful smell, old Ocean smiles."

She was thus enabled to leave the saloon and enjoy the fresh air on deck, occasionally. At length the Red Sea was entered, and only those who have been there in the month of August know how trying it is. Beyond that barren, desolate and uninviting coast arose many memories to stir her heart. On her right the Mohammedan crescent had first appeared, and her mind lingered on the zeal of the followers of the false prophet, which for so many centuries put to shame that of the messengers of the Cross!

Then to the left was Africa! A name so dear, as the scene of Alexander Mackay's labours, and of his sudden translation.

Little did she dream that somewhere near the Exodus crossing, well-nigh under the shadow of Sinai, she was, in like manner, to be translated to the land where the servants of Christ shall no longer have the sense of weariness. Her Heavenly Father judged that she had sufficiently long borne the burden and heat of the day, and after two days' unconsciousness she fell on sleep, and was buried at Suez.

> "Of all the thoughts of God that are
> Borne inward unto souls afar,
> Along the Psalmist's music deep,
> Now tell me if that any is,
> For gift or grace, surpassing this—
> He giveth His beloved sleep?"

After her death, Mr. Ruthquist received a parcel which she had forwarded to him from the wharf at Bombay. On a luggage label inside, evidently the only available paper at the time, she had written:—

"Jesus Christ, the same yesterday, and to-day, and for ever."

"They which live should not henceforth live unto themselves, but unto Him who died for them, and lived again."

> "My times are in Thy hand,
> My God! I wish them there;
> My life, my friends, my all, I leave
> Entirely to Thy care."

"I'll always trust in Thee."

The following letter, posted at Aden, was the first announcement which her parents received of her prospective home-coming. Some ten days elapsed, during which their lives were illumined with the thought of their speedy reunion, when the news reached them, through Pastor Montelins, Director of the Missionary Society at Stockholm, that she was gone!

STEAMER "ELEKTRA."
(Austrian Lloyd.)
August 29th, 1892, Near ADEN.

WELL, DEAREST FATHER, MOTHER, AND ALL!

Truth is stranger than fiction, and so it turns out that I am speeding on my way towards the home lands! My letter, explaining matters, enclosed by Maggie, has let you know how this has come about. We will not reach Trieste till about the 16th of September, I am told, and after that we have a long railway journey before us to Lübeck and Copenhagen; thence we "steam" to Karlskrona. From that we go by train (D.V.) to Eribro, . . . where the two little children are to be left, in the meantime. Having deposited, by God's continued help, my baby charge there, and rested a little, I will go to Stockholm, to see the Johannelund people and thence to visit the Nordforses, at Upsala (*all D.V.*) After this I shall hasten to Aberdeen to "speak in" upon you all ; but my time in Scotland is limited to a month, as, if the Committee decline to bring Johan home in April, I must hasten back to him, for it cost him much to let me go. At the latest I must be in India before Christmas, God permitting, for this is a sacred promise to Johan. All this sounds very stirring and romantic. The former it has already proved, the latter I hope it will yet prove, but no ordinary excitement, fatigue, and anxiety tell upon a weak body, and they have told upon mine hitherto. Things improve, however, as the days go on, and I am in hope that I will be enabled to hold out, and, above all, to bring the dear infant to Sweden, in pretty good health. He is decidedly fatter since we came on board ship, a week ago to-day, and my anxiety regarding him is much relieved. Mr. Karlsson takes entire charge of the elder child, Námá, a little girl barely two years old. . . . "Hitherto hath the Lord helped us." I hope to write again from some place on the Continent. Meantime, with dear love all round, and special birthday congratulations to dearest father,

I am, etc.

The extracts given below are from the last pages of her diary. There is no entry between August 13th and 31st.

May 25th. Yesterday I got the good news that an old pupil in Nagpoor to whom I had given a Bible, had died believing in Jesus, as Miss Miller (Zenana Missionary) thinks! To-day I was able to visit in three houses in the village, and give some comfort.

May 31st. Yesterday, Gustaf returned home, after having paid us a visit of three days. On Sunday night he preached from "Escape for thy life." To-day I visited the Zemindar's family, and the Daroga's.

June 2nd. Monsoon broke, and Johan and I were caught in it, just as we left Karabdool, where we had gone to hold a meeting (see p. 340).

June 5th. Had a nice letter from Nellie, from Mahablishwar—an echo to what I had been reading in Mrs. Vertue's little book, entitled, "Some Better Thing." *Amen!*

June 18*th*. To-day the new dispensary was finished, and partly taken possession of. We desire to thank God for prospering the work in connection with the building of it, at this trying season of the year.

June 20*th*. The new dispensary has been virtually opened, on behalf of a sick baby—"one of the least of these." May God add His blessing, which "maketh rich, and He addeth no sorrow with it."

June 27*th*. It was very touching, this evening, when the Zemindar's poor mother came running to Johan, and literally fell into his arms in her distress, on her son's account. May God graciously restore the widow's only son, if it be for His glory! The two words he uttered, when Johan went to see him the other day, were, "Allah" (God) and "Tanba" (repentance). God grant him repentance unto life!

June 30*th*. Got the sad news of the death of Mrs. Karlsson, of Saugor. (It occurred on the 25th, Monday, at ten o'clock at night.) It was remittent fever that carried her off. "It is the Lord."

June 31*st*. There was a continuous very heavy fall of rain in the night. The swollen river prevents the dâk (mail) from coming and going.

August 1*st*. To-day "the poor man" (Tuliya) was baptized by Gustaf in Chindwara.

August 5*th*. Went for a drive to the jungle, in

the Chindwara direction, and met the postman, with the mail-letter, and one from Mrs. Lindroth, lament-the death of her dear friend Mrs. Karlsson.

August 13*th*. To-day decides what Johan's and my near future is to be, for if Chensa brings back from Seoni the telegram, " Come," from Mr. Karlsson, I accompany him and the children to Sweden.

> "Wholly Thine, my Lord,
>   To go when Thou dost call,
>   Thine to yield my very self
>   In all things, great or small."

See hymn, No. 177, in "Sankey," which I have just sung.

August 31*st*. To-night finds me in the Red Sea, on board the *Elektra*, in charge of Mr. Karlsson's little baby, Ebenezer!

September 1st. To-day Miss F—— sails from London. She is probably on the sea now, as well as ourselves, and poor Mr. R——'s long "waiting-time" is nearly at an end! . . . Baby not quite well; I have just soothed him to sleep. . . . We are in the Red Sea, and it is airless. "Who, of God, is made unto us wisdom and righteousness, and sanctification and redemption." Amen.

The following is Mr. Karlsson's letter (translated from the Swedish) announcing Alexina's death to her husband.

THE RED SEA, ON BOARD THE ' ELEKTRA,"
September 5th, 1892.

DEAR BROTHER,—

Jesus said, "Blessed is he, whosoever shall not be offended in Me." You know that God is called "Wonderful," and wonderful He is, and many a time His dealings are very mysterious. If you will consider this you will do well. I am now going to thank you for the great sacrifice you made when you lent your wife to help me with my little children. She fulfilled her charge so faithfully and nicely, and seemed also to have had joy from it. But your sacrifice was great, and it became greater still than what was expected. Certainly you could not have expected that God so soon should have called home your beloved wife, but He has done so. Oh! how painful it is to me to have to give you this information. I cannot in words tell how I feel for you. May the Lord help you to bear this in patience. Saturday morning, Sept. 3rd, while we were drinking tea, your wife complained of having had a restless night, and that she felt very tired. I asked her to go to bed, and said that I would try to look after both the children while she was resting. This she did. At 8 a.m. I went into her cabin, and finding her feverish, I at once called the doctor.

* * * * *

By 4 p.m. she was quite unconscious. The doctor did all he could, and all were willing to help, but all was in vain. She remained immovable and unconscious up to 5.30 p.m. to-day (Sept. 5th), when her spirit fled. And now what shall I say for your comfort, if not this?—she has conquered, she is safe for ever. I am now left alone with my little ones, and my prospects are dark; but I hope the Lord will not take me away before I reach Sweden with the children. May the Lord help!

I am glad that I will not be obliged to sink your dear wife's remains in the sea, as I hope to bury her to-morrow at Suez. The coffin is already made, and I have dressed her in her own clothes, stockings and shoes, as well as I could. It is now late, and I am tired, so you must excuse this short letter. You may reasonably expect to hear more in detail, but I have my two little children, who take my time and strength. I will post this at Suez to-morrow, that you may hear as soon as possible, and be able to acquaint relations and friends. I cut off a lock of her hair, which I send."

Alexina so faithfully redeemed the time while she had opportunity, and was so ready to meet her Saviour, that it must have been a peaceful falling asleep and a joyous awakening in the presence of the King! "Now she," as Dr. Robertson Nicoll says of the sainted Professor Elmslie, "is in the haven, and we are far out at sea!"

Space forbids more than two letters (selected at random) from a multitude of those who loved her, and desired to make known their sympathy with the sorrowing relatives. The first is from a missionary in the field, the second from the Rev. J. Laidlaw, D.D., Professor of Theology, New College, Edinburgh.

NAGPOOR,
26th *September*, 1892.

MY DEAR MR. RUTHQUIST,—

The news contained in Mr. Danielsson's post card to Mr. Whitton has fallen like a bomb-shell in our midst. It is so sudden and startling and mysterious, that we are struck dumb in presence of a great sorrow. To all who knew your dear wife as well as we did, and who loved her deeply, it has come as a personal bereavement. My wife is weeping as for a sister. No loss has moved us like this for many a day. . . . But when we think of this sudden blow, and the awful loss it will be to you, we scarce know what to say. Our deepest sympathies also go out to Mrs. Danielsson, who has been bereaved of a sister beloved. God is able to sustain and uphold you all with the right hand of His righteousness, and we know He will do it. It is not easy to understand His dealings sometimes. One feels inclined to say, "If only she had not gone, she would have been in Amarwara still." But then we never can see very far before us. Our duty is to follow the path in which God seems to be pointing to us to go at the time, and to leave the consequences with Him. Both you and she believed that God was telling her to help those motherless children on the voyage to Sweden. Little did you think it was the road by which she was being led to glory. "What we know not now we shall know hereafter." The time is coming when our Father's way will be made plain, and then we shall see that it has been tracked with love.

We are all praying for you, and thinking very much about you.

We can only commit you and dear Mrs. Danielsson, and the rest, into the hands of One who is better able to dry up your tears than we can. Tell Mrs. Danielsson my wife will write her.

With our united warmest love and sympathy,

Yours in Christ,

JOHN DOUGLAS.

EDINBURGH,
8, MERCHISTON AVENUE,
7th November, 1892.

MY DEAR MRS. MACKAY,—

. . . By this time I trust the hand of our gracious Heavenly Father has somewhat soothed your sorrow, as His Spirit the Comforter only can. All friends who knew her must deeply feel for you and yours, that one so bright and loving and helpful has been so early taken. No doubt, when you gave her up to the mission field, you made a surrender once for all. Early death is always in the list of the missionary's possible sacrifices for Christ; they have counted life not dear for His work's sake. And so He has enrolled your Alexina, like her cousin of Uganda, in the noble roll of martyrs for Jesus and for suffering mankind. It is a high honour: only the Day will tell how high it is. We have our Lord's own word for it, that they who lose their life for His sake and the gospel's shall find it.

My wife and I feel much for you all in this deep trial. We have a warm recollection of her visit to us after we came to Edinburgh, on one of her journeys. Now on a journey of kindness and help, she has herself been taken into the heavenly rest. The good Lord comfort you all, and make her memory a blessing, such as only eternity can reveal. To have had a daughter so noble and self-sacrificing is a thing for you and your husband to praise God for. But to part with such an one, and make right use of the providence which takes her from you, needs special grace. May our heavenly Father grant it richly to you all. Excuse these hurried lines, and believe me, with much regard and sympathy,

Yours very sincerely,
JOHN LAIDLAW.

(A few Reminiscences by her Husband.)

AMARWARA, CHINDWARA, C. P., INDIA.
28th February, 1893.

When I came to India in 1885, I was one day looking through one of Mrs. Danielsson's albums in Narsingpûr, Central Provinces. Amongst the many photos I was especially struck with one, but I did not then know who it was. Soon after I was told that it was Miss Alexina Mackay, one of the Zenana missionaries in Nagpoor. Some months later she came to Chindwara, to stay with her sister during the hot weather. Then and there I made her acquaintance. Her lively and cheerful nature appeared to me as if she did not know much sorrow, of which this world is so full, but very soon I found in conversation, that she was well acquainted with sorrow, but that she had learned to cast all her burdens upon Him who had told her to do so. As she herself had tasted and seen the goodness of the Lord, she wanted others also to be happy. I cannot but with gratitude remember how she many a time tried to show me "a more excellent way" for a Christian, than to go looking sad and depressed, as if we had to carry our own burdens. The time came for her going back to her work in Nagpoor, which she did in a very cheerful spirit. Only then I began to realise what a help she had been to me by her words and bright Christian life. In June, 1886, we became engaged, and hoped to marry in 1887; but owing to a rule newly made by our Society, that a missionary has to be on the mission field for three years before he is allowed to marry, we had to wait till the autumn of 1888. The most of this time she spent in Scotland. In October, 1888, she came back to Bombay, where we were married. After a short visit to Punah, Nagpoor and Chindwara, we went on to Amarwara, in the Chindwara district, where we were going to labour, and share both joys and sorrows together. Many a one had felt for her, and spoken to her of the difficulties unavoidable in a lonely place like Amarwara, out in the jungle; but nothing of that kind could make her hesitate for a moment to go there, or anywhere, where the duties of her husband called him to be.

Amarwara is a village with about 1,500 inhabitants, situated twenty-four miles north of Chindwara, Central Provinces. The village is inhabited by Hindus of many castes, Gónds, and a good many Mohammedans. Many of the surrounding villages are inhabited by Gónds; and others by Gónds and Hindus. Alexina had not been many days in Amarwara before she went to see the women; and many a time she came with me to the surrounding villages.

Our first year in Amarwara was a very quiet but happy one. Early in 1889, the Misses Ainslie, late of St. Andrews, sent some money to us to be spent in mission work. As we felt the want of having a place of worship, we made up our minds to build, with the money put at our disposal, a house in which we could gather people to hear the word of God. It was soon set a-going, and within a couple of months the building was ready. In that church we have had meetings twice every Sunday, besides every evening in the week, when at home, except on Wednesdays. On those evenings we used to have meetings in the village. As a matter of course Alexina always led the singing, and much she did by her gift of song.

In November, 1889, God gave us a little daughter, who, as we thought, was to fill our cup of happiness.

After the restoration of the mother, who at the time seemed all but gone—the infant, alas! contrary to our fond expectations, after a brief life of twelve days, quietly passed away. The little one had, however, a mission to fulfil, for now we could share sorrow as never before, and heaven began to be more real to us, now that "a part of ourselves" was there —"only gone before," and the truth of the word, "Here we have no continuing city," seemed so applicable. In after years my wife used to say, "I do not think there is one day or one hour passes that I do not think of our darling Juanita; however, I begin to feel more reconciled to the loss. And why she was taken I will no doubt understand when I am in heaven." She tried to see many reasons for God's dealings with us in this way, but she could never feel quite satisfied. Sometimes she said, "Perhaps God wanted me to do more work amongst the women, and therefore He took her." At other times she said, "No doubt God has only shown His love in taking her, for I am not strong." And again she would say, "How free I am, compared with others, in going about with you, having nice changes here and there."

From December, 1889, to August, 1892, we worked together in and around Amarwara, with an occasional trip to see some of our friends. Our little home in Amarwara was, however, a happy and a peaceful one, as Alexina, with her bright and happy Christian spirit, wanted it to look nice and tidy; and when she was not away, telling the women of Jesus in the villages, or with me on an evangelistic tour she always found some good book to read, or some beautiful hymn to play and sing, or some little thing to do with her hands. She greatly disliked idleness in herself and others. She not only went to visit the women, but they used to come to see her also.

Many a time, when I had been away for a little, and came home, she was sorrounded by scores of women in the verandah of the bungalow, listening to her playing and singing, and eagerly taking in the wonderful story of Jesus and His love. But before going, the women, as a rule, wanted to see inside the bungalow, and she, in the same cheerful spirit, showed them one thing after another, and at the same time explained their use, not forgetting to tell them how God wanted us to make use of what He had given, but that we should never set our hearts on earthly things, so as to forget or dishonour the Giver, and above all, that we should not make idols of them, nor worship perishable things.

The women liked her, and she liked them, but she was not less loved by the children. It was an interesting scene, many a time, to watch when she was going about arranging shrubs and flowers in the compound, how children came running to help her, taking as much interest as herself in the on-goings, if not more; and when she felt tired, they would run for something for her to sit down and rest on, usually so many wanting to carry a little chair that the one tumbled above the other. Having now sat down they began some childlike talk, some asking, some listening, some examining her dress, shoes and stockings. Very frequently they wanted to see her foot, which request she granted them, and then to see how astonished they were to find a very white foot under a black stocking, was enough to amuse not only herself but others also.

As I have tried for some years to relieve some of the sick and suffering by giving medicine, there has been no lack of women, as well as men, coming from far distant places in order to get help. On these occasions my wife took a great interest in the welfare of their bodies and their souls, and then she learned to know and become known by many who otherwise never would have seen her. As this kind of work extended, we thought it desirable to get a dispensary. The same ladies who gave money for the meeting-house had sent some more afterwards to my wife. With this money and Rs. 100 given by a friend in India, we got a little dispensary built in May,

1892, where sick people could gather in an open verandah, and get some regular instruction before having their bodily wants ministered to. Alexina greatly rejoiced over these arrangements, and hoped to get many an opportunity of singing and speaking to those coming for medicine; but unexpectedly she got the call to take home to Sweden two little motherless children, which call she thought was from on high, and therefore she was willing to obey it, if, she said, I could spare her for three or four months. We resolved to help the poor sorrowing father, and many days had not passed before she was on her way to Bombay. On the 22nd of August, 1892, she left Bombay, but her voyage was cut short on the Red Sea, on the 5th of September, when she got the call to come up higher, to rest from her labours, and to receive the crown of life.

The news of her death came so unexpectedly to her nearest relatives and friends, that it was difficult for any one to realise that she was no longer amongst us.

When the news was made known in Amarwara, the women of the village came together in crowds, and one could see and hear them outstripping each other in weeping and lamentation, crying, "Oh, that she had only been allowed to die here, that we might have gone with her to the grave!"

I was told that an elderly man who often came to our bungalow, on hearing of her death, fainted, and that he did not taste food or water for a whole day and night. He came to me one day, quite overcome with emotion, and to comfort me he said, "I am sure Mem-Sahib will get a high birth next time; she will become a Brahman or a king, so perfect was she." This is the highest reward a man can get for good works, the Hindus think. A Mohammedan woman told me that she had dreamt, before any one knew of her death, how she saw Alexina passing the police station in Amarwara, and going towards the bungalow. She called to Alexina to come and sit down, but she answered, "I must go to my Sahib." The wonderful thing in the dream was that Alexina's face appeared shining as the sun, and therefore, the woman thought, there can be no doubt of her salvation! Still more strange it seems, that she herself anticipated that her days were to be few, for several times she said to me: "I am not going to live long." When I asked her why she said so, she answered, "It seems so to me." I used to say, "I do not like you to say so," then she would smilingly answer, "Well, I should not like to leave you yet." Many a time during her last year, she experienced more of that pure joy which comes from hearing and meditating on the word of God; and she used to say, "Oh, how I have enjoyed this sermon, text, or verse. On the evening of the last day she was in Amarwara, she called some women who used to come for instruction, saying, "I want to have them once more; who knows when I can have them next?" Her mind was very much taken up latterly with thinking of heaven, and how it would be there. On her way down to Nagpoor, to which place I accompanied her, she sang the whole way one beautiful hymn after the other, and several times in one day the twenty-third Psalm, and "My times are in Thy hand," etc.

The last words I heard from her lips, while tears filled her eyes, were: "I thank you so much for all your love to me; may God reward you for it." And so the train passed on.

She did not trust in anything in herself, nor rejoice in her own goodness and perfection. No! Christ and His love were hers, and Him she had loved and followed from her early childhood; and as the years passed, she learned to know and love Him more and more, and she herself could say, "I trust in Thee." It is so characteristic of her Christian faith that she wrote in her diary the day before she took ill: "Who of God is made unto us wisdom, and righteousness, and sanctification and redemption." Amen.

JOHAN RUTHQUIST.

Miss J. M. Small, Zenana Missionary, Nagpoor, writes:—

"How well I remember the first time I saw Alexina. We had just come to the end of a long railway journey, and were very tired. All the circle among whom we found ourselves were strangers to me, for I had only been in India a short time. But it was to a characteristic mission house we had come, and the welcome from the hostess, host and one zenana lady was as loving and cordial as it could be. During that visit I was much with her, who, in after years, was to become my dear friend and fellow worker. I remember days spent in the 'Little Bungalow,' afterwards to become so familiar, and several trips to the city, to be introduced to women to whom I could hardly speak at all, but who were in the course of a few years to become dear friends.

"Five years later I was appointed to take up her work during her absence on furlough. We were only a few days together on my arrival at Nagpoor, and our real intimacy began after her return. But I have heard much from those who were her fellow workers, about those first five years of her life among the women of India. Her earnest enthusiastic nature carried her through hard pioneering work, when physically she was often unfit for it. In those first days of zenana work in this city it was considered wise to do the work in the early morning, so, at an hour when even the most early risers were not astir, 'Pikoo' used to waken his mistress by loud rapping at her door, and after a very light 'chota hazree,' she was on her way to the city, hymn-book and little bag of fancy work in hand, ready to make any number of homes bright by her loving words and happy manner. Often she did not return for breakfast till twelve o'clock in the day. In addition to the books she required for her work she always carried with her a pile of little tracts, to be distributed to school-boys, or any one who would accept them. This system we had to stop afterwards, as we found it almost impossible to get along the streets, so persecuted were we by little urchins who only wanted a 'book' for the sake of getting something. But it shows her eager earnestness to make use of *every* opportunity. This was a feature in her character which always impressed one very much. A little group of people sitting in an open verandah, whether men or women, were seldom passed without an effort made to reach them, and in the houses where she taught she always did her utmost to gather servants and visitors round her as she sang or told her story. Although I differed from her on this subject, feeling I had come for the women, and feeling that they are best reached when alone, I could not but admire her spirit. In some parts of India, and in some houses in Nagpoor, her way would not have worked well, but there can be no doubt many heard the gospel from her lips, who would never have heard it but for her. She made friends with many a student, and it was a very common thing to see her in earnest conversation with one or more of them, whom she had induced to visit her in her own bungalow; and the visit generally wound up with a hymn or two. Sunday was always a well filled day. A class of big boys occupied her after the Marathi service, and when they had had their lesson, the sweeper woman was called to her side. In early years she had an early morning hour with a band of beggars, among whom were not a few lepers. Each one got one pice on leaving, and were expected to sit and listen for about half an hour. After having this service for a number of years she thought it was time to stop the pice, and as it was considered advisable to stop these diseased people from coming to the compound, this class was discontinued.

"Pikoo, her man-of-all-work, was not forgotten, and from his mistress he learned to read, and many things besides. Her zeal was worthy of imitation, and I can truly say she taught me many a lesson. She did not confine her energies to her own special work. Whenever she saw a need she was ready to do her best to supply it.

"Another feature in her character was her self-denying eagerness to make those around her happy. If it was in her power to make an evening bright for those who needed cheering, she was ready, however tired, to go and spend it with them. Perhaps, after singing a good deal in the course of her work, her voice was exhausted, and she was not able to do very much more, she would still make the effort, and sitting down at the harmonium, gratify this one and that one by singing their favourite songs. Then her stories were endless. Past experiences were recalled, sometimes very amusing ones, or else an account of her visiting during the day. She often talked till she was quite worn out. When she was in the room no other entertainer was necessary. A dear friend of hers told me with tears in her eyes how, when she was left alone, Alexina would come over, pen and paper in hand, to sit beside her, so that she might not feel dull and lonely. Another friend said, while she was away on furlough, 'There is quite a blank now she is away, and many miss her kind shake of the hand at the church door.' In the city many mourn for her, and we are quite sure that many of those to whom she so faithfully told of the Saviour's love will yet meet her where she is gone, and thank our Heavenly Father for having sent her to work in India.

(*From* "*The Indian Witness,*" *October* 22*nd,* 1892.)

"Most of your readers are acquainted with the thrilling story of Mackay of Uganda. Probably few are aware that two of his cousins have consecrated their lives to the cause of Christ in India. One is the wife of the Rev. G. Danielsson, of the Swedish Mission, Chindwara, the other, who is the subject of this sketch, after fifteen years of self-denying labour, finished her course in the Red Sea on the fifth of last month, and was buried at Suez.

"Alexina Mackay's early life was passed in a Scottish Free Church Manse, and her character was moulded by much the same influences as surrounded her better-known cousin. The secret of his heroism lay not so much in his intellectual gifts, though these were of a high order, as in his devotion to duty, his readiness to sacrifice himself for the good of others, and Christ-like compassion for the souls of men. Withal he possessed a bright, winning manner, which called forth the love of the natives, and a boundless store of fun, which rendered him a charming companion. Though the sphere of her labours was more obscure, these were the very qualities which shone so conspicuously in our departed friend.

"Miss Mackay was one of the lady pioneer workers in what has now become a flourishing and well-equipped branch of the Free Church Mission, Nagpoor. Until her marriage, four years ago, she with her bullock tonga was a familiar sight as she threaded the narrow lanes of the city, and entered the dingy houses like a beam of sunshine from the outside world. In her attempts to reach the women, rebuffs and rude speeches were a frequent experience, but her ready wit and unfailing courtesy generally disarmed opposition, and opened up a way for the introduction of her message. In common with other zenana workers, much of her time was spent in teaching her pupils how to read and sew. Her chief delight, however, was to gather the women in verandahs and courtyards, to whom she would sing Marathi hymns, and tell the story of the Cross. Such work involves a large amount of wear and tear, and calls for the exercise of much faith and patience. Her enthusiasm never flagged, and her belief in the fulfilment of God's promises never grew dim. Not a few in Nagpoor will cherish her memory and recall her bright visits, but like many another devoted missionary, she has had to pass away from earth without seeing much of the fruits of her toil. The time of reaping amongst the women of Nagpoor is not yet.

"It will come, and when the harvest is garnered, both sower and reaper will rejoice together.

"When Miss Mackay became the wife of the Rev.

Johan Ruthquist of the Swedish Mission, Amarwara, the crowded streets of Nagpoor were exchanged for a life of extreme loneliness amongst the villages in the uplands of the Chindwara district. It was no ordinary sacrifice for her to leave the many friends who loved her, with the prospect of no companionship outside her own household, but what she could find in the simple-hearted Gónds. Bravely did she gird herself to her new lot, and nobly did she second her husband in his work of teaching and preaching. Their happy, peaceful home was in itself an influence fitted to awaken a longing after a higher and purer life. A long career of untiring labour seemed to be before them, in which one hoped they might have the joy of gathering many golden sheaves. The Master had different thoughts regarding her. When we least expected it, she was called to the glory and brightness of eternity.

"Mrs. Ruthquist died at what she believed to be the post of duty, and in rendering services of love to the weak and helpless. By one swift, sudden stroke, a brother missionary had been robbed of his wife, and left with two young children. Once, for a few days, Mrs. Ruthquist had tasted the sweetness of clasping to her bosom a babe of her own. That hallowed memory quickened her sympathy for these bereaved ones. When, therefore, an appeal came to her for aid, it was characteristic of her that within less than a week she was on her way to Bombay to undertake the difficult and trying task of conducting them to their friends in Sweden. That accomplished, she meant to pay a short visit to her old home in Aberdeen, and be back to her husband and work before Christmas. Little did any of us dream that she had bid farewell to India for ever.

"Some years ago, a little boy, struck with her thin, wan face, as she lay on the sofa, resting one day, said as he quietly patted her:—'Auntie, when are you going to die?' The question was a startling one, but she quickly replied, 'I don't know, darling, but when I am very tired, and Jesus sees that my work is done, He will come for me.' We can answer that question now. The Red Sea in September has proved fatal to many a voyager. Mrs. Ruthquist has gone to swell the number. Mr. Karlsson, writing from Suez, tells us that she became ill on the 3rd of September. Remarking that she felt 'so tired' she went to bed. Soon after she passed into a state of unconsciousness, from which she never awakened. Jesus saw that her work was done, and as she was 'so tired,' He took her Home to rest for evermore. Many of us feel that a blank has been made in our lives that will not readily be filled. Her sorrowing husband writes :—'With her I seem to have lost all.

. . . She is now with Jesus, and that is enough for me. I have at times been able to share a little of the joy she is having, and I must say that only to taste a little of that joy is more than a mortal being can bear.'

"Amid the storm and stress of life, the perplexities of God's dealings with us in providence, 'the joy of the Lord is our strength.'

"It would help us greatly if we could ever keep our eyes fixed upon that vision of the future which arose before the old prophet Isaiah as he stood on his watch-tower, like some lonely sentinel waiting for the breaking of the morning. In front of him is a narrow path winding up the side of the hill of Zion which is crowned by the tabernacle of God. The name of it is 'the Way of Holiness.' It is crowded along its whole length with pilgrims. They are the 'ransomed of the Lord.' How do they occupy their time as they toil up the steep ascent? The prophet lends his ear to catch the sounds that are borne on the breeze. They are sounds of singing and mirth, 'joy and gladness.' As he continues to listen, however, he detects an undertone of 'sorrow and sighing,' which spoils the harmony of the music. He watches them for a little, until they reach the brow of the hill, and enter through the gates that lead into the sanctuary. Now they are in the presence of their Lord.

'They see the King in His beauty.' What triumphant strains are those which now reach him! Nothing but joy, nothing but gladness. They have obtained joy and gladness, and sorrow and sighing have fled away."

(*From* " *The Helpmeet*," *January*, 1893.)

"'Truth is stranger than fiction.' So wrote our dear friend, Mrs. Ruthquist, *née* Alexina Mackay, in announcing to her family her hope of paying them an unexpected visit, after conveying to Sweden the motherless babe of a fellow-missionary, which had been committed to her care. She intended to rejoin her husband at Amarwara by Christmas, but she added, 'always D.V.'

"Her letter was posted at Aden. Before reaching Suez she was seized with sudden illness, and after two days of unconsciousness, far from home or kindred, she passed away on the 5th of September. Her remains were laid to rest in the little English cemetery at Suez.

"She was the third child of the Rev. M. Mackay, formerly F. C. Minister of Fordyce; Mackay of Uganda was her cousin. From childhood it was her ambition to be a missionary, and she entered on the work with her whole heart when, in 1877, she joined our Zenana Mission at Nagpoor. Many of our readers will remember the lively and graphic accounts she gave of the work when home on furlough in 1882-3. After her return to India, as before, she was the life of the missionary circle at Nagpoor by her cheerful, obliging disposition. She resigned her connection with our Society—though not with mission work—in October, 1888, on her marriage with Mr. Ruthquist, of the Swedish Evangelical Mission, in Central India. Friends who saw her in Bombay on the eve of this last voyage thought her looking remarkably well; but she had never regained her former gaiety of spirit since the loss of her only child, a little daughter who died in infancy. Her heart seemed more than ever drawn towards the Heavenly Home, and she spent much time in meditation and prayer.

"Her memory will long be lovingly cherished by all who were associated with her."

Alexina's chief characteristics were humility, wonderful tact in conciliating people, her sunny disposition, which kept every one around her happy, her unselfishness, conscientiousness, and consideration for others. A friend, Mrs. Colonel Vertue, who knew her intimately in India, says:—"What struck me most in her was her individuality, for she was always *herself* at all times. Then, her ever ready sympathy and her capability of throwing herself heartily into the interests of others, forgetting her own for the time; her loving, bright, quick ways, which showed the ardent, brave spirit within, and her great powers of endurance, both mental and physical, which enabled her to do so much more than most people with stronger and more robust health, would have ventured to do."

But above all, and animating all, was her deep love for the Saviour, which began to show itself in early childhood, and so ever after

> "A sense of tune,
> A satisfied love meanwhile,
> Which nothing earthly could despoil,
> Sang on within her soul!"

www.ingramcontent.com/pod-product-compliance
Lightning Source LLC
Chambersburg PA
CBHW032022220426
43664CB00006B/332